# Connect to Your Career

by

**Suzann Connell, MEd, PhD**
Adjunct Faculty, College of Education
University of Phoenix
Los Angeles, California

**Julie Jaehne, MS**
Adjunct Faculty, College of Education
University of Houston
Houston, Texas

Publisher

**The Goodheart-Willcox Company, Inc.**
Tinley Park, IL
www.g-w.com

**The Goodheart-Willcox Company, Inc. Brand Disclaimer:** Brand names, company names, and illustrations for products and services included in this text are provided for educational purposes only and do not represent or imply endorsement or recommendation by the author or the publisher.

**The Goodheart-Willcox Company, Inc. Safety Notice:** The reader is expressly advised to carefully read, understand, and apply all safety precautions and warnings described in this book or that might also be indicated in undertaking the activities and exercises described herein to minimize risk of personal injury or injury to others. Common sense and good judgment should also be exercised and applied to help avoid all potential hazards. The reader should always refer to the appropriate manufacturer's technical information, directions, and recommendations; then proceed with care to follow specific equipment operating instructions. The reader should understand these notices and cautions are not exhaustive.

The publisher makes no warranty or representation whatsoever, either expressed or implied, including but not limited to equipment, procedures, and applications described or referred to herein, their quality, performance, merchantability, or fitness for a particular purpose. The publisher assumes no responsibility for any changes, errors, or omissions in this book. The publisher specifically disclaims any liability whatsoever, including any direct, indirect, incidental, consequential, special, or exemplary damages resulting, in whole or in part, from the reader's use or reliance upon the information, instructions, procedures, warnings, cautions, applications, or other matter contained in this book. The publisher assumes no responsibility for the activities of the reader.

**The Goodheart-Willcox Company, Inc. Internet Disclaimer:** The Internet resources and listings in this Goodheart-Willcox Publisher product are provided solely as a convenience to you. These resources and listings were reviewed at the time of publication to provide you with accurate, safe, and appropriate information. Goodheart-Willcox Publisher has no control over the referenced websites and, due to the dynamic nature of the Internet, is not responsible or liable for the content, products, or performance of links to other websites or resources. Goodheart-Willcox Publisher makes no representation, either expressed or implied, regarding the content of these websites, and such references do not constitute an endorsement or recommendation of the information or content presented. It is your responsibility to take all protective measures to guard against inappropriate content, viruses, or other destructive elements.

**Library of Congress Cataloging-in-Publication Data**

Connell, Suzann.
  Connect to your career / by Suzann Connell, PhD, Adjunct Faculty,
College of Education, University of Phoenix, Los Angeles, California,
Julie Jaehne, MS, Adjunct Faculty, College of Education, University
of Houston, Houston, Texas.
    p. cm.
Includes index.
ISBN 978-1-60525-906-8
1. Career development--Computer network resources. 2. Job
    hunting--Computer network resources. 3. Vocational guidance--
    Computer network resources. 4. Interviewing. 5. Online social
    networks. I. Jaehne, Julie Simon. II. Title.
HF5381.C8862 2014
650.14--dc23

2014000162

**The Best App for That images:**
Twitter app icon printed with permission from Twitter, Inc.
JobMo app icon printed with permission from Kiefer Consulting, Inc.
Nextdoor app icon printed with permission from Nextdoor.
JobCompass app icon printed with permission from JobCompass.
Dropbox app icon printed with permission from Dropbox.
Job Interview Questions and Answers app icon printed with permission from Career Confidential, LLC.
MySalaryCalc app icon printed with permission from Rumba Solutions.
HootSuite app icon printed with permission from HootSuite, Inc.

# From the Authors

Having a career you enjoy takes planning and then action. First, make a concentrated effort to identify your dream career. Second, expend time and energy to secure a job in your desired profession. More than likely, technology will be an essential part of your career-search process. It is important to know how to leverage technology to help you find the career of your dreams.

We designed *Connect to Your Career* with one overriding goal in mind: to help you understand how to use technology, such as social media, online job boards, and digital devices to connect to a career. Upon completing this book, you will able to:

- Build, and then protect, a professional online presence that will lead to employment.
- Develop professional networks to assist you in the job-search process.
- Practice job-specific and employability skills required by employers.
- Identify your skills, talents, and career strengths to develop a career plan.
- Create résumés and cover letters that convince employers to grant you an interview.
- Apply for jobs online and in-person and manage the job-search process.
- Prepare for various types of job interviews, including virtual interviews.
- Use post-interview techniques to help keep things in perspective.
- Evaluate job offers and respond to them in a professional manner.
- Develop an understanding of what employers expect so you can be successful at your new job.
- Prepare to take certification exams by answering practice certification questions.

*Connect to Your Career* is more than a book about how to get a job; it is a technology-driven 21st century reflection of how adults find and cultivate careers.

# About the Authors

**Suzann Connell** teaches technology, communications, and English courses for the University of Phoenix. The course curricula include career-development techniques, professional communication, writing, media writing, podcasting, and blog writing. Along with teaching, she is a freelance senior instructional designer. Suzann holds a master degree in education technology from Pepperdine University and a bachelor degree in training, design, and development from the University of Michigan.

**Julie Jaehne** has been an adjunct faculty member for 21 years at the University of Houston in the College of Education. Via distance learning, she has taught instructional technology courses and teacher certification courses. Julie also has extensive experience with the use of technology with kindergarten through 12th grade instruction. She is a published author of multiple computer application textbooks and tutorials. Julie holds a bachelor degree in business administration from Baylor University and a master degree in education with a concentration in occupational education from the University of Houston.

# Reviewers

The authors and publisher would like to thank the following individuals for their valuable input in the development of *Connect to Your Career*.

**Arin Baynard**
Career Development Coordinator
Seminole State College of Florida
Sanford, Florida

**Andrew M. Crain**
Career Consultant
The University of Georgia Career Center
Athens, Georgia

**Christy Dunston**
Career Counselor
University of North Carolina at Chapel Hill
    Career Services
Chapel Hill, North Carolina

**Amelia Maness-Gilliland, PhD**
Professor/Faculty, General Education
Colorado Technical University
Chicago, Illinois

**Anne Landon**
IMS Internship Coordinator & Assistant
    Director
Lycoming College
Williamsport, Pennsylvania

**Byron Lynn Morgan, PhD**
Lecturer, Management Department
Texas State University–Round Rock Campus
Round Rock, Texas

**Kevin Mess**
Computer Science Instructor
College of Southern Nevada
Las Vegas, Nevada

**Reid Smalley**
Executive Director of Workforce Development
Genesee Community College–The BEST Center
Batavia, New York

**Helen W. Spain, BS, MSEd**
Instructor, Office Administration/Medical
    Office Administration
Wake Technical Community College
Raleigh, North Carolina

**Marci Stone**
Adjunct College Professor
Fortis College
Salt Lake City, Utah

**Peter E. Veruki**
Director, Corporate Relations (Retired)
Vanderbilt University
Owen Graduate School of Management
Nashville, Tennessee

**Julie A. Willits**
Academic Advisor
The Pennsylvania State University
College of the Liberal Arts
University Park, Pennsylvania

**Amy Wolfgang**
Career Coach/Owner
Wolfgang Career Coaching
Austin, Texas

# Contents in Brief

# Table of Contents

Goodluz/Shutterstock.com

T-Design/Shutterstock.com

iofoto/Shutterstock.com

StockLite/Shutterstock.com

## Chapter 12

# Get Started

*Connect to Your Career* will help you get a head start on the career-search process. This text focuses on proven strategies that use technology as a tool to find the career that is the correct fit for you. You will be guided through the steps of creating your online presence, protecting your online identity, and networking in the 21st century. Integrated in this technology-centric approach are traditional résumés, as well as infographic résumés, that will capture the eye of an employer. The importance of certification is also discussed, as well as how to make the most of your career once you are a part of the workforce.

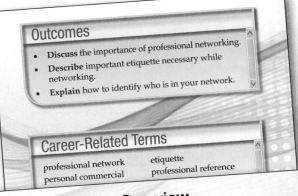

**Each chapter opener prepares you for the content that follows.** Outcomes define the goals you will accomplish after reading the chapter and completing the activities. **Career-Related Terms** introduce you to the terminology with which you will become familiar throughout your job-search process. The **Overview** sets the stage to prepare you for the topics that will be explored.

### Overview

Networking is a term used frequently in the workforce. When people interact with others in business situations, they are networking. Networking can be used to expand your list of professional contacts. These individuals may be able to assist you in advancing your career. Through networking, professionals can meet other colleagues in their field. Quite often these associates support each other in finding jobs and succeeding in the workplace.

Networking can be done formally by attending meetings or events or informally through conversations with someone you meet at work or at a social event. Networking can take place in person or online. Any communication that leads to career discussions can yield a new networking contact.

Approach the process in a serious manner. Use common sense and etiquette. Build your network and continue the process throughout your career.

**A portfolio is an important tool for the job-search process.** Every job seeker should consider creating a personal career portfolio. **Career Portfolio** activities in each chapter provide guidance to create a portfolio for use when exploring career opportunities. This process requires reflection on your accomplishments and your skill sets. Completing this activity will help you build confidence and identify who you are as a potential employee.

# Focus on Your Career

**Social Media for Your Career**

Vizualize.me is a graphic résumé-building program, which allows users to turn text into appealing charts for use in an...

**Exploring Certification**

Career Certification Skills—Using Reading Skills

Your classmate would like to get your feedback as she writes her r... you with a portion of her résumé to review. Read the education section respond to the questions that follow.

Education

...ge 2009 to 2010 Engineering Major
...ge 2008 to 2009 Culinary Arts Major

**The Best App for that**

Using your mobile device, conduct a search for the *Nextdoor* app. Nextdoor is a private social network to communicate with neighbors in local communities. Members post information about everyday events...

**What Employers Want**

Employers expect ethical communication. An ethical communicator uses honesty and accuracy to guide all communication. Communication must be truthful and presented in an unbiased manner. Facts should be given without distortion. If the information is an opinion, label it as such. Do not take cr...

**Special features spotlight information that is important for career preparation.** Practical tips help you focus on what is important as you look for a job.

- **What Employers Want** explores expectations for the workplace. By considering the employer's point of view, you can prepare for your career by developing positive behaviors to use on the job.

- **The Best App for That** recommends helpful smartphone apps. You will learn how to use your mobile devices as tools for the career-search process.

- **Social Media for Your Career** gives examples of social media sites that can double as online career networking hubs.

- **Exploring Certification** presents passages that sharpen your reading, locating information, and math skills. Completing these activities will hone these basic skills to help prepare you for professional certification.

**It is important to assess what you learn as you progress through the text.** Multiple opportunities are provided to confirm learning as you explore the content.

- **Connect to Your Career** activities take you beyond the classroom. Practical, realistic, interactive applications allow you to apply the concepts you learn to your job search. Activity files are available on the G-W Learning companion website.

- **E-Flash Card Activities** include each career-related term presented in the text. They are available on the G-W Learning companion website as well as the G-W Learning mobile site. Use the e-flash cards to reinforce what you learned and allow you to study on the go.

- **Review Your Knowledge** questions highlight basic concepts presented in the chapter so you can evaluate your understanding of the material.

- **Apply Your Knowledge** activities challenge you to integrate what you learned in the chapter with your own experiences and goals.

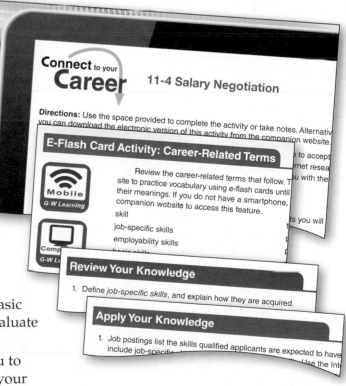

**Connect to your Career**    11-4 Salary Negotiation

**Directions:** Use the space provided to complete the activity or take notes. Alternativ... you can download the electronic version of this activity from the companion website.

**E-Flash Card Activity: Career-Related Terms**

Mobile
G-W Learning

Review the career-related terms that follow. T... site to practice vocabulary using e-flash cards until their meanings. If you do not have a smartphone, companion website to access this feature.

skill

job-specific skills

employability skills

**Review Your Knowledge**

1. Define *job-specific skills*, and explain how they are acquired.

**Apply Your Knowledge**

1. Job postings list the skills qualified applicants are expected to have include job-specific...

# Take Your Learning Online

**Technology is an important part of your everyday life.** The following technology-based resources and activities are available to support your learning and career-search process.

## G-W Learning Companion Website

The G-W Learning companion website for *Connect to Your Career* is a study reference that contains e-flash cards, matching activities, vocabulary games, and *Connect to Your Career* activity files.

G-W Learning companion website:

www.g-wlearning.com/careereducation/

## G-W Learning Mobile Site

The G-W Learning mobile site* is a study reference to use when you are on the go. The mobile site is easy to read, easy to use, and fine-tuned for quick access. E-flash cards and vocabulary games are available on this site. The content on the mobile site can also be accessed through the G-W Learning companion website.

G-W Learning mobile site:

www.m.g-wlearning.com

*Note: data rates may apply. Features accessed on the mobile site can be accessed without a smartphone via the G-W Learning companion website.

## G-W Online
## Engage. Apply. Succeed.

**Our collaborative learning environment is built for the way you study and communicate today.** G-W Online offers web-based instruction for purchase that supports the text and brings the content alive. An interactive online textbook, as well as reinforcement activities and assessment opportunities, provide independent learning that fits your personal style. Ask your instructor for more information.

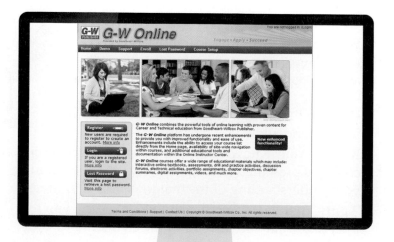

# Unit 1
# Preparing for Your Career

## Connecting to Your Career

### Why It Matters

The landscape for finding a job in the 21st century has experienced a change. Jobs are harder to find. There are fewer jobs available, and the competition is fierce. The Internet drives the job-search process as well as the application process. Savvy career seekers use the Internet as a strategic tool to reach an employment goal.

The first step in your career-search journey is to create your online presence. How will potential employers see you? Your online presence can help or harm your job-search process. While you perfect your online presence, you also must learn to protect your identity. There are hackers that want to steal your personal information. Once you have learned how to protect your identity, you are ready to make the most of your networking opportunities and connect to your career.

## Chapter 1

# Online Presence

## Outcomes

- **Discuss** how job seekers can create a positive online presence.
- **Create** a professional e-mail account.
- **Create** a LinkedIn account.
- **Create** a Twitter account.
- **Define** the purpose of a portfolio.
- **Explain** the importance of positive thinking.

## Career-Related Terms

| | |
|---|---|
| online presence | connection |
| secure password | microblog |
| career account profile | follower |
| networking | hashtag |
| freemium | portfolio |
| search engine optimization (SEO) | electronic portfolio |
| | self-talk |

You will see icons at various points throughout the chapter. These icons indicate that interactive activities are available on the *Connect to Your Career* companion website. Selected activities are also available on the *Connect to Your Career* mobile site. These activities will help you learn, practice, and expand your career knowledge and skills.

 Companion Website
www.g-wlearning.com/careereducation/

 Mobile Site
www.m.g-wlearning.com

# Overview

Think about it. The average person spends 30 percent of his or her time each day at work. Finding the career that will make you satisfied with your work life is probably at the top of your list of priorities. The first step in the career-search process starts with your online presence.

People learn many things on the Internet—current events, news, weather, social issues, and much more. Potential employers will explore the Internet to see what they can find about you. Although your name might not be the subject of millions of search engine trends, your name and the online results that it returns are important considerations during your job search.  An online presence can help to inform professionals in your field about your skills, qualifications, and talents. How will you stack up against other candidates?

# Creating Your Online Presence

Finding a career that is right for you can be an overwhelming task. You spend most of your waking hours working, so choosing a career is not to be taken lightly. A career is a lifelong pursuit. During your working years, you will more than likely change careers multiple times.

One of the first steps in the job-search process is to evaluate your online presence. An **online presence** is what the public can learn about a person from viewing his or her Internet activities. In today's workforce, your online presence can influence your success in the career-search process. Hiring managers often conduct independent research on job applicants to determine if the interview process should move forward.

Most people retain Facebook, Twitter, and Pinterest accounts to socialize and maintain relationships with friends and family. These are important aspects of online communication. However, since the Internet can reveal private communications to unwanted parties, a potential employer may be able to view private exchanges without your knowledge or consent just as anyone else could. Be aware of what you are posting on social websites, as these activities might appear when a search is conducted for your name.

For any personal social account that you have, change your privacy settings so that potential employers, or the public, cannot view pictures of your friends and family. Customize your privacy settings so only those whom you designate can visit your pages. However, remember that any photos or comments you post are potentially public and will never disappear. Do not post any photo or comment that would embarrass you if a potential employer lands on your page. Once information is posted on the Internet, you cannot hide or delete it.

Potential employers will enter your name in a search engine to see what your online presence reveals about you. This search will show if your online presence is positive, negative, nonexistent, or shared with someone else with the same name. Figure 1-1 shows each type of online presence.

A positive online presence can lead to employment opportunities. This occurs when a hiring manager enters your name into a search engine and discovers results such as links to well-written articles, a professional portfolio, and memberships to business networking sites. As a result, his or her impression of you can be positively influenced, even before an interview.

However, if a hiring manager enters your name into a search engine and begins to read negative press, his or her impression of you can change quickly. A negative online presence can harm your professional reputation and minimize your chances for potential job interviews. If you

| Types of Online Presence | |
| --- | --- |
| Positive | Search engine results reflect your professional accomplishments. |
| Negative | Search engine results reflect activities that negatively impact your chances of getting hired. |
| Nonexistent | A search engine returns no results that match your name. |
| Shared | Search engine results are an exact match to your name; however, the results are not about you, but about someone with your same name. |

Goodheart-Willcox Publisher

**Figure 1-1** The goal is to have a positive, professional online presence.

conduct an Internet search of your name, and the results are anything but positive, consider what you can do to reflect a more positive image.

You might think that searching for your name in a search engine where no results are returned is acceptable. Yet a nonexistent online presence denotes lack of technology skills, abilities, or lack of motivation or proactive thinking.

There are occasions when you may share the same name as another person. If this occurs, you will want to examine the results. If possible, think of how to differentiate your name in your online accounts by using a middle initial, for example. This way you have a unique online presence when someone conducts an Internet search for your name.

# Professional E-mail Account

Before you begin the career-exploration process, create a professional e-mail account. It is best to keep your personal and professional activities separate. Businesses use e-mail to communicate available jobs and to schedule interviews with job candidates. A separate e-mail account will enable you to manage communication for the job-search process and other professional business.

Examples of e-mail addresses are shown in Figure 1-2. How might an employer perceive applicants with these e-mail addresses? What would each of the e-mail accounts reflect about potential job candidates?

An e-mail address is a reflection of the owner of the e-mail account. For that reason, use your formal name for a professional e-mail account. Recruiters and human resource departments may sort job applicants by names that appear in the e-mail address. This is especially important for any follow-up contact an employer may have with a candidate. The employer expects to see an e-mail contact by name, not an unprofessional e-mail address.

To create your professional e-mail account, investigate free e-mail accounts with a provider whose name presents a more professional or business-like tone. For example, Yahoo offers

| Sample E-mail Addresses | |
| --- | --- |
| **Personal E-mail Address** | **Professional E-mail Address** |
| hockeystar@gmail.com | kevin.jones@ymail.com |
| sassy55555@yahoo.com | carol_smith@gmail.com |
| totallyrockin_thehouse@yahoo.com | jdouglas@rocketmail.com |

Goodheart-Willcox Publisher

**Figure 1-2** A professional e-mail account should be created to keep your business life separate from your social life.

## 1-1 Online Presence

**Directions:** Use the space provided to complete the activity or take notes. Alternatively, you can download the electronic version of this activity from the companion website.

1. Enter your name in the following search engines: Google, Bing, Ixquick, Dogpile, and Spokeo. Did you find multiple people with your name? If so, try entering your name and city to narrow the results.

2. What entries were displayed when you entered your name? Record the top four entries for each search engine.

3. Search engines do not always display the same results. Compare and contrast your findings from each search engine. What information is the same from one search engine to the next? What information is different?

4. An interviewer will attempt to visit profiles of job seekers to find information. Is there anything that you should change on those sites before the interviewing process begins?

Download the electronic version of this activity.

alternatives to @yahoo.com. You can select either @ymail or @rocketmail. Consider using your first name and last name separated by a period. If your name or a variation of it is not available from the selected provider, try using your first initial and last name or other combinations that reflect your legal name. If all combinations fail, consider switching providers. For example, if you do not find the name you prefer from Gmail, try opening a Yahoo e-mail account instead.

## Secure Password

You will need to create a secure password for your e-mail account. A **secure password** is a code used to access a private account or other private information, such as an e-mail account or computer network. Unauthorized users should not be able to easily identify or guess your password. You should not share your password with others. A password should be between 6 and 20 characters long and should be a combination of letters, numbers, and special characters. The safest password combinations are those that you create and that are unpredictable.

Consider the password strategies and examples in Figure 1-3.

Less secure, predictable passwords often contain the following data:

- common words
- birthday or anniversary date
- address
- favorite numbers
- repeated numbers or numbers in a sequence

After you create your professional e-mail account and establish a password, you are ready to create an account profile.

## Account Profile

When you set up a professional e-mail account, you may be prompted to complete a profile. A **career account profile** is information that describes who a person is in his or her professional life. Potential employers will use this information to learn more about you. Your professional online presence should reflect career activities that are separate from your family, friends, and social connections.

| Password Strategy 1 | |
|---|---|
| Start with a memorable sentence. | I will exercise more. |
| Remove the spaces and punctuation. | Iwillexercisemore |
| Capitalize or lowercase an unexpected letter. | iwilleXercisemore |
| Create a memorable, unique misspelling. | iwilXercisemor |
| Add numbers and symbols. | #iwilXercisemor2 |

| Password Strategy 2 | |
|---|---|
| Start with a memorable sentence. | My brother was accepted to Stanford University in 2013. |
| Use only the first letter of each word in the sentence. | M b w a t S U i 2013 |
| Remove the spaces and punctuation. | MbwatSUi2013 |
| Capitalize or lowercase unexpected letters. | mBwatSUi2013 |
| Add a symbol. | #mBwatSUi2013 |

Goodheart-Willcox Publisher

**Figure 1-3** These strategies can help you create a secure password.

Your profile will allow you to display a work-appropriate photograph. If you do not have a professional photograph, have a friend or family member take one that you can use temporarily. When taking the photo, remember these important tips.

- Dress appropriately to present a professional appearance.
- Have the photo taken from the shoulders to the top of your head. This type of photo is referred to as a *headshot*.
- Be aware of what is displayed behind you when you have your picture taken so that nothing detracts from your face.
- Avoid busy patterns in your attire and in the background.
- Smile showing your teeth.

After you upload your photo, the next step is to create a signature block. All e-mail accounts have a field for you to add a *professional signature block*. This feature automatically adds your signature each time you create a new e-mail or respond to a previous e-mail. Include your full name, phone number, and e-mail address in a readable size and font. It is important to make it as easy as possible for a potential employer to contact you. You may also include a job title under your name. If you do not have a permanent position, you can designate a job title that describes your skills, such as *Instructional Design Consultant,* until you find a permanent position. Figure 1-4 shows examples of professional signature blocks.

Have you ever created an account on a social networking site but did not complete your profile? For your professional e-mail account, be sure to complete your profile. A profile is a living

**The Best App** for that

*App* is the abbreviation for *application.* An app is a software program designed for one specific function. Some apps are free, while others have a nominal charge. Mobile apps can be loaded to a device such as a smartphone or a tablet computer. Download the free app for *LinkedIn* and *Twitter.*

document that you will need to update often, but an incomplete profile might give an employer the impression that you do not finish what you start.

# LinkedIn

Networking plays an important role in the career-search process. **Networking** is talking with people and establishing relationships that can lead to career growth or potential job opportunities. In order to build and expand your professional network, it is essential to create business profiles online. This is the beginning of the networking process.

LinkedIn is a professional networking site that provides static communication with professionals and is limited to closed groups and individual contacts. This professional networking site is used by more than 200 million people in the workforce for purposes of making new contacts and building business relationships. LinkedIn offers users space for posting and finding jobs that might not be advertised publicly.

LinkedIn's basic account type is a **freemium** model, which means users may utilize basic services without paying. For additional services and features, users can opt to purchase upgrades.

---

**Sample Signature Blocks**

| | |
|---|---|
| Shelley Jones | Rakesh Singh |
| Junior Accountant | Project Manager |
| (212) 555–1234 | (623) 555–4023 |
| sjones@email.com | rsingh@email.com |

Goodheart-Willcox Publisher

**Figure 1-4** Your professional signature block should be concise and complete.

# 1-2 Professional E-Mail Account

**Directions:** Use the space provided to complete the activity or take notes. Alternatively, you can download the electronic version of this activity from the companion website.

1.  If you have not already done so, create a professional e-mail account. Write down your new e-mail address.

2.  Complete your account by providing information for all of the required fields. Make certain the account profile is 100 percent complete.

3.  Since many users never read the user terms of agreement, they do not realize that e-mail is owned by the host company. Potentially, the e-mail provider has access to read or track communication sent and received without the user's permission. Do you think this is a violation of privacy? Explain why or why not.

4.  Add the URL for your e-mail provider to your favorites or bookmark it in your browser.

Download the electronic version of this activity.

There are several upgrade plans from which to select. When first joining LinkedIn, use the freemium model. As your career advances, you might wish to upgrade your account to utilize the premium features.

## Create an Account

In order to use LinkedIn, you need to create an account. To do this, navigate to www.LinkedIn.com in your browser. Provide your first and last name, professional e-mail address, and a password. Click the Join now button. LinkedIn will send a notification to the e-mail address you provided. Confirm that you received the e-mail by clicking the link inside the body of the received e-mail. That link will return you to the LinkedIn website. It is at this point that you can begin to populate your newly created account.

## Create a Profile

After you create an account, you will complete a profile similar to the one you created for your professional e-mail account. Your LinkedIn profile is a web page where you will describe your career history, education, and skills. As you complete your profile, LinkedIn will track your progress. Be diligent and make sure your profile is 100 percent complete.

The advantage of creating a profile on LinkedIn is that the site does the advertising for you through search engine optimization. **Search engine optimization (SEO)** is the process of indexing a website so it will rank higher on the list of returned results when a search is conducted. For example, large corporations are masters at making sure their websites are displayed at the top of a search results list. Because of LinkedIn's SEO, when a person searches your name, he or she will find your LinkedIn profile either at or near the top of the search results list.

When you create your profile, you will notice that LinkedIn creates a URL address, or link, for your account. You will have a chance to customize the link if you do not prefer the default provided for you. Once you have a LinkedIn URL, add it to your e-mail signature block for your professional e-mail account and your résumé.

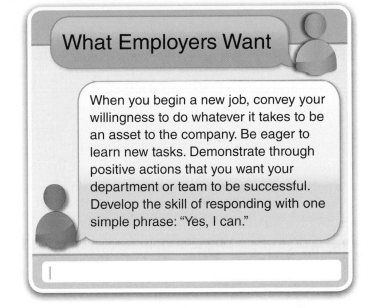

What Employers Want

When you begin a new job, convey your willingness to do whatever it takes to be an asset to the company. Be eager to learn new tasks. Demonstrate through positive actions that you want your department or team to be successful. Develop the skill of responding with one simple phrase: "Yes, I can."

### Headline

LinkedIn provides a space directly under your name for your professional headline. The headline includes four parts: your full name, your title, your geographic location, and your industry. After you have input your name, create the title portion of the headline. This is the opportunity to position yourself as you want others to see you. If you have a job, it is appropriate to use your current title and name of your employer, such as *Personal Banker at Southwest Mutual and Savings Bank*. If you do not have a permanent position, you can designate a job title that describes your skills, just as you did in your e-mail signature block. Think of the most convincing, succinct description of yourself that you would want an employer to read. Some examples of titles are as follows:

- Experienced Accountant
- Hotel Concierge
- Medical Assistant
- Personal Banker

As you begin completing the headline, LinkedIn will offer suggestions for pertinent words that might help you to frame your ideas.

Next, add your geographic area and your industry. This information helps employers who are searching for local candidates in a specific geographic location. Finally, add a professional photo, such as the headshot you used for your professional e-mail account.

## Activity

The Activity section is for you to update potential employers and your network regarding your professional pursuits. The updates are unlike Facebook or other social sites where it is acceptable to express emotions or your view on the day's activities. Use LinkedIn status updates to promote yourself in your professional life. Some examples of appropriate LinkedIn status updates include your activity on the site, such as becoming a member of a group or sharing a link to a news article relevant to your industry.

## Background and Experience

You will add your education, skills, specialties, contact information, certain work samples, and links to your blog, e-portfolio, or website. Add your academic courses, work experience, and professional activities, such as if you are building a new website. Avoid using vague words such as "smart" or "energetic" for your LinkedIn descriptors. Use only concrete words that will help market your talents. Remember, your writing style matters. Your work must be free of errors. Pay special attention to grammar, spelling, and punctuation. If potential employers or recruiters view a profile riddled with errors, they will move on to the next candidate.

Detail your work experience, even if the experience was a volunteer position. Provide information about the types of work that help the employer see you as a preferred job candidate. Create a notable series of statements that keep people reading about you.

Next, add specialties. The Specialties area of LinkedIn lists skills and job categories. Your connections will be able to *endorse*, or verify, that you have the skills listed. Many LinkedIn members who write blogs link to the blog in their profile. Those who view the profile are able to link to the blog directly from LinkedIn.

## Connections

The purpose of creating a profile is to share who you are as a professional. The best way to accomplish this is to make connections. **Connections** are people in an individual's network who are added only by invitation. People who are your connections agree to share their network with you.

The way to make a connection is to send an invitation. You can search for a person you know on LinkedIn. Once you see his or her profile, click the Connect button to send an invitation. On the full website, a window will open containing standard text inviting the person to connect. This is your chance to read the invitation and make changes to it before sending.

People who are your connections can view your entire profile without limits. People who are not your connections have a limited view of your profile. Therefore, it is advantageous to gain as many connections as possible. However, LinkedIn discourages spamming or sending invitations to total strangers. Members have the option to report unwarranted invitations to connect.

Connections are categorized as first, second, or third degree.

- A first-degree connection is a direct connection, mutually agreed upon by you and another member. You are able to view the entire profile of someone who is your first-degree connection, and he or she can see your entire profile.

- A second-degree connection means you are not directly connected to the other member, but you have a first-degree connection in common. You have a limited view of the profiles of your second-degree connections. You can connect with these users by clicking the Connect button.

- A third-degree connection is someone who is connected to one of your second-degree connections. You have a limited view of the profiles of your third-degree connections.

No connection means that LinkedIn did not detect any association from your profile, work experience, or education that you have in common with the other member.

Another way to communicate with other members is via messages from your LinkedIn inbox. Your *LinkedIn inbox* is your LinkedIn e-mail that will permit private communications with any member, even those with whom you are not connected. As you become familiar with your profile, look for your e-mail inbox. You have the ability to e-mail other connections within the system through your inbox.

## Groups

Once you complete your profile, you can join a variety of groups. Groups may be an *open group*, which means users do not have to be a member to read discussions. Other groups are *closed groups*, meaning you must ask for permission to join. An administrator of the group will receive your request to join and then view your profile. You will receive a notification if you gain permission to be involved.

Like other online groups, LinkedIn provides group members with a way to connect and sometimes share information with other members. You can build your LinkedIn connections by joining groups and contributing to discussions. Some groups are for exchanging information, while others are for recruiters hiring employees. Once you join groups on LinkedIn, you may send invitations to connect to others in the same group without being considered a spammer. One of the first groups to join, especially when unemployed, is a job seekers group. Select a group that is appropriate for you.

# Twitter

Twitter is a free, open networking site for professionals and nonprofessionals who communicate in real time. The purpose of networking on Twitter is to follow available job posts, as well as people's ideas, stories, opinions, and information. Twitter is a place where employers post jobs and job searchers visit to find employment opportunities.

Twitter communication is faster than e-mail. Twitter communication is considered micro-blogging. A **microblog** is short communication limited to a certain number of characters per post. When using Twitter, communication is referred to as a *Tweet*. Tweets are limited to 140 characters each. However, Twitter does not limit how often a user produces Tweets.

## Create an Account

To join Twitter, you must sign up for an account by navigating to www.Twitter.com. Locate the New to Twitter box and follow the instructions. Provide your full name, professional e-mail address, and a secure password. Click the Sign up for Twitter button. Similar to other accounts you have created, you will receive an e-mail confirmation. Click the link inside the body of the e-mail. The e-mail will confirm your Twitter account.

After you sign up, you can choose to see people you know who have already joined Twitter. If you choose to do this, provide your e-mail contact list to connect with people in your professional network.

### User Name

The three most prominent features others will see about you are your user name, your picture, and your profile. Users have the option of creating a unique Twitter name or using their e-mail address as their name. Create your Twitter name in a professional manner so recruiters can follow you. Although you are limited in characters, you have creative license when choosing a user name. Twitter user names are unique in that they feature the @ symbol as a prefix. On Twitter, brevity is essential. Consider the following examples:

- name with profession: @BobbyCrossWriter
- name with professional designation, such as *MBA*: @CrandallJonesMBA
- name with general location, such as *NYC*: @AmyMackNYC

### Bio

Twitter also provides a space for profile information. This information is referred to as a *bio*, short for biography. Write your bio providing a professional description of yourself. Your Twitter bio is limited to 160 characters. Next, upload your headshot as your photo.

## 1-3 LinkedIn Account

**Directions:** Use the space provided to complete the activity or take notes. Alternatively, you can download the electronic version of this activity from the companion website.

1. If you have not already done so, create a LinkedIn account by completing the "Getting Started" information.

2. Read the Terms of Agreement. What did you learn?

3. Complete a LinkedIn headline, including your full name, title, location, and industry. If you do not have a permanent position, write a title that succinctly describes your skills.

4. Complete the other sections of the profile. Review your account profile. Make certain it is 100 percent complete.

5. LinkedIn automatically creates a URL for your profile. Customize the link to fit your needs.

Download the electronic version of this activity.

## Followers

When using LinkedIn, you have connections. When using Twitter, you have followers who read your Tweets. **Followers** are Twitter members who view another user's Tweets in their own Twitter feed. When public profiles are used, you can follow anyone. At the same time, anyone can follow you without exchanging invitations. However, if desired, users may "block" a person. A private profile will allow you to approve follower requests. If you want to follow someone who has a private profile, you will have to send the user a follower request and wait for it to be approved.

You will want to gain followers and hold a professional audience through your Tweets. There are no advertisers allowed to promote or market items on the site directly. However, some individuals use Twitter to promote products and services via links. Users can Tweet using links that direct others to their professional portfolio and more information.

With the limited number of characters for each Tweet, users incorporate links to their blogs or websites by reducing the length of long links using URL shortening services, such as TinyURL. These services create shortened versions of long

# Career Portfolio

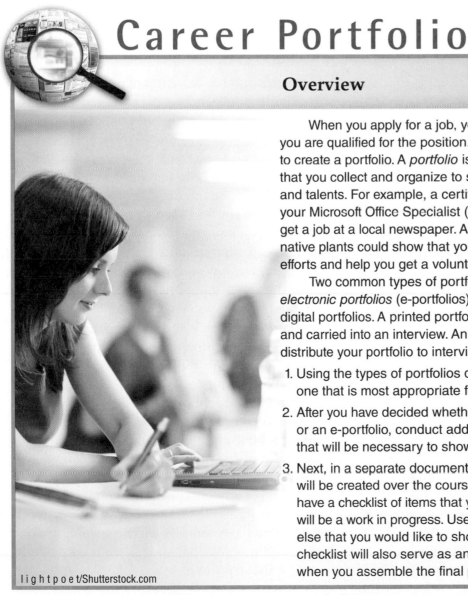

## Overview

When you apply for a job, you will need to show others how you are qualified for the position. In order to do this, you will need to create a portfolio. A *portfolio* is a selection of related materials that you collect and organize to show your job qualifications, skills, and talents. For example, a certificate showing you have completed your Microsoft Office Specialist (MOS) certification could help you get a job at a local newspaper. An essay you wrote about protecting native plants could show that you are serious about eco-friendly efforts and help you get a volunteer position at a park.

Two common types of portfolios are *printed portfolios* and *electronic portfolios* (e-portfolios). E-portfolios are sometimes called digital portfolios. A printed portfolio is placed in a binder or folder and carried into an interview. An e-portfolio is used to electronically distribute your portfolio to interviewers and hiring managers.

1. Using the types of portfolios described in Figure 1-5, select the one that is most appropriate for you.

2. After you have decided whether you will create a printed portfolio or an e-portfolio, conduct additional research on components that will be necessary to show your best qualifications.

3. Next, in a separate document, create a checklist. As this portfolio will be created over the course of this class, it will be helpful to have a checklist of items that you intend to include. This checklist will be a work in progress. Use it each time you think of something else that you would like to show a potential employer. This checklist will also serve as an outline for your table of contents when you assemble the final product.

lightpoet/Shutterstock.com

URLs for free. Using a shortened URL will help you direct followers to your blog or website and still have room to add a message. Twitter makes use of shortened URLs by automatically shortening URLs that are copied and pasted into a Tweet.

## Activity

Twitter accounts are similar to other social networking accounts. Have one for your social communication and a separate one for professional use. Keep your activity professional, and do not be tempted to Tweet about what you did on Friday night if it is not job related. You want to create Tweets that make people want to follow you. To build a professional following, read and comment about an article that you read, a project you are directing, or a course that you have completed. Brand yourself on Twitter as a proactive leader. Tweet frequently and focus on your intended audience.

Learn and use consistent hashtags. **Hashtags** are searchable keywords on Twitter that link users to all Tweets marked with the same hashtag keyword. Use hashtags anywhere in your Tweet—at the beginning, middle, or end. To make a word a hashtag, add the pound symbol (#) immediately before the word with no space between the symbol and the word. To make multiple words into a hashtag, precede it with the pound symbol and remove spaces between the words. Some examples of hashtags include the following:

- #hireme
- #greenjobs
- #careers
- #careermanagement
- #consultingjobs
- #ITjobs
- #jobpostings

When you begin to use Tweets to dialogue with followers, address them by using the @ symbol. For example, if you are engaged in several online conversations but want to respond only to Marie, begin the Tweet with @Marie. This convention is only appropriate when communicating on Twitter. In your formal employment searches, when you use e-mail, cover letters, or LinkedIn, remember to begin communication with a formal greeting and omit the @ symbol.

Twitter outpaces online job search sites with more than half a million Tweets each month for job listings alone. You can conduct searches for Tweeted available jobs on Twitter by using the hashtag #jobpostings. Twitter has become a popular way to network for jobs through companion sites as well. Websites, such as Tweetmyjobs.com, obtain available job listings from thousands of employers each day. There are aggregator job-posting sites, such as Twitterjobsearch.com, that combine Tweets and job announcements in one place and stores them in a searchable database.

# Portfolio

A **portfolio** is a selection of related materials an individual collects and organizes to show his or her qualifications, skills, and talents. As you begin establishing your online presence, it is a good idea to also start creating a portfolio. When you apply for a job, you will need to tell others about how you are qualified for the position. Showcasing examples of work you have completed or awards you have received is one way to communicate your qualifications.

Collect and save all documentation that demonstrates your accomplishments. Gather evidence for what you have accomplished during your work experience and during your academic career. Collect documentation from previous employers, concentrating on achievement certificates, recommendation letters, and other documents. Find school assignments, papers, or exams on which you scored well. Document work or school situations demonstrating your spoken or written proficiency in other languages. Include any publications you have written, and create a list of any organizations you have joined. In addition, gather evidence of academic or work projects you have completed. These items are perfect testimonials that strengthen your position as a potential employee.

## 1-4 Twitter Account

**Directions:** Use the space provided to complete the activity or take notes. Alternatively, you can download the electronic version of this activity from the companion website.

1. If you have not already done so, create a Twitter account by completing the "Sign Up for Twitter" steps.

2. Read the Terms of Service. What did you learn?

3. What user name did you select for your professional Twitter account? Write your user name here.

4. Complete the bio section for your Twitter account. Be sure your bio is a description that you want professionals to see.

5. What will you Tweet about to look for employment? What hashtags do you plan to use?

Download the electronic version of this activity.

Select documents that position you as a great candidate for a potential job. Examples of information to include are:

- honors and awards
- outstanding test scores
- courses related to your desired job or career
- certifications and diplomas
- volunteer work
- internships
- causes where you have active involvement
- patents
- leadership positions in organizations or jobs

You will also add a résumé, a list of references, and letters of recommendation. The items in your portfolio are not limited to this list. You may include any information that will illustrate why you are qualified for the position for which you are applying.

Organize all of your documentation using folders. You might find that you have a variety of documentation, both paper and electronic. It is suggested to use physical folders for your hard-copy documents as well as electronic folders on your computer for your electronic documents.

The two common types of portfolio publishing formats are hard copy and electronic. For hard-copy portfolios, the creator hand-carries the portfolio to job interviews to provide potential employers a chance to review pertinent work samples. Hard-copy portfolios are effective for original certificates, achievement awards, grade transcripts, and résumés.

An **electronic portfolio** contains data and content in analog form, such as video. Also known as *digital portfolios*, they contain data in computer-readable form. You may use a flash drive or CD that you leave behind with the interviewer, or you may use a hosting service. Some websites offer online portfolio-hosting services, some of which are free and others for which there is charge. Or, you may choose to create your own web page to post your portfolio. Through just one link, a potential employer has the opportunity to spend time looking through portfolio contents as desired.

Some common tools used to create an electronic portfolio are Microsoft Word, Microsoft PowerPoint, YouTube, or WordPress. It is a best practice to develop your portfolio using familiar software, rather than spend time learning a new program. Developing a portfolio is an ongoing process, so do not worry if you are uncertain about what to add. In most cases, people have more information and documentation than they realize. The goal is to keep it simple and relevant. Portfolios that are cluttered with too much data are often ignored.

An electronic portfolio has several advantages over a hard-copy portfolio. Electronic portfolios:

- provide unlimited space for documentation
- can be viewed any time
- can be updated or edited quickly and efficiently
- demonstrate technology skills

Types of professional portfolios vary, as shown in Figure 1-5. For example, if you are interested in pursuing work as a photographer, you will want a portfolio to display your photography skills. If your potential career involves writing, then much of your portfolio will highlight your written work. Select the type of portfolio you prefer to create to match your career goals.

# Positive Thinking

You have officially started the career-search process! Creating a professional e-mail account, professional networking accounts, and a portfolio are just the beginning. Approach connecting to a career as an adventure you cannot wait to start. It is up to you to make the adventure a pleasant one. The first step is to determine that the experience of creating a plan, gathering documentation, and completing all of the necessary steps to get in front of a hiring employer are doable. Remember that you are your own boss at this present moment. Would you want to work for you?

The way you approach the career-search process reveals who you are as a potential employee. This means you must finish what you start. Finish each lesson, each question, and

## Types of Portfolios

| Portfolio Type | Potential Uses |
|---|---|
| Showcase | Document high grades, awards, achievements, and milestones, as well as photography, video captures for musical performances, and public speaking |
| Process | Display progressive growth in academic skills highlighted with reflection pieces, such as original blogs, articles, or commentaries |
| Documentation | Demonstrate sustained academic success or work performance accomplishments |
| Hybrid | Display a combination of showcase, process, and documentation portfolios and include feedback from professional third-parties |
| Dossier | Exhibit an instructor's preparedness and effectiveness in the classroom, also referred to as a *teaching portfolio* |
| Professional | Display specifically work-related accomplishments, company workshops, or training programs completed successfully, along with valuable skills used on the job |

Goodheart-Willcox Publisher

**Figure 1-5** Consider your career goals as you decide which type of portfolio to use.

take the time to explore additional resources and links provided in this text. Do your best work, not mediocre work, or work just to turn in to an instructor. Work for you as your own boss. You will accomplish exactly what you decide to accomplish.

Be positive during the job-searching journey. Concentrate on your great qualities, which other candidates might not have. You are the right person for the job. Some common positive thoughts that you should focus on during the job search are as follows.

- I have capabilities that other candidates do not.
- I am a self starter.
- I demonstrate critical thinking skills.
- I have great judgment skills.
- I have awesome people skills.
- I can do this job.
- I will be able to find the work that I enjoy.
- Any employer would like me.
- Multiple employers would want to hire me.

Searching for a job can be a tedious process. Not every attempt will lead to an interview or job offer, but you should continue to be optimistic. Negative experiences can lead to negative thoughts.

If this occurs during the job-search process, manage your emotions carefully. Examples of some common negative thoughts include the following.

- I do not know what I want to do for a living, so I should not do anything just yet.
- I do not want to gather documentation.
- Many college graduates cannot find jobs; I will not either.
- School is a waste of time.
- Who would hire me?
- What if I am required to dress up for work when I hate dressing up?
- What if an employer finds out I was fired at a previous job?
- What if a new boss does not like me?

**Self-talk** is internal thoughts and feelings about one's self. Negative self-talk messages sometimes invade the thoughts of job candidates. In order to change negative self-talk to positive, start believing that an employer would like to have you as an employee.

Do you see how your thoughts affect your job-search performance? As you work on the steps necessary to obtain employment, practice positive self-talk.

# 1-5 Positive Thinking

**Directions:** Use the space provided to complete the activity or take notes. Alternatively, you can download the electronic version of this activity from the companion website.

1. Freewriting is an activity in which you write down thoughts and ideas without stopping. Consider thoughts you might have as you enter the career-search process. Freewrite about yourself as a job candidate for three minutes. Write down positive thoughts as you practice self talk. Note only positive qualities.

2. Next, write down the negative thoughts that might cross your mind as you begin the job-search process.

Download the electronic
version of this activity.

# Chapter Summary

- It is important to establish a positive online presence. Online presence is what the public can learn about you from viewing your Internet activities. Potential employers will enter your name in a search engine to see what your online presence reveals about you. This search will show if your online presence is positive, negative, nonexistent, or shared with someone else with the same name.

- Create a professional e-mail account to use for the job-search process. Keep your personal and professional activities separate. When creating an e-mail account, use your first and last name so that your name appears in the e-mail address. This helps recruiters recognize you when sorting through applicants. It is important to complete the career profile to project your professionalism.

- LinkedIn is a professional networking site that provides static communication with professionals. LinkedIn offers users space for posting and finding jobs that might not be advertised publicly.

- Twitter is a free, open site of professionals and nonprofessionals who communicate in real time. Twitter is a microblog site; microblogs are short communications limited number to a certain number of characters per post.

- A professional portfolio will showcase your qualifications, skills, and talents to potential employers. Collect and save documentation that demonstrates your accomplishments. Portfolios can be in hard copy or electronic format.

- The way you approach your career search reveals who you are as a potential employee. Staying positive is crucial to your success. Tell yourself that you are the right person for the job and that you will achieve your goals. Practice positive self-talk frequently to encourage yourself.

## E-Flash Card Activity: Career-Related Terms

Review the career-related terms that follow. Then visit the G-W mobile site to practice vocabulary using e-flash cards until you are able to recognize their meanings. If you do not have a smartphone, visit the G-W Learning companion website to access this feature.

| | |
|---|---|
| online presence | connection |
| secure password | microblog |
| career account profile | follower |
| networking | hashtag |
| freemium | portfolio |
| search engine optimization (SEO) | electronic portfolio |
| | self-talk |

## Review Your Knowledge

1. Explain the importance of a professional online presence.

2. Describe the process of setting up a professional e-mail account.

3. Define *networking*.

4. Describe the process of setting up a LinkedIn account.

5. Explain the importance of making connections on LinkedIn.

6. Explain how LinkedIn advertises for people who create an account.

7. Describe the process of setting up a Twitter account.

8. How can Twitter help in the job-search process?

9. Describe the purpose of a portfolio and the different types that are used by those applying for jobs.

10.  Define self-talk, and explain how you can change negative self-talk into positive self-talk.

## Apply Your Knowledge

1.  When considering you for a job, do you think it is appropriate for a potential employer to take into account what he or she reads about you online? Why or why not?

2.  List each of your social media accounts. Record the purpose and audience for each.

3.  How will you change the privacy settings of the social media accounts you have to communicate with friends and family? Even with these changes to your privacy settings, what would you change about what you post on social media sites?

4.  What are some of the ways you might change your current online presence to make a favorable impression on a potential employer?

5.  What elements did you add when you created a signature block for your e-mail account? Does your new signature block strengthen you as a job candidate?

6.  Search for jobs in your field using LinkedIn. Notice that some of the same words are used in job posts from different employers. List ten of these repeated words.

7.  After searching other LinkedIn profiles, what ideas did you gain for your own profile?

8. In the future, you will have a chance to develop online media to add to your LinkedIn profile. What would be appropriate for you to develop and add to your profile?

9. Why would recruiters Tweet about available jobs as opposed to uploading the information to a job board?

10. When you completed the activity on positive and negative thoughts, did you find you had a greater number of positive thoughts or negative thoughts when it comes to finding a job? Why?

## Exploring Certification

### Career Certification Skills—Using Reading Skills

*Career Certification Skills* questions are designed to help you prepare for formal certification test questions. Take your time and decide the best way to approach each activity.

Positive thinking can be a major challenge when you are looking for a job. However, it is one of the most important habits that you can develop. Make it a point to work on positive self-talk as you start your career journey. Reading about positive thinking can be inspirational. You can learn how to focus on the good things, rather than the negative.

1. Conduct an Internet search on positive thinking. List the titles, authors, and URLs for three articles.

2. In order to retain information that you read, it is necessary to focus and read with a purpose. As you read each article, determine the central ideas and review the conclusions made by the author. Summarize who, what, when, and where for each article and record the information for future reference.

## Career Certification Skills—Finding Information

You have taken a summer job as an assistant to a dietician in a doctor's office. A patient is concerned about cold season and wants know how to obtain the greatest amounts of vitamin C and fiber from fruit.

Using this chart, answer the following questions for your patient.

| Fruit | Calories | Vitamin C | Vitamin A | Dietary Fiber | Iron |
|---|---|---|---|---|---|
| | | (% daily values) | | | |
| Apple, 1 medium | 80 | 8 | 2 | 5 | 2 |
| Pineapple, 2 slices | 60 | 25 | 0 | 1 | 2 |
| Kiwi, 2 medium | 100 | 240 | 2 | 4 | 4 |
| Orange, 1 medium | 70 | 130 | 2 | 7 | 2 |
| Watermelon, 2 cups diced | 80 | 25 | 20 | 2 | 4 |

US Food and Drug Administration

1. Which fruit would you recommend as the highest source of vitamin C and highest amount of fiber?

2. Which fruit is the best source of iron, fiber, and vitamin C?

3. Compare and contrast the calories and vitamin C content of the pineapple and the watermelon.

## Career Certification Skills—Applying Math Skills

Imagine that over the past several days, you applied for many jobs each day, as shown in the following chart.

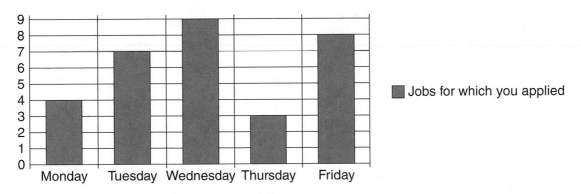

What is the average number of jobs you applied for each day? Select the correct answer. Show your calculations.

A. 7.8

B. 4.9

C. 5.0

D. 6.2

## Chapter 2

# Protecting Your Online Identity

## Outcomes

- **Explain** potential risks when searching for a job online.
- **Describe** how to recognize employment scams and how to report them.
- **List** ways to keep your identity safe when using websites.
- **Define** malware and ways to protect against it.
- **Explain** how to create and maintain a security plan.

## Career-Related Terms

| | |
|---|---|
| identity theft | phishing |
| multi-level marketing (MLM) | malware |
| Internet Protocol address | software virus |
| cookies | spyware |
| | firewall |

You will see icons at various points throughout the chapter. These icons indicate that interactive activities are available on the *Connect to Your Career* companion website. Selected activities are also available on the *Connect to Your Career* mobile site. These activities will help you learn, practice, and expand your career knowledge and skills.

Companion Website
www.g-wlearning.com/careereducation/

Mobile Site
www.m.g-wlearning.com

# Overview

The job-search process, as well as professional networking, can take place almost exclusively online. As you establish your online presence, it is important to know what takes place on the Internet. You must be aware of the ways in which you can prevent your identity from being stolen.

To prevent identity theft, do not provide information to people you do not know. Look out for employment scams, and be aware that simply visiting a website or clicking on a hyperlink can jeopardize your computer and the data that is stored on it. Create a security checklist to protect yourself and your computer—then use it.

## Online Risks

Technology has streamlined the career-search process. Applying for jobs online and networking with others can now be done without leaving your computer. However, it is important to be diligent in protecting your privacy. Do not be lulled into a false sense of security when communicating with others online, especially with those whom you do not know personally. This also applies to submitting information to websites that advertise job opportunities. In addition, avoid opening e-mails that look suspicious.

Your online identity is valuable to you and to criminals, so it should be protected. Many times the goal of an online criminal is to steal your identity. **Identity theft** is an illegal act that involves stealing someone's personal information and using that information to commit theft or fraud. There are many ways that your personal information can be stolen without you knowing it. A lost credit card or driver's license is a common way thieves are able to steal a person's identity. However, as computer technology advances, online identity theft becomes more prevalent. This form of fraud can happen any time you use your computer.

As you apply for positions during your job search, you will be requested to submit personal information via websites. Use common sense when deciding what personal details you share with strangers. Resist the urge to share too much information that could be stolen. Avoid listing a personal address on application forms or e-mail. Instead, provide your professional e-mail address as contact information. If a company requests your Social Security number before you are hired for a job, place all zeros in the spaces provided. You are *not* under obligation to provide this information anywhere online when searching or applying for a job.

If you suspect your identity has been stolen, visit the Federal Trade Commission website at www.idtheft.gov for guidance. Time is of the essence, so if this unfortunate situation happens to you, act immediately.

## Employment Scams

When you begin to apply for jobs online, you will visit many websites that are unfamiliar. While most of the sites will be legitimate, some might be designed to gain personal information for the purposes of compromising your identity. Those who are trying to commit identity theft have mastered the art of creating fake job ads to lure visitors onto their websites.

If you post your résumé on a website, there is a chance you will receive unsolicited e-mails from companies asking you to apply for a job. Research the company to make sure the posting is legitimate before responding.

## 2-1 Identity Theft

**Directions:** Use the space provided to complete the activity or take notes. Alternatively, you can download the electronic version of this activity from the companion website.

1. Identity theft can cause serious, ongoing problems affecting your credit and other areas of your life. If you think your identity has been stolen, there are several steps you should take immediately. Visit the Federal Trade Commission website at www.idtheft.gov. Read the information that pertains to reporting identity theft. Summarize the steps that should be taken if this should happen to you.

2. Next, on the same website, read about victim's rights. Summarize your findings.

3. What computer security steps does the Federal Trade Commission suggest that you take if you are a victim of identity theft?

Download the electronic version of this activity.

# Career Portfolio

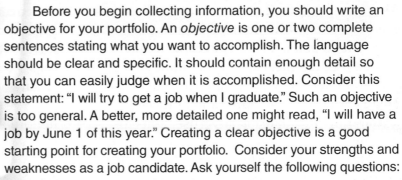

## Objective

Before you begin collecting information, you should write an objective for your portfolio. An *objective* is one or two complete sentences stating what you want to accomplish. The language should be clear and specific. It should contain enough detail so that you can easily judge when it is accomplished. Consider this statement: "I will try to get a job when I graduate." Such an objective is too general. A better, more detailed one might read, "I will have a job by June 1 of this year." Creating a clear objective is a good starting point for creating your portfolio. Consider your strengths and weaknesses as a job candidate. Ask yourself the following questions:

- Who is my audience? What do I want them to know about me?
- What is my message?
- What unique skills or experiences have I had? How can I demonstrate them?

1. Conduct research on the Internet to find articles about writing objectives. Also, look for articles that contain sample objectives for creating a portfolio.
2. Write an objective for creating your portfolio.

arek_malang/Shutterstock.com

## Recognizing Employment Scams

It is easy to become distracted when finding the perfect job advertisement on a website. Before you start submitting personal information, slow down and investigate the site. A legitimate website will list a physical address and additional information about the business. If you are unfamiliar with the organization, search for its name online. Evaluate what you find. Sometimes, conducting a search for the name of the business plus the word "scam" can reveal whether the business is legitimate.

Check the e-mail address for the company. For example, if the ad claims to be from a corporation but the contact e-mail address is a Yahoo address, something is wrong. Companies typically have their own URL that is a part of the e-mail address.

Another way to identify fraudulent employment advertising is to look for misspelled words and grammatical errors in the listings. Reputable companies sometimes make errors, but fraudulent advertisements are known for poorly written content.

One common type of employment fraud happens when criminals create phony employment ads and contact people using information they find online in résumés. After contact has been made with a potential applicant, the applicant is informed that in order to proceed with employment, the company needs to set up a direct deposit account. Unfortunately, many unsuspecting potential employees provide bank or PayPal™ account numbers, convinced they are dealing with a legitimate company. Criminals use many variations in payment-forwarding swindles. Never provide any bank account or payment information in preparation to obtain a job.

Do not send money to a potential employer for any reason. You should not be asked for any form of payment during the application process. A fraudulent company might insist that you pay for a background check or pay fees related to the application process. The request may include asking for a credit card number to cover these fees. Legitimate companies do not charge applicants to apply for a position. An applicant should never pay for an interview or for employment verification steps. Beware of anyone who requests a credit card during an application process.

Carefully evaluate job advertisements to determine whether they are legitimate. A good rule of thumb is "if it is too good to be true, it probably is." Job ads that make grandiose claims are usually not legitimate. Avoid any job posting that advertises making large amounts of money for little work or over a short period of time.

Be on the lookout for multi-level marketing companies. **Multi-level marketing (MLM) is** a business strategy in which employees are compensated for sales they personally generate and for the sales of the other salespeople they recruit. Another term for MLM is *pyramid scheme.* This term is applied because every person in the company has recruited those below him or her. If you are recruited by a representative to work in MLM, he or she will make money off your efforts. MLM companies often look like legitimate companies, but many fall into the category of "too good to be true." They often promise easy money for little work, which is rarely, if ever, true.

## Reporting Employment Scams

If you encounter a suspicious business or website when searching for jobs online, or are unfortunately the victim of a scam operation, report the incident. Reporting the incident helps law enforcement track down scammers and thieves. There are several agencies that are dedicated to the protection of job-seekers from such scams.

The *Internet Crime Complaint Center (IC3)* is a government organization that was established as a means to receive complaints of Internet-based crimes and report the incident of the crime to the appropriate local, state, or federal law enforcement

agency. The IC3 is a partnership between the Federal Bureau of Investigation (FBI) and the National White Collar Crime Center (NWC3).

Another federal organization that handles claims of online scams is the Federal Trade Commission. The *Federal Trade Commission (FTC)* is a government agency that focuses on consumer protection. The FTC addresses complaints regarding identity theft, business practices, work-at-home cons, job scams, and multi-level marketing schemes, among others.

The *Better Business Bureau (BBB)* is a nationwide, nonprofit agency dedicated to providing free business reliability reviews. The BBB gives businesses a rating of A+ through F. If you have suspicions about a company, you can check its rating with the BBB. It is possible that other people have also had negative experiences with the same company in the past. As a result, its rating can reveal whether you should get involved with the company.

## Websites

Each time you access a search engine or visit a web page, your computer's identity is revealed. Your name might not be visible to the public, but the computer's IP address is shown. The **Internet Protocol address,** known as an *IP address,* is a number used to identify an electronic device connected to the Internet. While

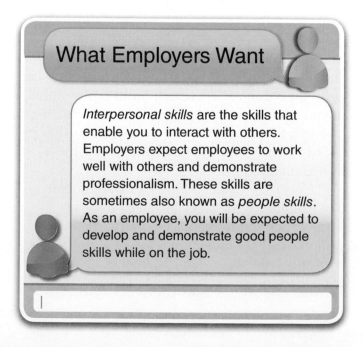

### What Employers Want

*Interpersonal skills* are the skills that enable you to interact with others. Employers expect employees to work well with others and demonstrate professionalism. These skills are sometimes also known as *people skills.* As an employee, you will be expected to develop and demonstrate good people skills while on the job.

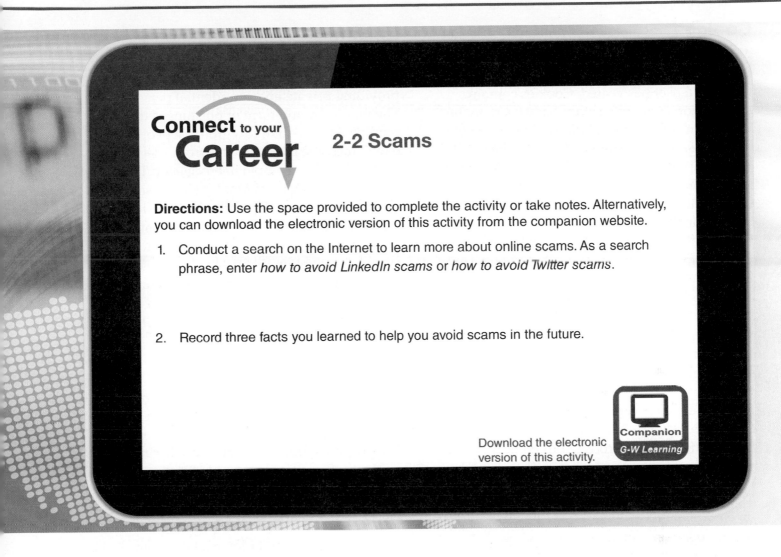

**Connect** to your **Career**

**2-2 Scams**

**Directions:** Use the space provided to complete the activity or take notes. Alternatively, you can download the electronic version of this activity from the companion website.

1. Conduct a search on the Internet to learn more about online scams. As a search phrase, enter *how to avoid LinkedIn scams* or *how to avoid Twitter scams*.

2. Record three facts you learned to help you avoid scams in the future.

Download the electronic version of this activity.

Companion
G-W Learning

your personal information, such as your name and address, cannot be easily discovered, an IP address can reveal your approximate geographic location based on your Internet service provider. Any e-mails you send from your computer or mobile devices have an IP address attached to them, so use caution when doing so.

If you are uploading documents to a website, make sure the site is secure with a URL that begins https. The "s" stands for secure. This is not 100 percent foolproof, but generally is a sign of protection. Secure websites may also display an icon somewhere in the browser to indicate the communication is secure. Be wary of uploading applications, résumés, and cover letters to sites that do not display the protection. One way to protect your online identity is to ensure that you are only transmitting data over secure web pages.

Public Wi-Fi hotspots should be avoided. While convenient, these networks are generally not secure and put your computer devices at risk for being hacked, therefore inadvertently exposing data. Hackers are able to create "fake" hotspots in locations where free or paid public Wi-Fi exists. Users unknowingly connect to the fake network, allowing the hacker access to any data being transmitted over that connection. The signal with the best strength may not always be the legitimate hotspot. An easy way to avoid fake hotspots is to check with an employee of the business providing the Wi-Fi to get the name of the network and the access key. For example, hotels will generally not ask for a credit card number when logging into Wi-Fi because they already have the card number on file. If a Wi-Fi authentication screen is asking for credit card information, confirm that the Wi-Fi is legitimate.

## Cookies

**Cookies** are bits of data stored on your computer that record information about the websites a user has visited. Cookies contain information about where you have been on the Internet and the personal information you enter on a website. Some advertisers place them onto your computer without your knowledge or consent. Most cookies are from legitimate websites and will not harm your computer. Marketers use the information for research and selling purposes. If a hacker gains access to the cookies stored on your computer, you are at risk. They can be used to steal personal information you have entered on a website. Cookies also can be used to target you for a scam based on your Internet history.

As a precaution, there are ways to protect your computer from cookies. One way is to opt out of accepting them. Some Internet browsers allow you to opt out of cookies by setting a preference that says to *accept* cookies or *never accept* cookies. Check your browser for specific instructions.

Another way to protect your computer is to delete cookies on a regular basis. They can be removed by selecting the **Tools** or **Settings** menu from your browser, and then **Options**. Depending on the version of the browser, you can select an option that will automatically delete the cookies. Still another way to remove them is to run a disk cleanup from the **Start** menu.

## Phishing

**Phishing** is the use of fraudulent e-mails and copies of valid websites to trick people into providing private and confidential personal data. The most common form of phishing is done by sending a fake e-mail to a group of people. The e-mail message looks like it is from a legitimate source, such as an employment agency. The e-mail asks for certain information, such as a social security number or bank account information, or it provides a link to a web page. The linked web page looks real, but its sole purpose is to collect private information that is then used to commit fraud. Never open an e-mail attachment that you are not expecting. It is better to send an e-mail asking about the attachment before opening.

# Malware

**Malware**, short for *malicious software*, is a term given to software programs that are intended to damage, destroy, or steal data on a computer. The purpose of malware can be to disrupt your productivity, gain access to all of your personal data, or to compromise your online identity. Malware comes in many forms, including viruses, spyware, Trojan horses, and worms.

Beware of an invitation to click on a website link for more information about a job advertisement. A large percentage of websites contain malware.

# Social Media for Your Career

YouTube is a video-sharing website where you can learn and share just about anything. There is a wealth of professional and business information contained in videos posted there. YouTube allows you to search by keywords, such as *career skills*, and view the search results. You will find a variety of career-related tips and techniques, such as "how to develop a personal brand" or "how to prepare an elevator speech." YouTube allows you to gather ideas for your chosen career field while learning how to increase your technology skills.

One click can activate a code, and your computer could be hacked or infected. An illegitimate website may encourage visitors to download applications or templates that contain malware.

A **software virus** is a computer program designed to negatively impact a computer system. A virus may destroy data on the computer, cause programs on your computer to malfunction, or collect information and transmit it to some other location. Viruses can be introduced onto your computer by downloading virus-infected programs from an e-mail or from a website. **Spyware** is software that spies on a computer. Spyware can capture information such as Internet activity, e-mail messages and contacts, usernames, passwords, bank account information, and credit card information. Often, affected users will not be aware that spyware is on their computer.

Virus protection software purchased from a reputable company will help protect a computer. Virus protection software is also referred to as *antivirus* or *antimalware* software. Once installed, adjust the setting so that the software runs on a regular basis. By selecting this option, the software updates itself with the latest virus programs, scans the computer for viruses, and deletes them from the computer. After every Internet session, it is advisable to scan your computer with your virus protection software.

Your virus protection software should also have a firewall. A **firewall** is a program that monitors information coming into a computer and helps assure that only safe information gets through.

# Create and Maintain a Security Plan

Fortunately, there are steps you can take to protect yourself while applying for jobs online. If you have any suspicions about communicating with someone or giving your information via a website, do not proceed. Investigate the person or the company with whom you are dealing. You may be able to avoid a scam before it is too late.

Your online identity is yours alone. When your information becomes public, it becomes vulnerable to identity theft. Your bank account numbers, credit card numbers, Social Security number, address, and birthday are information hackers hope to gain. In order to protect your online identity, develop a multi-tiered security plan. Use the security plan checklist as shown in Figure 2-1 as a tool.

Plan to protect your mobile devices from hackers. Consider downloading and running antivirus software for your mobile device. Even though most are not susceptible to viruses, check with your provider on a regular basis in the event that conditions change. Because you rely on your mobile devices, it is important to guard them against theft and viruses that would disrupt your primary means of communication.

## Security Checklist

- ☐ Secure passwords created for computer
- ☐ Secure passwords created for mobile device
- ☐ Password information stored in a safe place
- ☐ Antivirus protection software installed and running
- ☐ Data back-up completed
- ☐ Internet browser updated
- ☐ Security settings set to high
- ☐ Windows automatic updates in *on* position
- ☐ Pop-up blocker turned on
- ☐ Suspicious e-mails deleted
- ☐ Unknown links avoided
- ☐ Cookies deleted
- ☐ Firewall turned on
- ☐ Wireless router password set
- ☐ Flash drives checked for viruses before using
- ☐ Automatic wireless connections disabled
- ☐ Free public hotspots avoided
- ☐ Public hotspots or wireless connections used with caution
- ☐ Privacy settings on for social networks

Goodheart-Willcox Publisher

**Figure 2-1** Consider the items in the security checklist as you develop a security plan for your computer and mobile device.

## 2-3 Malware

**Directions:** Use the space provided to complete the activity or take notes. Alternatively, you can download the electronic version of this activity from the companion website.

1.  Conduct Internet research on the latest malware protection software. Recommend five software programs you would consider using on your computer. List the name of each program and its cost.

2.  Conduct Internet research on how to protect your mobile device against malware. What did you find?

3.  Write the make and model of your mobile device. Visit the site of your service provider or the company that manufactures the device. Search the site to find current information on malware that may affect your mobile device. Is your device susceptible to viruses?

Download the electronic version of this activity.

Put a plan in place to protect your mobile devices from theft. You carry them with you almost everywhere you go. However, if you become careless and leave them in an unexpected location, your identity can be stolen before you know it. You may also be stuck with a large telephone bill. To protect your mobile device from use by a thief, create a password to lock it. Have the number of your mobile device in a safe place so that if the unexpected happens, you can contact your service provider.

## Secure Passwords

Recall the strategies you learned in Chapter 1 for creating secure passwords. Implement these strategies when you create a password for an online account. Passwords are grouped into categories: weak, medium, and strong. Figure 2-2 describes these three levels of password strength.

Unfortunately, many people have weak passwords for even their most important accounts, such as banking or credit card accounts. When creating new passwords, keep these tips in mind.

- *Do not* be careless or in a hurry.
- *Do not* use passwords that contain information that can be easily guessed by someone who has access to other parts of your personal information, such as your birthday.
- *Do not* use the same passwords for multiple accounts or profiles.
- *Do not* use the same password for secure and nonsecure sources. For example, if you have favorite game or music sites that require passwords, do not use the same password for your bank account.

**The Best App for that**

*JobMo* is an app that provides you with the ability to search for available jobs close to your home. You can search and apply for jobs through the app. Salary information and trends for your selected jobs are also available.

To protect your identity while applying for jobs online, remember to do the following.

- *Do* change your passwords often.
- *Do* use at least 10 characters with an unpredictable capitalization, a number, and a symbol.
- *Do* record your passwords on a dedicated hard-copy document to keep track of them and the accounts for which they are used.

| Password Strength | |
|---|---|
| **Strength** | **Description** |
| Weak | Contains one easy to remember word, uses lowercase letters with no symbols, usually six to eight characters in length |
| Medium | Contains one uppercase letter in a lowercase word and one number or symbol, usually eight characters in length |
| Strong | Contains a mixture of uppercase and lowercase random letters, numbers, and symbols and is 10 characters or longer |

**Figure 2-2** Creating secure passwords should be part of your security plan.

- *Do* create a dedicated hard-copy document with an abbreviation of the account name, the password, and the date that you created the password.
- *Do* record the security questions that you answered to create an account and how the account system will contact you if you forget your password.
- *Do* keep your records of password information on a hard-copy document that is not on the computer where you use the passwords.

## Security Settings

Become acquainted with the security settings and security features of your browser when accessing the Internet from your computer. First, look for a menu called **Tools**, **Settings**, or something similar. Within this menu, locate your web browser's security features, sometimes called Internet options, Privacy settings, or Security. Change your settings to protect your computer and your information. Enabling a *pop-up blocker* prevents your web browser from allowing you to see pop-up ads, which often contain malware.

## Back Up Your Computer

An important part of a security plan is backing up the data on your computer. If a virus invades your computer or the hard disk crashes, it may be too late to retrieve your files and computer programs.

Put a plan in place to do regular backups. Decide on a storage device and method for backing up your files.  Place the backup in a fireproof container and store it at a location other than your home, if possible.

**Connect** to your **Career**    2-4 Security Plan

**Directions:** Use the space provided to complete the activity or take notes. Alternatively, you can download the electronic version of this activity from the companion website.

1. Use the example in this text to create your own personal computer security plan on a seperate sheet of paper or in a word processing document. Personalize the form to fit your own needs. Add provisions for your mobile devices also.

2. If you have not already done so, create a hard-copy document of your passwords. Include all the documentation that is necessary to protect as well as recover your passwords. **Do not** write the information on this document. Create a separate hard-copy document and put it in a safe place.

Download the electronic version of this activity.

Companion
*G-W Learning*

## Chapter Summary

- You should be aware of online risks while searching and applying for jobs and networking with others. It is important to be diligent in protecting your identity while online to avoid identity theft.

- When you apply for jobs online, you will visit many unfamiliar websites. While most of the sites are legitimate, some might be designed for the purpose of compromising your identity. Be aware of employment scams and learn how to avoid being a part of a scam. If you think you have identified an employment scam, report it to an appropriate government office.

- There are risks associated when using the Internet to search for a job. Be aware that your IP address shares information about your computer. Only upload documents to sites that are secure. Protect your computer from cookies by deleting them on a regular basis. Also, be aware of phishing schemes that lure you into giving your personal information for purpose of defrauding you.

- *Malware* is a term given to software programs that are intended to damage, destroy, or steal data on a computer. Malware comes in many forms including viruses, spyware, Trojan horses, and worms. Using antivirus software can help protect your computer.

- Create and maintain a security plan to protect your computer. Your plan should include secure passwords, maintaining security settings, and backing up your files. By doing this, you can help secure your equipment and data.

## E-Flash Card Activity: Career-Related Terms

Review the career-related terms that follow. Then visit the G-W mobile site to practice vocabulary using e-flash cards until you are able to recognize their meanings. If you do not have a smartphone, visit the G-W Learning companion website to access this feature.

identity theft

multi-level marketing (MLM)

Internet Protocol address

cookies

phishing

malware

software virus

spyware

firewall

## Review Your Knowledge

1. Define *identity theft*.

2. Describe three ways to recognize an employment scam.

3. What is a computer's IP address?

4. Name two ways to protect your computer from cookies.

5. What is malware?

6. Describe two types of malware.

7. What is phishing?

8. Explain the benefits of creating a security plan.

9. Why is it important to use antivirus software?

10. Compare and contrast a weak password and a strong password.

## Apply Your Knowledge

1. Make a list of Internet activities that can possibly put your online identity at risk. What can you do to safeguard your identity?

2. What are some reasons a hacker would want to obtain your online identity?

3. How could you confirm a company's information before applying for a job?

4. Why might it be an inefficient use of your time to get involved with a multi-level marketing company?

5. How would you know if your computer had a virus?

6. What is the best way to protect your e-mail account from being hacked?

7. What would you do if you received an e-mail from an unknown source with a subject line of, "Hey, check this out!"

8. Have you ever come across a job advertisement that looked suspicious? What caused you to suspect that it might be a scam? Explain.

9. Security settings may be found in different locations on different types of Internet browsers. Describe how to find the security settings on the Internet browser you use in your job search.

10. When is the best time to use a security plan to protect your computer? Why?

## Exploring Certification

### Career Certification Skills—Using Reading Skills

A friend is impressed that you can receive your professional e-mail on your smartphone and get a unique tone when e-mail arrives. This person asks for your help with forwarding e-mail to a smartphone. Your friend would like you to send him the directions.

1. Directions must be followed in sequence. Create a set of numbered directive steps in order that detail each step necessary to forward e-mail to a smartphone. Include logging in using a password and logging out when complete.

2. Create a separate set of directions on how to create a unique tone for e-mail received from the professional e-mail account. Use clear, coherent sentences to convey your directions.

### Career Certification Skills—Finding Information

Many work environments involve teams of people from different departments working together to complete a project. At your new job, each person must complete his or her task according to the schedule documented in the following chart to finish the project on time.

| | Week 1 | Week 2 | Week 3 | Week 4 | Week 5 | Week 6 |
|---|---|---|---|---|---|---|
| **Wireframe created** | Engineering | | | | | |
| **Wireframe reviewed** | | Marketing | | | | |
| **Wireframe approved** | | | Exec Committee | | | |
| **Launch plan created** | | | Marketing | | | |
| **Design plan created** | | | Design | | | |
| **Design plan reviewed** | | | | Marketing | | |
| **Design plan approved** | | | | | Exec Committee | |
| **Design implemented** | | | | | | Design |
| **Content written** | | | | Copywriting | | |
| **Site infrastructure developed** | | | | Engineering | | |
| **Content reviewed** | | | | | Marketing | |
| **Content uploaded to website** | | | | | Engineering | |
| **Website tested** | | | | | | Marketing |

Goodheart-Willcox Publisher

Using the schedule, answer these questions.

1. What is due from the engineering department on week four?


2. What week would be the best for someone in marketing to take a vacation?


3. On week three, what is the design department responsible for completing?


## Career Certification Skills— Applying Math Skills

You have a job selling posters for an online bookstore. Your job is to calculate taxes and shipping costs for each order. Your first customer of the day orders a poster priced at $12.95. The customer needs the item shipped from the United States via airmail to Ontario, Canada. Canadian sales tax, which is 15 percent, applies to this transaction. The shipping cost, which is $6.40, will be added after the tax is calculated. What is the total cost of the item including tax and shipping?  Select the correct answer. Show your calculations.

A. $19.56

B. $18.24

C. $21.29

D. $52.37

## Chapter 3

# Networking for Your Career

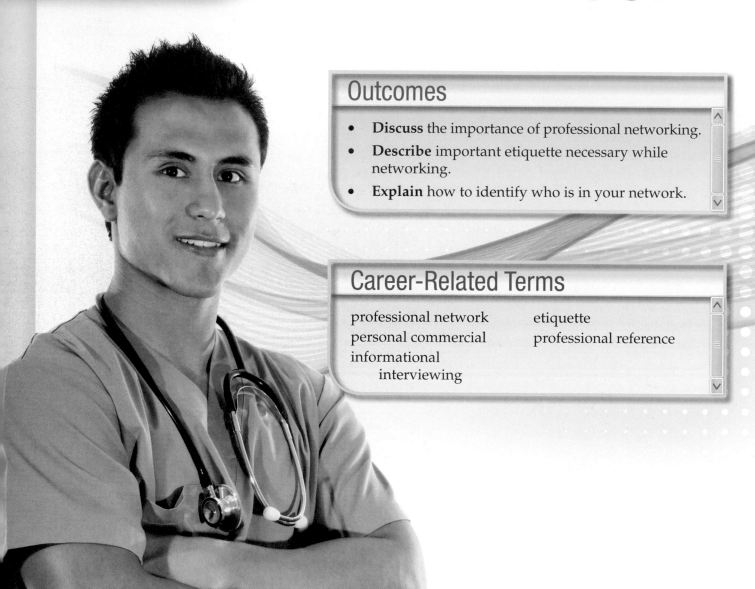

## Outcomes

- **Discuss** the importance of professional networking.
- **Describe** important etiquette necessary while networking.
- **Explain** how to identify who is in your network.

## Career-Related Terms

professional network
personal commercial
informational
   interviewing

etiquette
professional reference

You will see icons at various points throughout the chapter. These icons indicate that interactive activities are available on the *Connect to Your Career* companion website. Selected activities are also available on the *Connect to Your Career* mobile site. These activities will help you learn, practice, and expand your career knowledge and skills.

Companion Website
www.g-wlearning.com/careereducation/

Mobile Site
www.m.g-wlearning.com

# Overview

Networking is a term used frequently in the workforce. When people interact with others in business situations, they are networking. Networking can be used to expand your list of professional contacts. These individuals may be able to assist you in advancing your career. Through networking, professionals can meet other colleagues in their field. Quite often these associates support each other in finding jobs and succeeding in the workplace.

Networking can be done formally by attending meetings or events or informally through conversations with someone you meet at work or at a social event. Networking can take place in person or online. Any communication that leads to career discussions can yield a new networking contact.

Approach the process in a serious manner. Use common sense and etiquette. Build your network and continue the process throughout your career.

# Professional Networking

As you begin your job-search process, you will find that the more people you know, the greater your odds will be for finding job leads. As you will recall from Chapter 1, *networking* is talking with people and establishing relationships that can lead to potential career or job opportunities. It is the process of creating new contacts with a goal to give and receive support while building relationships. You probably already have a personal network that includes your friends and family. These are the people with whom you socialize and build personal relationships. As you begin your career, you will develop a professional network. A **professional network** consists of those people who support an individual in his or her career and other business endeavors. Professionals network to help each other by exchanging career information and job opportunities.

Networking can help you find jobs that may not be advertised to the public. Knowing someone at a company who has information about a job opening can lead to contact with a hiring manager. A person in your professional network may help you get an interview or give you good advice about a company that may lead to a job opportunity.

As you prepare to network, the Department of Workforce Development suggests that job seekers create a personal commercial. A **personal commercial**, also known as an *elevator speech*, is a rehearsed introduction that includes brief information about a person's background and a snapshot of his or her career goals. It is suggested that you develop a 30- to 60- second commercial about yourself to give to people with whom you have face-to-face contact. A commercial must be short, as if you could recite it on an elevator going from one floor to the next. Your brief statement should review major points from your résumé. Chances are you will not recite your speech verbatim. Yet, there is value in being prepared with a concise message that promotes who you are and your abilities. A commercial makes the most of the few seconds you may have when you meet a potential networking contact.

Consider filming your commercial and posting it online to a website such as YouTube, and then include the link to your video in your online communication. This can be an effective way to network.

Learning to network is one of the most important pieces of career advice a job seeker should take. Practice networking often. You will gain experience in social settings and learn by doing. Your networking begins now.

## 3-1 Personal Commercial

**Directions:** Use the space provided to complete the activity or take notes. Alternatively, you can download the electronic version of this activity from the companion website.

1. A *personal commercial* is a rehearsed introduction that includes who you are and a snapshot of your career goals. Summarize who you are and your major career goals in one or two sentences.

2. Your brief statement should review the major points from your résumé. Summarize the points of your résumé you want to include in your personal commercial. Be succinct.

3. Practice your message aloud. Try to memorize it. Time yourself. How long is your personal commercial?

4. Do an Internet search for *15-Second Pitch (Elevator Speech)*. Select a video that focuses on a personal commercial. Take the time to watch it. What important tips did you learn from the video?

5. Film yourself giving your commercial, and then watch the video. Does your commercial sound natural? What did you learn about your speech from watching the video?

Download the electronic version of this activity.

## Face-to-Face Networking

Face-to-face networking can begin anywhere you meet with individuals or groups of people. Never discount an opportunity to connect with someone who can share information that may help you in your career. Informal opportunities might start with people in your social network. By initiating a conversation about career topics, someone in your social network might connect you with another who eventually becomes part of your professional network.

Consider asking the career development director at your university or your favorite instructor to be part of your network. These people have come to know you during your formal education. Through your interactions with them, they may have become mentors or other respected sources of advice. Call on these individuals to help guide you through the career-search process.

Attending meetings such as an alumni event or professional association event is a good place to network. Begin by researching organizations that reflect your career goals. For example, if you are a marketer, check the American Marketing Association website for meetings open to the public. These meetings provide opportunities to meet people in your profession.

Conducting informational interviews is an important activity that can give you insight to your profession. **Informational interviewing** is a strategy used to interview and ask for advice and direction from a professional, rather than

# Career Portfolio

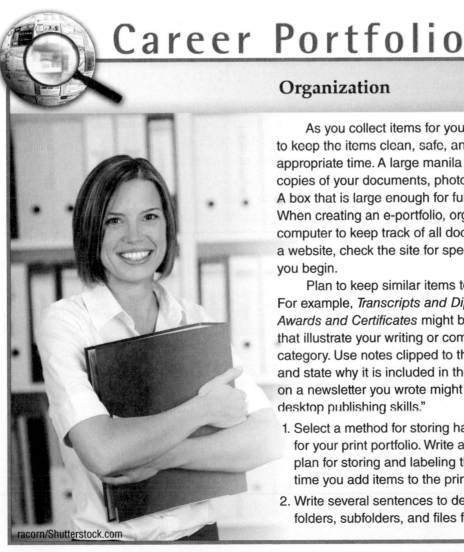

## Organization

As you collect items for your portfolio, you will need a method to keep the items clean, safe, and organized for assembly at the appropriate time. A large manila envelope works well to keep hard copies of your documents, photographs, awards, and other items. A box that is large enough for full-size documents will work also. When creating an e-portfolio, organize a filing system on your computer to keep track of all documents. If you are going to use a website, check the site for specifications on file formats before you begin.

Plan to keep similar items together and label the categories. For example, *Transcripts and Diplomas* might be one category. *Awards and Certificates* might be another category. Documents that illustrate your writing or computer skills may fit into another category. Use notes clipped to the documents to identify each item and state why it is included in the portfolio. For example, a note on a newsletter you wrote might say, "Newsletter that illustrates desktop publishing skills."

1. Select a method for storing hard-copy items you will be collecting for your print portfolio. Write a paragraph that describes your plan for storing and labeling the items. Refer to this plan each time you add items to the printed portfolio.

2. Write several sentences to describe how you will name the folders, subfolders, and files for your e-portfolio.

asking for a job opportunity. This can lead to networking opportunities and better prepare you for the job-search process. By talking with someone in your field, you can learn more about what is expected, types of jobs available, and other inside information about an industry. Communicate with those who are familiar with employment opportunities and events. In addition, remember to follow up with your contact person after an interview. Always send a thank-you message to show appreciation for his or her time.

## Online Networking

Do not limit yourself to face-to-face networking opportunities as it will be necessary to connect with others online as well. Once you have created a professional social media account, such as a LinkedIn or Twitter account, you are ready to begin connecting with others online. LinkedIn and Twitter are only two of many free sites you can join that provide the opportunity to network with others.

When networking on LinkedIn, follow connections of those with whom you wish to network. Comment on and support their posts. Pay attention to others, and exchange information that you know. Use your LinkedIn profile to connect with groups and to comment on articles or news stories relevant to your industry. Learn from your connections and build relationships. When networking on Twitter, Tweet regularly. Consider uploading your résumé using seven to ten Tweets. Follow those who follow you, and support their Tweets by sharing them with others.

It may be helpful to establish a blog. Possible blog topics might be your job-search process and experiences or your professional contributions to a career field or industry. Blogging is one way to draw positive attention and showcase your communication skills.

Online networking only works if you are active online. Check your professional media pages every day for updates. When people connect with you, respond promptly and professionally. Thank people when it is appropriate.

**The Best App for that**

Using your mobile device, conduct a search for the *Nextdoor* app. Nextdoor is a private social network to communicate with neighbors in local communities. Members post information about everyday events, including local employment opportunities. How could this app help a job seeker?

# Networking Etiquette

There are rules of networking that should be followed, both in person and online. All networking requires polite exchanges referred to as etiquette. **Etiquette** is consideration for others. You use etiquette every day. For example, you wait your turn in line when making purchases. You obey traffic signals. When networking, you wait and then proceed in concert with others.

Professional communication is the most important part of any contact with new people. Never cold-call strangers and ask them to be a part of your network. Be respectful as to how you approach other professionals.

When you are speaking with someone face-to-face, use good communication and listening skills and avoid slang or unprofessional language. If you are communicating via e-mail, apply the rules of grammar and use proper formatting. Remember, you are making an impression that can help build your career.

# 3-2 Informational Interview

**Directions:** Use the space provided to complete the activity or take notes. Alternatively, you can download the electronic version of this activity from the companion website.

1. Research companies in your area with which you would like to conduct an informational interview. Select one. Record the company name and address, industry, and human resources contact information.

2. Schedule an informational interview. Record the pertinent information for the interview.

3. Create a list of ten questions to ask at the informational interview.

4. Make a list of the follow-up activities you will pursue after the informational interview.

Download the electronic
version of this activity.

Networking requires confidence and the ability to market oneself. Being tentative is a networking obstacle. When others ask, let them know your career goals. This may lead to an opportunity to share your career-search activities. It is acceptable to let others know that you are seeking employment but remain sensitive to each person's reaction when you do so. Do not dominate a person's time with long conversations either in person or online. Be brief and polite.

Communicate your skills and expertise clearly along with your career goals. There is no point to reach out to people if they are unclear about your career potential and goals. If a person does not respond offering a known job opportunity, quickly close the topic with a phrase such as, "If you hear of anything, please let me know," and move the conversation in a new direction. If a person responds positively, it is acceptable to send an e-mail that reminds him or her of the details of the conversation along with your résumé.

Resist becoming a self-centered network that only *receives* information. Networking involves supporting others and should be reciprocated. Focus on others while listening and learning. Self-centered networkers face the chances of being rejected. Networking begins at the pre-career stage and becomes a permanent part of socialization. Your network will evolve and might include thousands of individuals over your lifetime.

## In-Person Etiquette

Before you begin face-to-face networking, create business cards. Model a business card from a professional in your field or do online research to find a format that is appropriate for you. Similar to the signature block for your professional e-mail address, include your full name, your phone number, and e-mail address. If you have a LinkedIn account, consider adding the link. It is important to designate a job title that describes your skills, such as *Instructional Design Consultant*. Without a title, the person to whom you give the business card may not remember the field or type of position in which you are interested. To protect your personal information, avoid including an address.

If you are attending a formal meeting, be on time. Turn off your cell phone, and place it out of sight. Dress the part of a professional and be prepared to interact and ask questions. Be friendly and outgoing with people you meet. When meeting a new person, extend your hand for a handshake and make eye contact. Provide your full name. Learn new names, and remember each person to the best of your ability. Express an interest in the person and his or her job. Ask for a business card, and offer one in return.

Immediately after an event or meeting, jot down notes on each business card that you collect. Your notes might be as simple as physical features or details you learned about the person. Send an e-mail acknowledging the conversation to make sure your name stays on that person's radar.

## Online Etiquette

As you begin networking online, it is still important to interact appropriately. Etiquette is just as important for online communication as it is for face-to-face contact. Positive, professional communication leads to positive online networking experiences. Avoid being negative, ranting, or venting about any individual or company. Negative or poorly written online communication could influence a potential hiring manager to decline interviewing you.

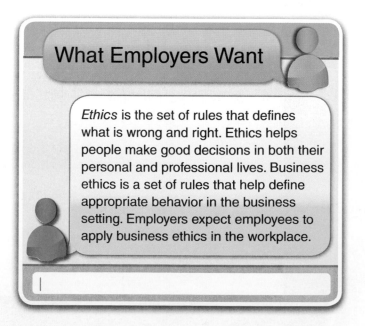

### What Employers Want

*Ethics* is the set of rules that defines what is wrong and right. Ethics helps people make good decisions in both their personal and professional lives. Business ethics is a set of rules that help define appropriate behavior in the business setting. Employers expect employees to apply business ethics in the workplace.

**3-3 Business Cards**

**Directions:** Use the space provided to complete the activity or take notes. Alternatively, you can download the electronic version of this activity from the companion website.

1.  Conduct an Internet search for *business cards + (your industry)*. Review the results. Are there any common design elements or specific information typically included? Select a style that you would like to use.

2.  Record the information you will include on your business card. Include your full name, job title, phone number, e-mail address, LinkedIn URL, and any other information.

3.  Describe your plan for having business cards printed. Will you order them online, visit a printing shop, or use your own printer?

Download the electronic version of this activity.

Complete your profiles so that people with whom you are networking can learn who you are. Incomplete profiles give the impression that you do not finish what you start. Use your online profiles to promote your personal brand and highlight your career strengths. When appropriate, change your status headline to "seeking employment."

As you begin networking online, it is important to be respectful of others. People value their time, and professional networking is no exception. Avoid sending unsolicited e-mails stating that you need a job. However, it is appropriate to send e-mails asking for job-search strategies or leads. Do not flood a person's account with comments, questions, and other communications. One or two skillfully worded questions or comments spread over a period of time are enough to grab someone's attention. If you are hoping to engage someone online and he or she does not reply, do not persist. Not everyone checks their professional accounts for updates every day. It may be a matter of time before you get a response. However, lack of communication may imply that he or she is not interested in communicating with you. If you do not receive replies, find someone else who will be beneficial to your professional network.

Although networking online can give you many new insights into the careers of people you know, privacy must be respected. Avoid sending e-mail to strangers inviting them to join your network. Sending unsolicited e-mail, connection requests on LinkedIn, and other online communications to people you do not know is unacceptable. This could be perceived as spam. If there is a person you do not know but want to add to your network, ask for an introduction from someone in your network who knows that person. Join groups in your field. A group membership status will help you get introductions and make new connections.

# Identify Your Network

As you build your network, be proactive. Create a list of those whom you consider part of your professional network. Each person you meet may or may not become a part of your network. For those people whom you consider part of your network, note each person's name, contact information, industry, when you met him or her, and any other important contact information. You might create a spreadsheet of the details. Include these in your contact list on your smartphone or tablet computer. It is important to have this information available at all times.

From this networking contact list, you will create a list of three to five professional references. A **professional reference** is a person who is ready and willing to recommend an individual for a job if requested. Select people from your professional network who are familiar with your professional strengths. Then, have a conversation with those people to be certain they would be comfortable if called on to vouch for your skills or experience. Not everyone wants to be in this position, so do not pressure someone to accept.

Once you have a list of people who have agreed to accept this responsibility, create a professional document. At the top of the document, add your name and "Professional References." List each person and contact information. When you begin interviewing, you will be requested to submit this document. You can also make it part of your portfolio.

 **3-4 Your Professional Network**

**Directions:** Use the space provided to complete the activity or take notes. Alternatively, you can download the electronic version of this activity from the companion website.

1. As you identify your network, consider creating a tracking document to keep your contacts organized and updated. One method is to use a spreadsheet program. Open a spreadsheet and create columns with the following headings: contact name; phone number; e-mail address; position title; company name, address, and URL; industry; where you met; year you met; willing to be a reference? (yes/no).

2. Fill out the spreadsheet with information about the people in your network.

3. Transfer this data to your mobile device so you can have each person's contact information available at all times.

Download the electronic version of this activity.

## Chapter Summary

- As you begin your career search, professional networking will become an important activity. Your professional network is made up of those people who support you in your career and business activities.

- Etiquette is necessary when networking. Use common sense and manners when you are communicating with someone as a networking contact.

- After networking for a period of time, you will identify those who are in your network. From this list of people, you will develop a list of professional references that will help you as you apply for positions.

## E-Flash Card Activity: Career-Related Terms

Review the career-related terms that follow. Then visit the G-W mobile site to practice vocabulary using e-flash cards until you are able to recognize their meanings. If you do not have a smartphone, visit the G-W Learning companion website to access this feature.

professional network                          etiquette

personal commercial                           professional reference

informational interviewing

## Review Your Knowledge

1. Define the term *professional network*. Why is it important to have one?

2. Explain why you should create a personal commercial.

3. Describe how someone in your personal social network can lead to a professional network connection.

4.  What is informational interviewing?

5.  Why is etiquette important when networking?

6.  Describe how being a self-centered network does *not* help your career.

7.  Give three tips for in-person networking.

8.  Give three tips for online networking.

9.  What are some behaviors that are not accepted when networking online?

10.  Describe the process of creating a list of professional references.

## Apply Your Knowledge

1.  Professional networking can start with your personal network.  What are some precautions to take before including friends and family as part of your professional network?

2.  Explain how a personal commercial can help build your personal brand.

3.  What are some actions that you will take to prepare for face-to-face networking?

4.  Make a list of events that you might attend in the next few weeks that would be beneficial for networking. Why did you select these activities?

5.  Informational interviews are often overlooked for their importance.  Research one company with which you would like to have an informational interview.  What criteria did you use to select a company?

6.  Explain your strategy for networking online.

7.  Describe how you can use proper etiquette when networking in person and online.

8.  Why is it important to have a personal business card even if you are not currently employed?

9.  Professional references generally say good things about the person for whom they are speaking. You would not give names of people who would say bad things. Why are personal references important?

10. Why do you think it is important to get permission from your professional references before giving out their names and contact information?

## Exploring Certification

### Career Certification Skills— Using Reading Skills

You have received an e-mail response from someone you recently met at a networking event. This person has several contacts in your chosen industry. She would like to meet with you again. Read the e-mail message, and respond to the questions that follow.

---

**E-mail**

Thank you for your e-mail. It was great to meet you at the State University alumni dinner last weekend. I am interested in hearing more about your volunteer work with the city. My company is looking to become more community-minded.

I would like to meet you for lunch to discuss your experiences. I am available on Tuesdays and Thursdays from 1:00 p.m. for one hour and Fridays at noon for one to two hours. Please call my main office number and schedule an appointment with the assistant for the day that works best for you. After we have a meeting on my calendar, I will be in touch with the address of the restaurant where we will have lunch.

---

1. When is this person available to meet with you?

2. How should you get in touch with this person to schedule a lunch meeting?

### Career Certification Skills—Applying Math Skills

As a computer account manager, you had $4,365 in sales this month. Your monthly expenses include taxes, which are 30 percent of your total sales, and insurance, which is $135 per month. How much did you make this month after taxes and insurance? Select the correct answer. Show your calculations.

A. $2,920.50

B. $4,365.00

C. $4,000.00

D. $3,250.00

## Career Certification Skills—Finding Information

You have taken a job at a local television channel as an assistant to the weather reporter. Your job includes learning how to read a barometer. Your supervisor has provided you with a barometer and these notes:

- Mercury readings higher than 30.20 with steady pressure indicate fair weather.

- Mercury readings under 29.80 with falling pressure indicate rain.

- Mercury readings under 29.80 with rising pressure indicate the weather is clearing.

The red needle is manually set to show the previous reading. The black needle automatically shows the current reading. The difference between the red and the black indicates rising or falling pressure. No difference indicates steady pressure.

Using the barometer, answer the following questions.

1. To which number is the black needle pointing?


2. Is the pressure rising, falling, or remaining steady?


3. What does the current reading indicate about the weather?

# Unit 2

# Essential Skills for Your Career

4  Workplace Skills
5  Your Career Strengths

## Connecting to Your Career

### Why It Matters

To be successful in the workplace, employees must possess a variety of skills. Job-specific skills are necessary to perform tasks related to a position. Transferrable skills, which involve critical thinking and personal skills, are also required. All of these skills enable an employee to work effectively with coworkers and supervisors. In some industries, certification may be essential in order to qualify for employment.

The job-search process requires that you assess your skills and qualifications as you apply for positions. Evaluating your aptitudes, skills, abilities, and values will help you market yourself and become a successful candidate for employment. Once your evaluation is complete, you will be ready to set goals and create a plan that can take you one step closer to your career.

## Chapter 4

# Workplace Skills

## Outcomes

- **Describe** types of workplace skills.
- **Explain** certification and its importance to employees as well as employers.

## Career-Related Terms

| | |
|---|---|
| skill | thinking skills |
| job-specific skills | people skills |
| employability skills | personal qualities |
| basic skills | certification |

You will see icons at various points throughout the chapter. These icons indicate that interactive activities are available on the *Connect to Your Career* companion website. Selected activities are also available on the *Connect to Your Career* mobile site. These activities will help you learn, practice, and expand your career knowledge and skills.

Companion Website

www.g-wlearning.com/careereducation/

Mobile Site

www.m.g-wlearning.com

Andresr/Shutterstock.com

# Overview

Successful employees have job-specific skills as well as employability skills. Job-specific skills are unique to a certain job and are required in order to complete the tasks associated with it. Employability skills, called *foundation* or *transferrable skills*, are essential for working effectively with coworkers and supervisors. These skills enable you to solve problems and communicate with others. They include basic skills, thinking skills, people skills, and personal qualities.

In some industries, certification is essential in order to qualify for employment or to stay employed. Certification confirms that an individual has acquired knowledge and mastered skills for a specified area. Earning certification can help you be competitive in the workplace and move ahead in your career.

## Skills for the Workplace

Employers look for potential employees who can help make their companies successful. There are many criteria used to sort through the hundreds of résumés submitted for open positions. Finding a potential employee with the required educational background and experience are usually the first criteria employers use when screening applications. For example, an employer looking to fill a position for a nurse will confirm that the candidate is truly qualified for the position. The applicant's degree and work experience will be reviewed to confirm the individual has job-specific skills. A **skill** is something an individual does well. **Job-specific skills** are critical skills necessary to perform the required work-related tasks of a position. Job-specific skills are acquired through work experience and education or training. Without them, the individual would be unlikely to perform the job successfully.

As you apply for positions, potential employers will ask you questions related to your employability skills. **Employability skills** are applicable skills used to help an individual find a job, perform in the workplace, and gain success in a job or career. Employability skills are also known as *foundation skills* or *transferrable skills*. You have already acquired many of these skills in school. However, some of these skills are gained through life experience, such as working at a job or interacting with others in social situations. These skills are not specific to one career, but rather transferrable to any position for which you might have.

Finding a candidate with foundation skills is crucial in today's workplace. Transferrable skills can be categorized as basic skills, thinking skills, people skills, and personal qualities.

## Basic Skills

**Basic skills** are the fundamental skills necessary to effectively function in society. These skills include reading, writing, speaking, and listening. They also include knowing how to apply mathematics and technology skills.

- *Reading.* Reading involves acquiring meaning from written words and symbols to evaluate their accuracy and validity. Reading skills allow you to *locate information* in various forms, including in books, on the Internet, and in pictures such as graphs. Reading also helps you comprehend and evaluate material to ensure understanding and form judgments.

- *Writing.* Writing is using written words to express your ideas and opinions. Writing skills enable you to communicate effectively on paper or while using a computer. Writing requires you to edit and revise written communication for accuracy, emphasis, and for audience. Effective *business writing* is required in the workplace.

- *Speaking.* Speaking is communicating ideas verbally. Speaking skills enable you to present information clearly, maximize word choices, control your tone of voice, and adjust your message for your audience.

- *Listening.* Listening is hearing what others say and evaluating their messages for information. When you use listening skills, you pay attention to what other people are saying and understand the points being made.

- *Mathematics.* Mathematics is the study of numbers and their relationships. Mathematics skills enable you to use numbers to evaluate information and detect patterns so that decisions can be made.

- *Technology.* Technology skills include how to use social media, software, and basic computer systems. Using technology skills is necessary to be productive in the workplace.

## Thinking Skills

**Thinking skills** are those skills that help people solve problems. Even if you are unable to find a solution, thinking skills help you assess a situation and identify the options. Examples of thinking skills include decision making, creative thinking, problem solving, visualization, and reasoning.

- *Decision making.* Decision making is the process of analyzing a situation and evaluating possible outcomes in order to choose the best solution. Decision-making skills enable you to weigh pros and cons in order to solve problems.

- *Creative thinking.* Creative thinking involves developing or designing unusual and clever ideas about a given topic or situation. When you use creative-thinking skills, you develop unique or different ways to solve a problem.

- *Problem solving.* Problem solving is implementing a solution in the most efficient manner. Problem-solving skills help you carry out a plan or implement new processes to achieve a desired outcome.

- *Visualization.* Visualization is the ability to form mental images. Visualization skills allow you to imagine how something will function or appear prior to an actual process.

- *Reasoning.* Reasoning is the ability to combine pieces of information or apply general rules to specific problems. Reasoning skills enable you to reach conclusions based on what you already know.

## Social Media for Your Career

Vine is a social media app launched by Twitter. This video-sharing tool is designed to develop short videos that may be linked together in a continuous loop. The videos are viewable directly in your Twitter feed. Your name, photo, and bio transfer directly from your Twitter account to Vine when you launch the app. Use Vine to pitch your skills and talents, along with your Twitter résumé, via short films.

## People Skills

**People skills** are the skills that enable people to develop and maintain working relationships with others. These skills have a significant impact on your relationships with others in the workplace. Examples of people skills include social perceptiveness, negotiation, leadership, teamwork, and cultural competence.

- *Social perceptiveness*. Social perceptiveness is being aware of others' feelings and understanding why they may act a certain way. Socially perceptive people exhibit kindness and understanding. They take an interest in their coworkers and who they are. However, it is important to balance social perceptiveness with the ability to assert yourself politely and professionally when appropriate.

- *Negotiation*. Negotiation is discussing various positions of an issue and reconciling differences of opinion. The key to negotiating is being able to pinpoint the common goals among each position. This prepares everyone to argue the facts from his or her point of view and reach a compromise.

- *Leadership*. Leadership is the ability to influence or inspire other people. In the workplace, leaders encourage others and coordinate activities to reach goals.

- *Teamwork*. Teamwork is working cooperatively with other people. Important aspects of teamwork include encouraging each other, building mutual trust and respect, and cooperation among team members.

- *Cultural competence*. Cultural competence is respecting all people regardless of age, national origin, gender, or ability. Being culturally competent enables you to interact effectively with all people in the workplace.

## Personal Qualities

**Personal qualities** are the characteristics that make up an individual's personality. Examples of personal qualities include self-esteem, self-management, and responsibility. Having *self-esteem*

**The Best App for that**

Many websites offer career assessments to assist job seekers in evaluating their interests and targeting a career. Many of these sites are free, and the apps can be downloaded to a mobile device for easy access. An example of free a career assessment app is *Career Test*.

is having confidence in yourself and your abilities. *Self-management* is the ability to work independently without supervision. *Responsibility* is being trusted to complete duties or tasks.

Employers look for employees who are flexible and can adjust in a positive manner to work situations as they change. This includes being professional, having a positive attitude, and above all, being ethical. Positive ethics are an important work quality that all employers expect their employees to possess.

## Certification

The workplace is more competitive today than in recent history. Career seekers must prepare themselves in every way possible in order to compete for the few prime jobs that are available. One way you can get an edge on the competition is to earn a certification in your area of expertise.

**Certification** is a professional status earned by an individual after passing an exam focused on a specific body of knowledge. The individual generally prepares for the exam by taking

## 4-1 Workplace Skills

**Directions:** Use the space provided to complete the activity or take notes. Alternatively, you can download the electronic version of this activity from the companion website.

1. As your job search progresses, you will decide the type of position for which you will apply. The job may have a specific title, such as teacher. Alternatively, you may be looking for a position in a functional area, such as marketing. Marketing positions have many job titles, such as marketing assistant, marketing manager, or promotions manager, to name a few. Write down the job title or area for which you are interested.

2. For the job position you identified, list some of the job-specific skills that are necessary to perform the requirements of the job.

3. Next, select one of the foundation skills that you consider most important for this position. The foundation skills are basic skills, thinking skills, people skills, and personal qualities. Write a paragraph that supports your opinion of why these skills are necessary for that job.

Download the electronic version of this activity.

classes and studying content that will be tested. Certification programs are usually sponsored by associations or vendors. There are many types of certifications in most industries and trades, as shown in Figure 4-1.

Some jobs require a candidate to have a professional certification in order to be employed. For example, a financial planning agency might require a financial planner to be certified as a qualification for the job. Other employers may prefer, but not require, certification. For example, an individual may have a degree in accounting and be employable with that degree alone. However, some accounting firms may favor hiring accountants who are certified public accountants (CPA).

There are certifications that must be renewed on a regular basis. For example, if you earned one of the many certifications sponsored by Microsoft, the certification is only valid for one specific version of software. When the next version is released, you must take another exam to be certified for the update.

Other certifications require regular continuing education classes to ensure individuals are current with up-to-date information in the profession. These classes are known as *continuing education* for which *continuing education units* (CEUs) are earned. If you are a teacher, your school system may require that you earn a specified number of CEUs every year to keep your teaching certification up-to-date.

Some certifications are not subject-specific but attest that the individual has employability skills. These certifications confirm that the person who earned the certificate possesses the skills to be a contributing employee. The focus of these certifications is on workplace skills. Individuals who earn this type of certification have demonstrated they possess the qualities necessary to become an effective employee.

## Benefits of Certification

Hundreds of applications are submitted to employers each day for a limited number of open positions. Many criteria are used to screen these submissions, and certification has become

| Certifications by Industry |
|---|
| **Administrative**<br>Certified Professional Secretary (CPS)<br>Certified Administrative Professional (CAP) |
| **Automotive**<br>ASE Certified Medium/Heavy Truck Technicians<br>ASE Master Certified Automobile Technician |
| **Financial Planning**<br>Certified Financial Planner (CFP) |
| **Health Support**<br>Certified EKG/ECG Technician (CET)<br>Certified Nurse Technician (CNT) |
| **Hospitality**<br>Certified Hospitality Accountant Executive (CHAE)<br>Certified Hospitality Supervisor (CHS) |
| **Human Resources**<br>Professional in Human Resources (PHR)<br>Senior Professional in Human Resources (SPHR) |
| **Information Technology**<br>Cisco Certified Network Professional<br>Microsoft Certified Systems Administrator<br>Sun Certified Java Programmer |
| **Internal Auditing**<br>Certified Internal Auditor (CIA)<br>Certification in Control Self-Assessment (CCSA) |
| **Manufacturing**<br>Certified Manufacturing Technologist (CMfgT)<br>Certified Engineering Manager (CEM) |
| **Project Management**<br>Project Management Professional (PMP)<br>Certified Associate in Project Management (CAPM) |
| **Real Estate**<br>Certified Commercial Real Estate Appraiser (CCRA)<br>Certified Residential Specialist (CRS) |
| **Workplace Safety**<br>Certified Environmental Health and Safety Management Specialist (EHS)<br>Certified Safety Auditor (SAC) |
| **Workplace Skills**<br>National Career Readiness Certificate (NCRC) |

Goodheart-Willcox Publisher

**Figure 4-1** Certifications are available in many different industries.

one of them. For employers, certification takes the guesswork out of determining whether a candidate is qualified for a position. Anyone can say that he or she has a skill, but the certification confirms it. The certificate earned proves the holder met the required qualifications. Employers no longer have to rely on a candidate's evaluation of his or her own skills.

For the employee, certification offers many of the following advantages.

- Certification is often voluntary. Those who seek it demonstrate ambition and dedication to a career.

- Certification provides personal achievement and accomplishment. Working to be recognized in your career area provides pride.

- Certification may give you priority when interviewing for jobs as well as when being promoted on the job.

- Certification may increase your salary. Some companies offer higher salaries for those who are certified.

# Career Portfolio

## Documents

Goodluz/Shutterstock.com

Your portfolio will include documents that you have collected as well as those you have created. An example of a collected document is a certificate. Any collected documents that highlight your skills and qualifications should be included. To add these to your printed portfolio, photocopy the documents. To add to your e-portfolio, scan the items.

For the files you create, decide which file formats to use. You can use the default format to save your documents. For example, use Microsoft Word format for letters and essays or the Microsoft Excel format for spreadsheets. Someone reviewing your e-portfolio would need to have the same or a compatible program to open these files. Another option is to save created documents as PDF or HTML files. Keep in mind that having all of the files in the same format can make viewing easier for others who need to review your portfolio.

When creating your e-portfolio, check the site where it is hosted for specifications on file formats and how to upload the documents.

1. Identify documents you have *collected* that will be included in your portfolio.

2. Identify documents you have *created* that will be included in your portfolio.

3. Begin the process of photocopying these for your print portfolio. Next, scan each collected document for inclusion in your e-portfolio. Save created documents in an appropriate format.

Becoming certified in your career area can allow your résumé to stand out from others. Hundreds of job seekers applying for the same position may all have similar work experience and education. However, certification proves that you have the skills needed on the job, and this distinction can put you at the top of the list of acceptable candidates. Research certification options in your chosen career field or areas of interest to decide if a certification is right for you. There might be many available in your career field. Conducting the research can help you decide which is best for you and your career plans.

## How to Earn Certification

To earn certification in a specified area, it is important to prepare for the exam you select. There are several ways to accomplish this goal. One way is to take formal test-prep classes that cover the important topics tested on the exam. These classes are usually offered at local colleges, universities, and businesses. Some classes are offered online. Be prepared to pay a fee for attending these classes.

The materials used in these classes are specifically developed to prepare individuals for the exam. The organization offering the certification may publish training materials used for exam preparation. Alternatively, companies working with the certification organization may prepare study materials.

Another way to prepare for the exam is to purchase exam-preparation materials from a bookstore or online. There are many books available for those who wish to study without taking a formal class.

In addition to training materials, practice tests are often available as preparation tools. For

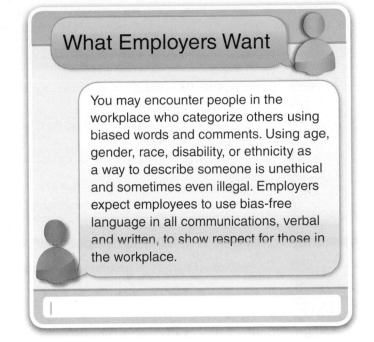

**What Employers Want**

You may encounter people in the workplace who categorize others using biased words and comments. Using age, gender, race, disability, or ethnicity as a way to describe someone is unethical and sometimes even illegal. Employers expect employees to use bias-free language in all communications, verbal and written, to show respect for those in the workplace.

each type of certification area, the test will usually have a specific format. Typical test formats include matching, multiple choice, or short answer. Before you take an exam, be aware of the test format so that you are not surprised on exam day. Practice exams are an effective way to prepare. Many of these practice tests are available online. If you are taking a formal class, practice tests will more than likely be a part of the curriculum.

A certification exam is usually administered by an official testing organization. These testing organizations have been approved by the certification sponsor. Do not take a certification exam at a location that is not an official test center. It will be necessary to pre-register for the exam, and in most cases, there will be an exam fee. Be prepared to show identification, such as a driver's license, when you arrive for the test.

## 4-2 Certification Options

**Directions:** Use the space provided to complete the activity or take notes. Alternatively, you can download the electronic version of this activity from the companion website.

1.  Is certification necessary or available for the career you want to pursue? If yes, list the name of the certification, the agency or company that issues the certification, and other pertinent information you need to know before sitting for the exam.

2.  If certification is not required for your chosen career, research a certification that might be helpful in moving you forward professionally. Some certifications are applicable to a variety of jobs and career fields. Conduct research on a certification that can be applied to a variety of job titles, and note pertinent information about the certification.

Download the electronic version of this activity.

## Chapter Summary

- A skill is something an individual does well. Job-specific skills are critical skills necessary to perform the required, work-related tasks of a position. Employability skills, also known as foundation skills, are applicable skills used to help a worker find a job, perform in the workplace, and gain success in a job or career. Foundation skills can be categorized as basic skills, thinking skills, people skills, and personal qualities.

- One of the ways to get an edge on the competition during your job search is to earn a certification in your area of expertise. Certification attests to workplace skills that an individual possesses. For the employer, certification helps identify qualified employees. For the employee, it confirms that the individual can perform in a position and can be a competitive advantage. There are various types of certification available for specific careers, as well as general certification that proves workplace competencies.

## E-Flash Card Activity: Career-Related Terms

Review the career-related terms that follow. Then visit the G-W mobile site to practice vocabulary using e-flash cards until you are able to recognize their meanings. If you do not have a smartphone, visit the G-W Learning companion website to access this feature.

| | |
|---|---|
| skill | thinking skills |
| job-specific skills | people skills |
| employability skills | personal qualities |
| basic skills | certification |

## Review Your Knowledge

1. Define *job-specific skills*, and explain how they are acquired.

2. Why are employability skills also considered transferrable or foundation skills?

3. What are basic skills? Provide some examples.

4. Compare and contrast thinking skills and people skills.

5. List examples of thinking skills.

6. Why does an employer expect employees to have people skills?

7. Define *personal qualities*.

8. How can certification help an individual compete for a position?

9. Explain continuing education.

10. Why is certification important to an employer?

## Apply Your Knowledge

1. Job postings list the skills qualified applicants are expected to have. Often the skills listed include job-specific skills as well as employability skills. Use the Internet to locate a job posting in your area of interest. List the job-specific skills mentioned in the posting. Next, list the employability skills requested.

2. Transferrable skills are skills that you have acquired in school or working in another career field. Consider the skills you have gained throughout your life. Describe how the skills you learned in one situation, such as in school or at a part-time job, can transfer to your chosen career field.

3. Identify someone you know who has been working in his or her industry at least five years. Interview this person to learn more about employability skills. How have these skills helped him or her advance in the workplace?

4. Basic skills are necessary to perform nearly any job. Basic skills include reading, writing, speaking, listening, mathematics, and technology. Write two or three sentences describing how each of these skills is important in your chosen career field.

5. Thinking skills are important employability skills. Conduct an Internet search on *improving thinking skills*. Select two or three articles from your search results. As you read them, make notes about how you can improve your thinking skills.

6. People skills enable you to work with others successfully. Select one or two people skills from the list in this chapter. Describe how you can improve the skills you select as you progress through your job search.

7. Employers look for positive personal qualities in job candidates. Explain why self-esteem, self-management, and responsibility are important qualities for any employee.

8. Continuing education units are required in some professions. Conduct an Internet search on *continuing education units*. What did you find?

9. Certification can make you stand out as a job applicant. Research the certifications available in your chosen career field. Select one that interests you. Note the title of the certification and how to achieve it.

10. Using the certification you selected, explain how you can fit it into plans for your career.

## Exploring Certification

### Career Certification Skills—Using Reading Skills

You are in charge of the student activity programs at a small college. You are taking 26 students to a play. Read the theater's policy on accommodating groups, and respond to the questions that follow.

**Group Accommodation Policy**

In order to receive a discounted group rate, a group must have a minimum of 20 people. The theater requires at least four weeks' notice ahead of the performance date to accommodate a group. Seating can be reserved in advance once the number for your group has been determined. The group will then have up to two weeks to present payment. Payment for the total number of tickets purchased can be made in one of the following forms: a school or organization check, a money order, or credit card. Cash is not accepted.

If informed six weeks ahead of the date of the performance, a backstage tour can be arranged for your group. The 20-minute tour takes place immediately following the performance. The tour will be conducted by the theater manager or someone on the theater management staff. Please inform us at the time of your reservation if any members of your group will require special accommodations.

1. How far in advance must you schedule your group event in order to receive the group rate and go on the backstage tour?

2. You plan to send a thank-you note to the tour guide for providing such an informative backstage tour. To whose office will you direct the note?

### Career Certification Skills—Finding Information

You have taken a volunteer job at a local animal rescue organization. You are providing your supervisor with information for her report.

| | Animal Statistic Table: Seattle Animal Shelter Annual Report | Dog | Cat | Total |
|---|---|---|---|---|
| A | Beginning Shelter Count | 54 | 210 | 264 |
| B | Intake from the Public | | | |
| | Healthy | 1,023 | 1,270 | 2,293 |
| | Treatable–Rehabilitatable | 9 | 30 | 39 |
| | Treatable–Manageable | 45 | 91 | 136 |
| | Untreatable–Unhealthy | 136 | 190 | 326 |
| | **Subtotal Intake from the Public** | 1,213 | 1,518 | 2,794 |

Source: http://www.seattle.gov/animalshelter

Using this table, answer the following questions.

1. Which type of animal was taken in most during this time period?

2. Of the total number of unhealthy and untreatable animals that come to the rescue site, what percentage of them are cats?

3. What is the total number of cats and dogs taken in by the organization from the public?

## Career Certification Skills—Applying Math Skills

The sports team you coach has a cylindrical water container that is 1.5 feet in diameter on the inside. At halftime, the depth of the water in the container is 1 foot. If 1 cubic foot of space holds 7.48 gallons, about how many gallons of water are currently in the tank? Select the correct answer. Show your calculations.

A. 13

B. 10

C. 7.48

D. 74

## Chapter 5

# Your Career Strengths

## Outcomes

- **Conduct** a personal career inventory.
- **Create** a personal brand.
- **Develop** a plan for your career.

## Career-Related Terms

| | |
|---|---|
| job | value |
| career | personal brand |
| aptitude | emerging occupation |
| soft skill | Occupational Information |
| hard skill | Network (O*NET) |
| keyword | career plan |
| ability | technology plan |

You will see icons at various points throughout the chapter. These icons indicate that interactive activities are available on the *Connect to Your Career* companion website. Selected activities are also available on the *Connect to Your Career* mobile site. These activities will help you learn, practice, and expand your career knowledge and skills.

Companion Website
www.g-wlearning.com/careereducation/

Mobile Site
www.m.g-wlearning.com

Bogdan Brasoveanu/Shutterstock.com

# Overview

As you begin the job-search process, you will complete many self-assessments that will help you evaluate your qualifications for employment. Employers look for well-rounded individuals who can help accomplish the goals of the business. Potential employees must have the skill set that matches the company's needs.

A career inventory is the first step in evaluating your aptitudes, skills, abilities, and values. Through this assessment, you can focus your energy on what is necessary for you to become a successful candidate for employment. Once your inventory is complete, you will be ready to set goals and create a plan that can move you closer to your career.

# Personal Career Inventory

A **job** is short-term employment for compensation. A **career** is a long-term progression in one particular field with opportunities for growth and advancement. At different times in your life, you will need a job to help pay your way through school or to meet other obligations. However, once you get into college, you will probably make plans for a career. Careers require long-term planning. They are life-long endeavors that utilize particular skills and expertise. A career generally requires more education than a job. Before beginning a career, many people often accept part-time jobs or internships.

You can prepare for the job- or career-search process by taking a personal career inventory. A *personal career inventory* provides information about your interests. It is an efficient way to learn about your natural aptitudes, skills, abilities, and values. It is important to apply for jobs in which you will be successful. It is equally important to apply for jobs that match aptitudes, skills, abilities, and values. Which are you seeking—a job or a career?

## Aptitudes

An **aptitude** is a characteristic that an individual has developed naturally. If you have an aptitude for something, you are able to learn it easily and perform it well. Some aptitudes are cognitive, or mental. Other aptitudes are physical. For example, some college students have an aptitude for math, while others have an aptitude for ballet. Within both the cognitive and physical categories, aptitudes manifest themselves in familiar areas, such as mechanics, art, computers, logic, music, writing, or socialization. Different jobs require different aptitudes.

One key to job success is to find work in an area that matches your aptitudes. Your aptitudes can provide you with clues on how to begin a job-search process. In order to plan your career, experts suggest that you select career opportunities that match your strongest characteristics.

Successful men and women who are experts in their fields probably found work that matched their natural tendencies or aptitudes. Natural interests can relate to your career goals. For example, you may have an aptitude for one or more of the following:

- mathematics
- drawing
- writing
- sports
- repairing machines

Experiences from the past can indicate future direction. If you have ever started a new job but quit soon after you were hired, chances are that your aptitudes and the job were mismatched. Some people begin a job or career and then realize that it was not as they had imagined. As you begin planning for a career,

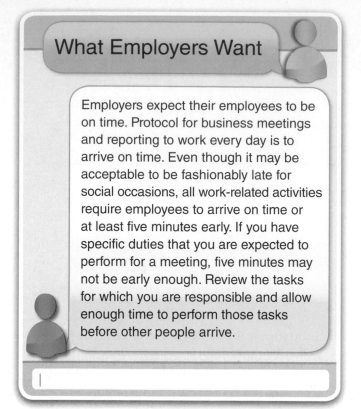

## What Employers Want

Employers expect their employees to be on time. Protocol for business meetings and reporting to work every day is to arrive on time. Even though it may be acceptable to be fashionably late for social occasions, all work-related activities require employees to arrive on time or at least five minutes early. If you have specific duties that you are expected to perform for a meeting, five minutes may not be early enough. Review the tasks for which you are responsible and allow enough time to perform those tasks before other people arrive.

consider those things that are of interest to you. What do you like to do? What tasks or activities do you perform easily? Sometimes students take classes and discover what they like or dislike.

You probably received better grades in classes that were most interesting to you. The subjects of these classes can lead to a possible career direction. Finding work that you enjoy begins with finding work where you are best suited.

Read the job posting in Figure 5-1. In this job posting, the employer is looking for a candidate with a strong mechanical aptitude. At times, employers ask for a specific aptitude as opposed to formal training.

Various tests can help you identify your aptitudes. An *informal aptitude test* helps distinguish your personality type and skill set. Your work preferences, natural tendencies, and socialization style can be measured. Tests such as these provide you with opportunities to practice test taking.

You might have taken a *formal aptitude placement test*, such as the SAT or ACT college placement exams. These tests are used to measure overall achievement and compare performance to others.

Do not worry if you are uncertain about identifying any particular aptitudes. Sometimes it takes additional consideration and opportunities to uncover natural tendencies. Continue to identify areas that interest you in your academic track and in your career.

---

### Quality Maintenance Technician II

**Company Name:** Sears Import

| | |
|---|---|
| **Job Type:** Full Time | **Required Travel:** Frequent |
| **Duration:** Permanent | **Salary:** Commensurate with experience |

**Location:** Banning, California, USA

**Job Description**
The Quality Maintenance Technician II (QMTII) will provide unit-level support for maintenance and safety standards, to include the performance of preventative maintenance checks, and review of in-store maintenance procedures as assigned, in full-line stores and off-mall stores. The QMTII assists the assigned stores in maintaining the standards and disciplines needed to provide a high level of customer satisfaction while minimizing energy usage. The person seeking this position should be a self-starter, be proficient in completing tasks in the required time frame, and have a strong mechanical aptitude. Daily travel is required. This position reports to the District Facilities Manager.

**Figure 5-1** Employers may request specific aptitudes as well as formal training.

## 5-1 Aptitudes Inventory

**Directions:** Use the space provided to complete the activity or take notes. Alternatively, you can download the electronic version of this activity from the companion website.

1. The following words are examples of recognized aptitudes: budgeting, persuasion, photography, and studying. However, there are many more. Make a list of common aptitudes with which you are familiar.

2. Next, make a list of aptitudes that you think are your strongest. Rank your top five personal aptitudes 1–5, with the number 1 aptitude as the strongest.

3. Which one of your top five aptitudes would you most want to demonstrate to an employer? Why do you think that aptitude is important for career success?

4. Conduct an Internet search for *career aptitude tests*. For example, CareerColleges.com offers a free online career aptitude test. Select one aptitude test, and complete it.

5. After completing the test, summarize the results. What did you find out about yourself?

Download the electronic version of this activity.

## Skills

*Skills* are things that you do well. Unlike aptitudes, which come naturally, you can develop your skills over time. However, skills fluctuate. You either gain or lose them with time. You are not born with skills; you have to work at them consistently. For example, if you practice piano every day and then stop for an entire year, what would be the outcome? It is likely that you will lose much of your piano-playing skills. Skills are classified as either soft skills or hard skills.

**Soft skills** involve behaviors that a person uses to relate to others, and they are not easy to measure. Examples of soft skills include leadership, charisma, tact, personal and professional time management, conflict resolution, and professionalism. Soft skills may also include employability skills.

**Hard skills** are measureable and can be observed. Some hard skills include software and technology skills, speaking or writing in a foreign language, keyboarding, programming, and designing. Skills can also be both physical and mental. Hard skills may also be job-specific skills that are required to perform as an employee.

Employers include skills as part of specific job requirements. They select words that best describe the position they are looking to fill. These specific words are known as keywords. **Keywords** are words that specifically relate to the functions of the position for which the employer is hiring. For example, an employer might post an advertisement including keywords that describe someone who has developed time-management skills. Another employer might post an ad for someone with social skills. *Social skills* are those skills that enable a person to work well with others.

Skills can also be verbal. Maybe you have a gift for public speaking or leadership. Skills can include knowledge. You may be able to recite the periodic table of the elements. Do not underestimate or discount your skills. When it comes to focusing on your career, you might be wondering how aptitudes relate to skills.

**The Best App for that**

Using your mobile device, conduct a search for the *iPQ Career Planner* app. iPQ Career Planner provides information for career planning. By taking the assessment offered within the app, you can identify the skills you have that might help you find a job. How do you think this could help you in your job search?

Consider a college student who has always enjoyed music and has an aptitude for music. Maybe he or she developed musical skills and took lessons to support that internal motivation. For this student, the aptitude and skills match. It might be fitting that he or she would consider a career search in a music field, opposed to another field of study.

However, what if a student has an aptitude for music, but has never taken the opportunity to develop skills as a musician? Quite possibly, he or she might have to settle for a career that is not an ideal match. If career aptitudes and career skills do not coincide perfectly, you may need to diversify your job search in order to locate an employer who is looking for your unique set of qualities.

Skills are marketable commodities. Figure 5-2 lists examples of some of the skills that employers look for in today's job market. To market yourself, you need to identify your skill sets in terms of employability.

**5-2 Skills Inventory**

**Directions:** Use the space provided to complete the activity or take notes. Alternatively, you can download the electronic version of this activity from the companion website.

1. The following words are examples of recognized soft skills: ethical, hard working, innovative, loyal, personable, and reliable. However, there are many more. Make a list of your five strongest soft skills and rank them 1–5, with the number 1 skill as the strongest.

2. Describe why your number 1 ranked skill is your strongest soft skill.

3. The following are examples of recognized hard skills: computer literate, follows directions, manages deadlines, mathematical skills, research skills, and written communication. However, there are many more. Make a list of your five strongest hard skills and rank them 1–5, with the number 1 skill as the strongest.

4. Describe why your number 1 ranked skill is your strongest hard skill.

Download the electronic
version of this activity.

---

**Skills Employers Seek**

- analytical
- communication
- critical thinking
- interpersonal
- leadership
- organization
- presentation
- problem solving
- project management
- research
- technology
- web development

**Figure 5-2** Can you identify which skills are soft skills and which ones are hard skills?

## Abilities

**Ability** is a mastery of a skill or the capacity to do something. Having aptitudes and skills is supported or limited by your abilities. For instance, the college student who has musical aptitude and skill might not have the ability to perform under pressure in musical concerts.

Your aptitudes and skills are just the beginning of what employers seek. An employer will list a variety of abilities as part of a job posting. Examples of must-have abilities in job postings often include the following:

- work long hours without tiring
- assist others with little or no direction
- effectively handle multiple projects
- implement visual designs
- think logically
- speak multiple languages

# Career Portfolio

## Soft Skills and Hard Skills

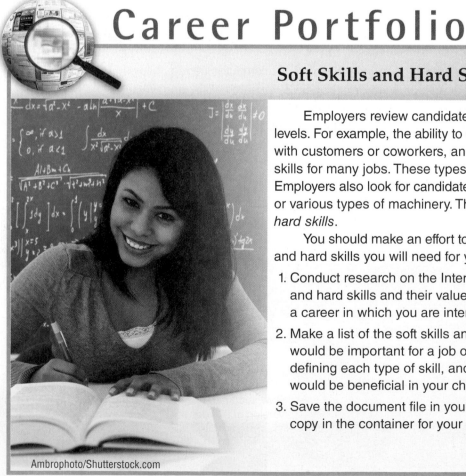

Ambrophoto/Shutterstock.com

Employers review candidates for various positions and skill levels. For example, the ability to communicate effectively, get along with customers or coworkers, and solve problems are all important skills for many jobs. These types of skills are often called *soft skills*. Employers also look for candidates who can use software programs or various types of machinery. These abilities are often called *hard skills*.

You should make an effort to learn about and develop soft skills and hard skills you will need for your chosen career area.

1. Conduct research on the Internet to find articles about soft skills and hard skills and their value in helping employees succeed in a career in which you are interested.

2. Make a list of the soft skills and hard skills you possess that would be important for a job or career area. Write a paragraph defining each type of skill, and explain why you think these skills would be beneficial in your chosen career.

3. Save the document file in your e-portfolio folder. Place a printed copy in the container for your print portfolio.

## 5-3 Abilities Assessment

**Directions:** Use the space provided to complete the activity or take notes. Alternatively, you can download the electronic version of this activity from the companion website.

1. Recall your top five aptitudes from Activity 5-1. How do these five aptitudes translate into your abilities? For example, you may have an aptitude for persuasion, which may translate to an ability to sell products to customers. List your top five aptitudes and an ability that you have developed for each.

2. Do you have other aptitudes that could be developed into new abilities?

3. Consider other abilities you have. Which of your abilities would be desired qualities an employer might look for in a candidate?

Download the electronic version of this activity.

Confirm that you have the ability to perform all requirements of any job before you apply. You might qualify for many points of a job position or posting. However, if you are missing one of the must-have abilities, you might need to continue looking for other opportunities.

## Values

**Values** are beliefs about the things that matter most to an individual. A value represents your beliefs in yourself and how you wish to work and live. Values affect every part of your life, including the way you engage in relationships and make work decisions. Some of your values change with time and others remain constant. Values that are not likely to change are those that steer you in the direction of your career.

Examples of values include believing in working hard or the importance of caring for others. Other examples of values include:

- perfection
- equality
- harmony
- determination
- teamwork
- status

All people hold values, but many have not taken the time to identify them. It is possible to share values. Think about what you value, not only in working relationships but also in working environments. It is important to identify your values so that you can focus on finding a career that is a good match for you.

## 5-4 Values Assessment

**Directions:** Use the space provided to complete the activity or take notes. Alternatively, you can download the electronic version of this activity from the companion website.

1. There are many examples of recognized values, such as ambition, family, and integrity. The list of values is endless. Make a list of ten personal values that are important to you.

2. Next, rank each value in your list with the most important marked as number 1. How do you think your personal values will affect your job search and your future career?

Download the electronic version of this activity.

# Your Personal Brand

Once you have identified your aptitudes, skills, abilities, and values, you are ready to develop a personal brand. A **personal brand** is a snapshot of who an individual wants to be as a professional. It showcases your aptitudes, skills, abilities, and values. Your personal brand is a statement that reflects the value you bring to a company in exchange for a salary upon which you and the company agree.

You are familiar with product brands, such as the iPhone and the Kindle. You have knowledge of corporate brands, such as Apple and Microsoft. When you consider each brand, your mind fills in the details of the logo, products, corporate culture, and reputation. Corporations hire thousands of full-time staff to promote and protect brand names. When a potential employer reads your personal brand statement, you want him or her to imagine how you would be an asset to the company.

Create a personal brand to promote and market yourself as a unique job candidate. When you begin writing your personal brand statement, you should use words that best describe your aptitudes, skills, abilities, and values. These words become your *brand keywords*, and they will help you create a memorable statement. As you begin writing your brand statement, consider using a maximum of four brand keywords. Focus on producing one sentence that best describes who you are. Figure 5-3 illustrates examples of brand keywords that reflect an individual's personal career inventory. Review the personal brand statements in Figure 5-4. Notice that each statement is succinct, uses brand keywords, and

**Brand Keywords**

- dedicated
- dependable
- ethical
- hard-working
- honest
- honorable
- passionate
- punctual
- reliable
- team contributor

Goodheart-Willcox Publisher

**Figure 5-3** Words that best describe your aptitudes, skills, abilities, and values become your brand keywords.

reflects the image the person wants to project to potential employers.

Brand yourself as the professional you want to become. Your brand determines how you will market yourself. Use it in your professional online profiles, résumés, and cover letters.

# Planning Your Career

Conducting a personal career inventory and developing your personal brand reveal your career strengths and aspirations. Use this knowledge to help you decide on a career path. A *career path* is a person's progression in his or her professional field. In your educational experience, you may have been introduced to career paths that categorize various jobs common in the workforce. As you will see in Figure 5-5, career paths are broad categories that focus on specific skills and competencies for various types of jobs. Within each career path, specific industries are referenced. Selecting a career path involves choosing which is best suited to your aptitudes, skills, abilities, and values, and then selecting an industry within it.

**Personal Brand Statements**

- Through a unique combination of math expertise and problem solving, I am an *honest*, *ethical*, and *dedicated* accountant who enjoys being a *team contributor*.

- I am a *dependable*, *hard-working* concierge who is *passionate* about serving guests in the most positive and professional way.

- My previous employers describe me as a *reliable* project manager, because I leave no project detail to chance.

Goodheart-Willcox Publisher

**Figure 5-4** An effective personal brand statement reflects the value you bring to a company.

## 5-5 Personal Brand

**Directions:** Use the space provided to complete the activity or take notes. Alternatively, you can download the electronic version of this activity from the companion website.

1.  Conduct an Internet search for *personal branding*. Select your favorite website and read about the importance of a personal brand, how to write your own statement, and how a personal brand statement will help you market yourself. Record your findings in the space that follows.

2.  Make a list of keywords that you will use to write your personal brand statement.

3.  Using your keywords, write a statement that represents your personal brand. This statement will not be static. You will revise it as you progress through your career. You will use this statement in your career-search activities.

Download the electronic version of this activity.

## Career Paths

**Agriculture, Food & Natural Resources**
Food Products and Processing Systems
Plant Systems
Animal Systems
Power, Structural & Technical Systems
Natural Resources Systems
Environmental Service Systems
Agribusiness Systems

**Architecture & Construction**
Design/Pre-Construction
Construction
Maintenance/Operations

**Arts, Audio/Video Technology & Communications**
Audio and Video Technology and Film
Printing Technology
Visual Arts
Performing Arts
Journalism and Broadcasting
Telecommunications

**Business Management & Administration**
General Management
Business Information Management
Human Resources Management
Operations Management
Administrative Support

**Education & Training**
Administration and Administrative Support
Professional Support Services
Teaching/Training

**Finance**
Securities & Investments
Business Finance
Banking Services
Insurance

**Government & Public Administration**
Government
National Security
Foreign Service
Planning
Revenue and Taxation
Regulation
Public Management and Administration

**Health Science**
Therapeutic Services
Diagnostic Services
Health Informatics
Support Services
Biotechnology Research and Development

**Hospitality & Tourism**
Restaurants and Food/Beverage Services
Lodging
Travel & Tourism
Recreation, Amusements & Attractions

**Human Services**
Early Childhood Development & Services
Counseling & Mental Health Services
Family & Community Services
Personal Care Services
Consumer Services

**Information Technology**
Network Systems
Information Support and Services
Web and Digital Communications
Programming and Software Development

**Law, Public Safety, Corrections & Security**
Correction Services
Emergency and Fire Management Services
Security & Protective Services
Law Enforcement Services
Legal Services

**Manufacturing**
Production
Manufacturing Production Process Development
Maintenance, Installation & Repair
Quality Assurance
Logistics & Inventory Control
Health, Safety and Environmental Assurance

**Marketing**
Marketing Management
Professional Sales
Merchandising
Marketing Communications
Marketing Research

**Science, Technology, Engineering & Mathematics**
Engineering and Technology
Science and Math

**Transportation, Distribution & Logistics**
Transportation Operations
Logistics Planning and Management Services
Warehousing and Distribution Center Operations
Facility and Mobile Equipment Maintenance
Transportation Systems/Infrastructure Planning, Management, and Regulation
Health, Safety and Environmental Management
Sales and Service

Goodheart-Willcox Publisher; Information source: www.careervision.org

**Figure 5-5** Select a career path that is best suited to your aptitudes, skills, abilities, and values.

With each passing decade, employment trends evolve. It is your task to predict future employment options in the career field of your choice. One of the ways to analyze the future employment outlook is to compare yesterday's job trends with current market advertisements. The federal government and many states compile and publish data for emerging occupations. **Emerging occupations** are new occupations that have developed or changed due to technological or other advancements. For example, in the past a clerk filed hard-copy papers into file cabinets. That job has changed to an emerging occupation for IT professionals who clean up and defragment files stored on a computer. Additional new and emerging occupations include:

- genetics counselor
- hearing aid specialist
- information security analyst
- ophthalmic medical technician
- robotics engineer
- sustainability specialist
- transportation security screener
- wind turbine service technician

As you begin planning your career, take advantage of the many career resources that are available. **Occupational Information Network (O*NET)** is one resource that provides descriptions of in-demand industry areas in emerging occupations. O*NET OnLine is a tool job seekers can use for career exploration and job analysis.

The US Department of Labor is another resource for job seekers. Through the Department of Labor, users can view job information, hourly standards for jobs, wage information, and occupational safety information. According to the Department of Labor, in-demand industries are vital to our economy's health. Some in-demand industries include the ones shown in Figure 5-6.

In Chapter 1, you began creating your professional online presence and wrote career profiles for various professional networking accounts. Now that you have learned about career paths, take time to incorporate these titles into your online career profiles. Figure 5-7 shows examples of career paths and summary words that you can

### In-Demand Industries

| | |
|---|---|
| Advanced manufacturing | Green economy |
| Aerospace | Health care |
| Automotive | Homeland security |
| Biotechnology | Hospitality |
| Construction | Information technology |
| Education | Nanotechnology |
| Energy | Retail trade |
| Financial services | Transportation |
| Geospatial technology | |

Goodheart-Willcox Publisher

**Figure 5-6** Certain industries experience more growth than others.

use to personalize your profiles. As you learn more about marketing yourself as a potential employee, revisit your networking accounts, and update them regularly. Be strategic in your choice of careers and only use those that apply to your career interest. Focus on the areas for which you are best suited. For example, if you are interested in teaching, you might use teaching or training in your descriptions. If you have a Twitter account, you might use #teaching or #training.

Next, look for LinkedIn groups to join and follow to look for jobs and networking opportunities. In the search box on LinkedIn, "teaching," returns results for groups of *Higher Education Teaching and Learning* and *The Teaching Professor.* Each has thousands of members with whom you can interact. These are results from those who are advertising for teaching jobs, as well as specific member profiles of those involved in teaching. Twitter will generate similar results when you search for your career field of interest proceeded with a hashtag.

## Career Plans

Now you are ready to start setting career goals. What does it take to find a job? In today's job market, the outdated process of writing and mailing a résumé does not work efficiently or quickly. Just as the workforce has changed over

## 5-6 Emerging Occupations

**Directions:** Use the space provided to complete the activity or take notes. Alternatively, you can download the electronic version of this activity from the companion website.

1. Use O*NET (www.onetcenter.org) to research emerging occupations. Consider your aptitudes, skills, abilities, and values when researching the occupations.

2. Select two occupations that interest you. List them.

3. Make notes on the details of the two emerging occupations you selected, including the industry, job description, tasks associated with the job, salary range, required education level, and technology used in the position.

4. What aptitudes, skills, abilities, and values do you have that make you well suited to these careers?

5. Which one of the two emerging occupations you researched would you be more likely to pursue? Explain why.

Download the electronic version of this activity.

Companion
G-W Learning

## Career Path Summary Words

| Career Path | LinkedIn Profile Summary Words | Twitter Profile Hashtags |
|---|---|---|
| Information Technology | Network Systems<br>Information Technology<br>Digital Communications<br>Programming<br>Software Development | #digitalmedia<br>#HTML<br>#IT<br>#networkdesign<br>#programming<br>#software |
| Education & Training | Administration<br>Certification<br>Education<br>Teaching<br>Training | #certification<br>#education<br>#highereducation<br>#kthrough12<br>#educationadministration<br>#teaching |
| Health Science | Biotechnology<br>Diagnostics<br>Nursing<br>Public Health and Safety<br>Therapy Services | #biotechnology<br>#diagnostics<br>#health<br>#publicservices<br>#publicsafety<br>#registerednurse |
| Business Management & Administration | Administrative Support<br>Business Information Management<br>General Management<br>Human Resources Management<br>Operations Management | #accounting<br>#administration<br>#businessmanagement<br>#businessservices<br>#finance<br>#marketing |

Goodheart-Willcox Publisher

**Figure 5-7** Your online presence should include summary words that correspond to your selected career path.

the years, the methods of gaining employment have changed as well. Finding a job in today's economy requires organization and a plan before you begin.

Where are you in the job-search process? From the beginning, it is critical to establish goals and priorities. The best type of goal setting begins with a two- to four-year career plan. A **career plan** is documentation of where a person is today in the job-search process and where he or she would like to be in two to four years. Your career plan begins today. Your current situation, whether you are a student or prospective employee, is the perfect starting point. You will document your work in this course as milestones toward your ultimate career goals.

The benefits of creating a career plan include self-reflection, career goal setting, and a commitment to complete the tasks you start. It is important to create a career plan so that you can reflect on your progress, practice setting goals, and create a roadmap to help you accomplish your goals. You will add deadlines and resources that you will need to accomplish your tasks. Without goals, you are less likely to advance in the job-search process. Make it a practice to review and update your plan at least twice a year.

Some common items in a typical two- to four-year career plan are shown in Figure 5-8. You will notice that these items fall into some general categories, such as academic goals, job-search goals, and goals to research careers. It is helpful to draft your goals before writing your plan.

## Action Items for Career Plan

**Year 1**
- Monitor and maintain a strong grade point average (GPA)
- Evaluate skills, abilities, and aptitudes
- Establish short-term job goals and long-term career goals
- Determine which courses are required to meet career goals
- Create a résumé
- Create online career profiles
- Visit online resources such as O*NET Online
- Target a specific job to obtain
- Use social media for professional networking

**Year 2**
- Continue to update online career profiles
- Update résumé to reflect current career position
- Recruit current coworkers for professional references
- Expand knowledge of technology and learn new software
- Set goals for position titles and salary increases

**Year 3**
- Evaluate satisfaction with current job
- Update career portfolio
- Investigate corporations to gain long-term employment
- Attend employee workshops
- Review existing and potential employee benefits including 401(k) plans
- Map out future career goals

**Year 4**
- Write a statement of career for the next 10 years
- Set a goal for financial independence
- Determine which long-term assets to acquire, such as housing
- Evaluate professional life in comparison with your personal goals
- Network as a professional in field of expertise
- Determine if additional academic training or certification is necessary

Goodheart-Willcox Publisher

**Figure 5-8** Action items to include in a career plan are often academic goals, job-search goals, and career-research goals.

Once you have drafted action items that are important for your future, you can start writing your actual career plan. There is no right or wrong way to format this document. Figure 5-9 shows an example of a template you could use to get started.

## Technology Plan

It is likely that you use a great deal more technology than your parents did when they were your age. You might not realize that the technology you use to communicate with friends, such as social media, texting, taking photographs, and conducting research, translate into proficient and employable skills. In addition to a host of technology tools at your disposal, you probably rely on apps to navigate directions, check the weather, or even purchase movie tickets. Do not take your knowledge of technology for granted.

Fortune 500 companies employ technology-savvy individuals for social media positions. These employees are hired for tasks such as maintaining Twitter accounts and blogs for their

 **5-7 Career Plan**

**Directions:** Use the space provided to complete the activity or take notes. Alternatively, you can download the electronic version of this activity from the companion website.

1. Review Figure 5-8, and identify items to include in a two- to four-year career plan. This will be a starting point for writing your career plan.

2. Using the Internet, research examples of career plans and directions on how to write a career plan. Keep in mind that there is more than one way to write a career plan. Find an example that you like. Use this example and your answers from the previous question to write an actual career plan. This document will evolve as you progress through this text.

Download the electronic version of this activity.

| Career Plan Template | | | |
|---|---|---|---|
| Career Plan: Year 1 | | | |
| Career Item | Specific Action to Take | Target Completion Date | Actual Completion Date |
| | | | |
| | | | |
| | | | |

Goodheart-Willcox Publisher

**Figure 5-9** A career-plan template should include a place to record a plan of action and a completion date for each career item.

companies. How would you like your job duties to include responding to customers via Twitter?

Career seekers often develop a technology plan to prepare them for future employment. A **technology plan** is documentation of software and other technology a person knows today and needs to know in the future.

A technology plan begins with identifying a specific technology and then determining your skill level. The plan reveals the technology knowledge you have and use on a daily basis. You will use this plan with your current proficiencies as part of the data you gather to organize your job search. The technology plan also helps identify gaps that you need to fill during the next two to four years. This gives you an opportunity to research what is needed in your career so that you may identify new skills that will be necessary for you to be successful.

A sample technology plan is illustrated in Figure 5-10.

| Technology Plan | | | | | | |
|---|---|---|---|---|---|---|
| | Current Proficiency Level | | | Desired Level of Accomplishment | | |
| Technology | Novice | Experienced User | Expert | Novice | Experienced User | Expert |
| Blogger | X | | | | | X |
| Facebook | | X | | | | X |
| Instagram | X | | | | X | |
| LinkedIn | X | | | | | X |
| Microsoft Word | X | | | | X | |
| Pinterest | X | | | | X | |
| Twitter | | X | | | | X |
| Tumblr | X | | | | X | |
| YouTube | X | | | | X | |

Goodheart-Willcox Publisher

**Figure 5-10** A technology plan can help you focus on the technology that you need to learn in order to accomplish your career goals.

## 5-8 Technology Plan

**Directions:** Use the space provided to complete the activity or take notes. Alternatively, you can download the electronic version of this activity from the companion website.

1. Review the technology plan in Figure 5-10. List all of the software programs of which you have a working knowledge.

2. Next, indicate the level of proficiency you desire for each type of technology.

3. Of the types of technology at which you are already an expert or experienced user, which ones do you think will be the most useful in your career? Distinguish those in your list.

4. Choose three technologies at which you are a novice. How can you become an expert?

Download the electronic
version of this activity.

# Chapter Summary

- A job is short-term employment for compensation. A career is a long-term progression in one particular field with opportunities for growth and advancement. Conducting a personal career inventory is the best way to prepare for finding a job or a career. You will likely be successful in a job that matches your aptitudes, skills, abilities, and values.

- A personal brand is a snapshot of who you are as a professional, showcasing your aptitudes, skills, and abilities. Brand yourself as the professional you want to become.

- Planning for your career allows you to reflect on your progress and set goals to accomplish in the future. Documentation of where you are today in the job-search process and where you would like to see your career in two to four years is a career plan. Creating a technology plan allows you to inventory the software and technology you already know and your skill level for each one.

## E-Flash Card Activity: Career-Related Terms

Review the career-related terms that follow. Then visit the G-W mobile site to practice vocabulary using e-flash cards until you are able to recognize their meanings. If you do not have a smartphone, visit the G-W Learning companion website to access this feature.

| | |
|---|---|
| job | value |
| career | personal brand |
| aptitude | emerging occupation |
| soft skill | Occupational Information Network (O*NET) |
| hard skill | career plan |
| keyword | technology plan |
| ability | |

## Review Your Knowledge

1. Explain the difference between a job and a career.

2. What is a *personal career inventory*? How can it help you prepare for a job or career?

3. Define *aptitude*. How can aptitudes lead to job success?

4. What are *skills*? Define the two types of skills, and give examples of each type.

5. What is an *ability*? How does it differ from an aptitude or skill?

6. Define *values*. Explain how your values may affect your career choices.

7. Discuss the importance of a personal brand and how to create your personal brand statement.

8. What are *emerging occupations*?

9. What are the benefits of creating a career plan?

10. What is the purpose of a technology plan?

## Apply Your Knowledge

1. How does the measuring of aptitudes, skills, abilities, and values help you to find enjoyable employment?

2. Identify which of your natural aptitudes is your strongest. How could it translate into a career?

3. Explain the correlation between your *abilities* and your *skills*.

4. What new abilities would you need to develop in order to work at your dream job or career?

5. Develop a personal brand statement for a person you know or a famous person.

6. In what way is a career plan like a map of future work-related goals?

7. It is common to become uncertain regarding items on a career plan four years into the future. When this happens, what resources might help you to develop long-term career goals?

8. Some job seekers think that getting a job is the end of the career journey, yet that can be when developing a career plan takes place. Why is a first job not necessarily the job that a candidate will keep for a lifetime?

9. Name three jobs for which your current technology skills may qualify you.

10. In this chapter, you completed a career plan, a technology plan, and began gathering materials for a portfolio. Of these activities, which is the most natural for you to do? Why?

## Exploring Certification

### Career Certification Skills—Using Reading Skills

You completed your technology plan. This plan highlights areas in which you might have found gaps between your current skills and the skills required for your desired career.

1. Research emerging technologies and apps in your desired field and determine which technology skills might benefit you as a new job candidate. Make a list of your findings.

2. Write one to two paragraphs describing the application of the technology, which companies are most likely to use the technology, and how you would learn the technology to become an acceptable job candidate. Update the technology plan you created in Activity 5-8 accordingly.

### Career Certification Skills—Finding Information

Completing a two- to four-year career plan will pay dividends as you start the job search process. It will be important to regularly review the plan that you just created and evaluate where you need assistance or direction to reach your goals.

1. Research articles on career plans and their importance. As you read the articles, consider the writer's purpose as well as your purpose for reading the article. When you are finished, evaluate what you have read.

2. Review the career plan you wrote in Activity 5-7. Highlight the areas where you would like guidance to accomplish your goals.

3. Take your career plan to a guidance counselor, mentor, or someone else who can give you unbiased feedback. What did you learn from this experience?

### Career Certification Skills—Applying Math Skills

You are an office assistant at a doctor's office. A patient's bill for a checkup totals $105. The patient's health insurance requires the patient to pay only 20 percent of the total bill. How much will the patient's insurance pay for the checkup? Select the correct answer. Show your calculations.

A. $86

B. $87

C. $84

D. $83

# Unit 3 Application Process

## Connecting to Your Career

### Why It Matters

One of the first challenges you will face as a job seeker is persuading a potential employer to believe you are the perfect candidate for a position. In most cases, your résumé will be the key to this process. Once you identify a job opening, you must create a résumé that convinces the reader to invite you for an interview. The résumé should be stellar and perfect in form. Along with the résumé, you will submit a cover letter. If you are required to complete a formal application form, it should be as presentable as your résumé and cover letter.

Corporation websites, job lists, and a job boards will be valuable sources for finding advertisements for positions. Make these resources work for you by adopting the Sunday Evening Plan. Update your online presence on a regular basis and manage the application process.

# Résumés

## Outcomes

- **Explain** the purpose of a résumé.
- **Discuss** the importance of keywords.
- **Describe** sections of the résumé.
- **List** types of résumé formats.
- **Describe** various ways to save a résumé.
- **Discuss** the importance of customizing a résumé for specific positions.

## Career-Related Terms

| | |
|---|---|
| résumé | career profile |
| résumé template | timeline résumé |
| trending | skills résumé |
| heading | visual résumé |
| career objective | infographic résumé |

You will see icons at various points throughout the chapter. These icons indicate that interactive activities are available on the *Connect to Your Career* companion website. Selected activities are also available on the *Connect to Your Career* mobile site. These activities will help you learn, practice, and expand your career knowledge and skills.

 Companion Website
www.g-wlearning.com/careereducation/

 Mobile Site
www.m.g-wlearning.com

# Overview

When you are seeking employment, the résumé you prepare is an important first step in getting an interview. You get one chance to impress the reader, so your résumé must make a strong and positive statement about who you are. You must persuade the potential employer that your skills and experience fit the position he or she is seeking to fill.

A good résumé is a marketing tool that sells you as the perfect candidate for a position. What makes a good résumé? First, it must be well-written and presented in an organized manner. Second, it must have searchable keywords. Finally, it must have content that entices the reader to invite you for an interview.

# Résumé

A **résumé** is a written document that lists an individual's qualifications for a job, including education and work experience. It can be the first impression most employers will have prior to meeting you. A résumé is a glimpse into a candidate's professional preparation and pertinent qualifications for work. Its chief purpose is to convince a potential employer that your experiences and skills match the qualifications of the job. Think of a résumé as a powerful summary of who you are and why you would be an asset as an employee.

After a résumé is created, it should be formatted as both a hard copy and an electronic document. Even though we live in a technological society, there is still the need for hard copy documents. For example, it is appropriate to bring hard copies of your résumé to an interview. You do not want to miss the opportunity to put your information in front of the interviewer and his or her colleagues.

The electronic version of the document, commonly called an *e-résumé*, can be used to apply for positions online. Candidates can also e-mail an e-résumé to apply for a job.

Both versions of a résumé follow a standard process. A résumé must be well-written and free of errors. The information should be organized in a way that highlights your qualifications. This will allow a potential employer to see that your skills match the job requirements. It is

worth spending time to perfect your résumé. It is the gateway for a potential interview and, ultimately, to a great job.

When creating a résumé, consider using a résumé template to get the process started. A **résumé template** is a pre-formatted word processing document that contains a standard layout with adequate margins of white space. Templates look balanced on a page and contain pre-selected fonts, bullet points, headers, footers, and sometimes separator lines. They are documents designed to give a résumé a professional look and feel. It can be easier to use a template and customize it for your personal needs rather than to start from scratch.

When reviewing the many available templates, consider the following:

- adequate white space and margins
- font that is black in color
- headings that are larger than the body text
- no elaborate headings, text boxes, or tables

Take advantage of the myriad of free templates available online from Microsoft, Google docs, and other online resources, and save them as documents on your computer.

# Keywords

As you begin sifting through job ads, you will notice certain words that are used frequently. These repeated words often include specific terms related to the position, such as *leadership*, *degree*, and *specialist*, to list a few. These are known as

# 6-1 Résumé Templates

**Directions:** Use the space provided to complete the activity or take notes. Alternatively, you can download the electronic version of this activity from the companion website.

1. Conduct an Internet search for *résumé templates*. Record several URLs of templates you would consider using.

2. Which template do you prefer? Why? Would you consider using this template to create your own résumé?

Download the electronic version of this activity.

keywords. As explained in Chapter 5, *keywords* are words that relate to the functions of the open position. Most keywords are nouns or noun phrases, not verbs. Examples of keywords are shown in Figure 6-1.

Employers use keywords in job advertisements to describe the duties associated with requirements for open positions. The use of keywords helps employers find candidates who have the skills or talents for which they seek. They select keywords that are important to the job and then look for those words in the résumés candidates submit. This can help in finding potential matches for the job opening. Read the job advertisement in Figure 6-2, and note the following keywords used.

- journal entries
- monthly reconciliation of bank accounts
- tax schedules
- bank draws
- project reports
- workflow timing
- process and procedure improvements
- honesty
- responsibility
- integrity
- fulfillment of commitments

Practice reading job advertisements and identifying keywords that you will use in your résumé. Using the right combination of keywords is the way to become visible to an employer or recruiter. A résumé and account profile should include the exact same keywords that employers use in the advertisement for the job for which you are applying.

**Keywords**

| | | | |
|---|---|---|---|
| Accounts payable | Credit management | Investments | Retail |
| Advocacy | Curriculum | Leadership | Risk management |
| Balance sheet | development | Logistics | Sales experience |
| Banking | Customer service | Manager | Social media |
| Benefits | Data analysis | Mandarin Chinese | management |
| administration | Data entry | Marketing | Spanish |
| Bilingual | Debt refinancing | Microsoft Word | Spreadsheet expertise |
| Billing | Editing | Networking | Statistics |
| Biotechnology | Education | Patient services | Supervisor |
| Budget analysis | Engineer | Payroll | Surveying |
| Business | Financial planning | Planning | Team building |
| development | Health and safety | Product | Telecommunications |
| Business to | Health care | representation | Underwriting |
| business (B2B) | High-tech industry | Professional | Video editing |
| Certified public | HTML5 | Project management | Web design |
| accountant | Information | Public relations | Written communication |
| Collections | technology | Real estate | skills |
| Construction | | | |

Goodheart-Willcox Publisher

**Figure 6-1** Use keywords that are appropriate for the job to which you are applying.

The job-search process has transitioned from employers reading hard-copy résumés to computer software programs that scan electronic résumés for keywords. Before technology became prominent in job searching, action verbs were used in résumés because humans read each one individually. A job candidate appeared action-oriented by using action verbs.

With the hundreds of résumés and job postings available online, often humans do not sort or read résumés at the beginning stages of the recruitment process. Instead, computer programs scan the content for keywords to expedite the screening process. *Automatic data tracking (ADT) software* is used to scan résumés for keywords. The software is used by employers and recruiters to sort through résumés and flag the ones that match the keywords for which they are looking.

Résumés with the correct keywords trigger responses, while résumés without matching keywords are ignored. If your résumé lacks keywords associated with a specific job, you decrease your chances of having your résumé flagged during the early stage of the screening

## What Employers Want

*Etiquette* is the art of using good manners and polite behavior in any situation. It is also the absence of destructive workplace behaviors, such as negative comments and conversations. Employers expect appropriate etiquette in the workplace. When interacting with coworkers, clients, and any other business professional, employees should show respect and courtesy, and maintain a pleasant demeanor.

## Essential Duties and Responsibilities

- Assist in the monthly close process by preparing journal entries, reports, analysis, and supporting schedules, as needed, under the directions of management
- Perform monthly reconciliations of bank accounts
- Assist in the preparation of tax schedules
- Assist with bank draws, file uploads, and project reports
- Concurrently perform multiple assignments and self-manage schedule to determine workflow timing and duration
- Perform special projects under the direction of management, and respond appropriately to requests from other company personnel
- Apply principles of accounting and use judgment and professional skills in determining appropriate procedures for preparation and maintenance of accounting records, transaction research, and reporting
- Identify opportunities for process and procedure improvements and work with management to implement
- Demonstrate honesty, responsibility, integrity, and fulfillment of commitments

Goodheart-Willcox Publisher

**Figure 6-2** Practice finding keywords in job postings.

process. Remember to constantly update your résumé for online job applications. Keep the following tips in mind.

- Keywords change over time; keywords used six months ago may have evolved or become obsolete.
- Most keywords are nouns and noun phrases, not verbs.
- Using keywords alone as a list in your résumé will not create an effective job-search tool.
- Incorporate the keywords for your specific career into effective but brief sentences.
- Keywords might include skills as well as experience.

**Trending** refers to keywords and phrases that have the highest number of searches in any given day. Many Internet search engines, such as Yahoo, list what is trending, as do social media websites like Twitter. Trending information is saved, and the data are tabulated. These tabulations are ranked and posted on the sites. For example, if you conduct a search for "technology jobs," the search engine will rank your search terms and offer the most popular results for the job posting keyword phrase. If

enough employers use consistent wording for job posts, search engine robots will categorize those and record how often they are repeated.

As employers' needs change, keywords related to a job will also change. For example, during the hot summer months, employers might be looking for summer lifeguards. The keyword *lifeguard* would be popular, or currently trending. In the colder winter months, this is likely to change. Instead, keyword trends during the winter months would include *seasonal retail help*. Consider the job for which you are applying. In many cases, the keywords on your résumé should match what is trending.

In addition, as job seekers enter terms into search engines to find open positions, those terms are also tabulated. For example, if a candidate is looking for an accounting job, Google will list keywords that are most popular at the moment.

In order to know which keywords will have ADT software finding your résumé quickly, conduct research on trending keywords in your career field. For example, for an entry-level position in a corporation, you might think of the words *clerk* or *receptionist*. However, as you begin to research, you might learn that the phrase *front desk assistant* is the preferred terminology for the same position.

## 6-2 Résumé Keywords

**Directions:** Use the space provided to complete the activity or take notes. Alternatively, you can download the electronic version of this activity from the companion website.

1.  Research keywords that are used in your preferred industry or career field. Review job advertisements, conduct an Internet search, or use any other resources that will help you create a solid list of keywords.

2.  Consider your top ten keywords. Why do you think these are important to use in your résumé?

Download the electronic version of this activity.

# Sections of a Résumé

Résumés have standard sections employers expect to see. Some sections, however, are optional and should be included only if they apply to you and the position you are seeking.

When deciding how to format each section, consider the overall length of the résumé. Will it be one page or two? Typically, a recent graduate should have a one-page résumé, while those with several years of experience may have a two-page résumé. Remember to allow adequate white space on the page for readability. Also, consider how the résumé will be presented or sent to the employer. Will it be printed, e-mailed, or uploaded to a website?

Take into consideration how the potential employer will be reading your résumé. If it is posted to your personal website or attached to an e-mail, it will be read on a computer screen. The headings should be clear without being distracting. Be conservative, and do not use fancy or whimsical typefaces. The same applies if you are submitting a hard-copy résumé.

## Heading

A **heading** provides a person's full name, phone number, e-mail address, and geographic location. A heading is a standard part of all résumés. Never omit the heading, as it is the most prominent feature that identifies you. At a quick glance, a potential employer can learn your geographic location or proximity to the job location and your personal contact information.

In most cases, the first line of a heading is your formal given name. Avoid using nicknames and abbreviations. It is acceptable to use only your first name and last name. The middle name or initial is optional.

On a hard copy résumé, add your street address to the heading. The employer will need your exact address. A phone number follows, beginning with the area code. There is no need to indicate whether the number is a mobile or land line. It is obvious that it is the preferred phone number. Add your e-mail address next. If you have created a LinkedIn account, you may wish to include the URL.

On an e-résumé, follow the hard copy instructions of placing your name on the first line. *Do not* add the exact street or home address to the heading. It is likely that an e-résumé will be posted on the Internet, so it is unnecessary and possibly unwise to list your exact street address and city. It is acceptable and recommended to use a general geographic area and your zip code. Provide a major city near your home or a general metropolitan area in close proximity to where you reside. Your phone number, e-mail address, and LinkedIn URL follow. Notice the differences between the headings of a hard copy résumé and an e-résumé as shown in Figure 6-3.

## Career Objective and Career Profile

After creating the heading for a résumé, the next sections are often the career objective and profile. A **career objective** is a brief statement that explains an individual's career goals to an employer. A **career profile** details an individual's

---

### Sample Résumé Headings

**Hard Copy Résumé**

Shelley Jones
111 Main Street
Baltimore, MD 21202
555-555-1234
sjones@e-mail.com
www.linkedin.com/in/shelley-jones

**E-Résumé**

Shelley Jones
Greater Baltimore Area 21202
555-555-1234
sjones@e-mail.com
www.linkedin.com/in/shelley-jones

**Figure 6-3** The heading for a printed résumé should include an exact street address. An e-résumé should provide the general geographic location only.

# Career Portfolio

Andrey_Popov/Shutterstock.com

## Technical Skills

Your portfolio should not only showcase your academic accomplishments, but the technical skills you have, too. Are you exceptionally knowledgeable regarding computers? Do you have a talent for playing a musical instrument?

Technical skills are very important. Interviewers will want to know what technical skills you have.

1. Write a paper describing the technical skills you have acquired. Describe the skill, your level of competence, and any other information that will showcase your skill level.

2. Save the document file in your e-portfolio folder.

3. Place a printed copy in your container for your print portfolio.

accomplishments, skills, and current career level. The objective tells the employer what you want; the profile tells the employer who you are. The objective and the profile will be customized for each position. Keywords will play an important role in these two sections to show you are qualified for the position.

In some instances, it may be preferable to omit these two sections. For example, if you are still in school, you may not have enough professional experience to write a strong career profile. You have the option to eliminate these two sections rather than try to write sentences that are irrelevant.

## Career Objective

An objective articulates the type of job you want to secure. Some consider an objective on a résumé optional, but people who review résumés often read the objective before the education and work experience. If the objective matches a job opening, the person reading will continue to read the résumé. A hiring manager wants to find candidates who announce a clear desire to work in a particular position. A basic rule of thumb when creating a résumé objective is to write one or two lines that summarize your goal.

**Objective** College graduate seeking concierge position in the hotel lobby to utilize customer service skills and create the ultimate guest experience.

Note how the applicant accomplished the following in the objective:

- stated the desired job position: "concierge"

- included the preferred department in which to work: "in the hotel lobby"

- noted a hard or soft skill: "to utilize customer service skills"

- added a goal: "create the ultimate guest experience"

It is important to keep the objective brief and professional. Avoid the use of the first or second person in your statement. For example, avoid an objective that reads, "*I am* a college graduate seeking a concierge position in the hotel lobby to utilize *my* customer service skills to create the ultimate guest experience."

Even if you do not have extensive experience in a desired field, create the objective for the job that you desire. Applying for multiple positions will require customizing a résumé for each job. You will also adjust the objective to meet the requirements of the position. Do not feel locked in with the first objective you create.

## Career Profile

The profile, also known as a *qualification summary*, tells who you are. It details a candidate's qualities in the present tense. A career profile is lengthier than an objective as it provides the potential employer with a synopsis of the benefits the company will gain from having you as an employee.

The profile is a brief summary of your entire résumé. Write it using active rather than passive voice. If you have work experience that strengthens your résumé, use your work experience first, even if the work was performed on a volunteer basis. Consider this order for the content of your profile.

1. Strongest work experience
2. Hard skills
3. Soft skills
4. Abilities
5. Aptitudes

Compose your profile using complete, short, and powerful sentences. The profile should not exceed one-third of the space for the total résumé which is equivalent to five to six lines.

**Profile** Bi-lingual, top contributor, and provider of consistent information to guests. Responds to queries, gives directions, and makes detailed reservations and recommendations. Utilizes and shares knowledge of local events and venues in addition to local transportation options. Personable and engaging in casual conversation with guests.

## Experience

Your past and current jobs or internships will make up the experience section of your résumé. Detail the name of the company or organization, followed by the city and state. Include the start and end dates of employment. If still employed, reflect that with the word "present," such as "August 2014 to present."

Under the company information and dates, specify the position held and describe the work experience. Use these descriptions to weave in the keywords that you identified. The use of appropriate keywords will trigger a match for job-related search criteria. For example, if a job recruiter is looking for an accountant, the software will search for résumés on the Internet that include keywords such as *ledger accounts*, *balance sheets*, *financial audits*, *operational data*, and *reconciling discrepancies*. Do not list random keywords.

Once appropriate keywords are discovered, the résumé will be flagged. What happens to wonderful résumés that do not contain a single matched keyword? They are passed over. A skillfully written résumé with keywords woven into the content will be a successful résumé.

## Education

Most often, education is included on a résumé immediately following work experience. However, if you are a recent graduate without much work experience, you may consider listing your education first, followed by experience.

The label of this section can be changed from "Education" to "Relevant Coursework" or "Relevant Education." If you are still in school, indicate the number of years you have attended and provide your expected graduation date. List the courses you have taken that are most relevant to the position for which you are applying. Include any training, workshops, or seminars you have completed, even if you participated in classes for a previous employer.

If you are no longer a student, list your education beginning with the most recent diploma or degree earned. Include colleges as well as business or technical schools. Graduates should indicate the year a degree or diploma was earned, type of degree received, major subject, and minor

## 6-3 Résumé Heading, Objective, and Profile

**Directions:** Use the space provided to complete the activity or take notes. Alternatively, you can download the electronic version of this activity from the companion website.

1. Create two headings that you might use for your personal résumé. One should be for an e-résumé and one for a hard copy. Later, you will transfer this information to your résumé.

2. Create a career objective for your résumé. Use the information provided in the chapter as a guide. You will transfer this information to your résumé.

3. Create a career profile for your résumé. You will transfer this information to your résumé.

Download the electronic version of this activity.

subject, if any. Also, list any certifications earned, special courses or training programs completed, or any other related educational achievements. If you have earned multiple degrees, such as an associate degree and a bachelor degree, list the conferred degrees separately. Provide the official school name, city, state, degree conferred, and year that the degree was conferred. If you are an outstanding scholar in your college career, or if you have achieved other academic recognition or rewards, add them to you résumé.

College students have an implied high school diploma or GED, so adding high school information is optional. Consider adding high school information only when there are outstanding achievements or honors and awards to highlight.

## Special Skills

The *Special Skills* section of your résumé is an opportunity to focus the reader's attention on the skills you have gained in school or from previous jobs. These skills may not be noted or highlighted in other sections of your résumé. You are likely to see soft skills, hard skills, transferrable skills, and job-specific skills in a job posting. For purposes of a searchable résumé scanned by ADT robots, list all of the required skills that you possess under *Specials Skills*. These may include skills related to technology, language, management, or other areas of expertise an employer might look for in a candidate. Your goal is to list top skills that will transition you from candidate to employee.

Carefully review the advertisement for the job you are seeking and focus on the required skills. If you have the relevant experience, use the same words to describe it. Do not stretch the truth. Only use the keywords that fit your background.

# Résumé Formats

After you finish gathering information for your résumé, you are ready to decide on a format. A **timeline résumé** emphasizes employers and work experience with each. A **skills résumé** lists work experience according to categories of skills or achievements rather than by employer. Some candidates find that the best strategy is to use both, or a combination of the two. This is called a *combination résumé*. Like all aspects of the résumé, organize the information in a way that displays your strengths as a job candidate.

## Timeline Résumé

A timeline résumé, also known as a *chronological résumé*, is shown in Figure 6-4 on page 110. If your most recent work experiences are the best qualifications you possess when applying for a job, use the timeline résumé. Place information in reverse chronological order with the most recent information first.

On a timeline résumé, add beginning dates and end dates for each job listed under the *Experience* section of the résumé. Use one of the following options to format the dates:

- month and year: September 2015
- month, day, and year: September 1, 2015
- year only: 2015

Remember that the résumé presents a broad overview of your experience to an employer and is the vehicle to gain an interview. The exact duration of your work at a particular job might be of interest in detail to a potential employer later. However, at the résumé stage, your task is to display information accurately without giving an employer an initial negative impression. For example, if you only worked at an organization for two months, you might want to state just the year, such as "2014 to 2014" as opposed to "November 2014 to December 2014." Using a two-month time period is not necessary if you want to emphasize the skills you gained as an employee, rather than the fact that you were employed as seasonal help.

## Skills Résumé

A skills résumé is also referred to as a *functional résumé*. A skills résumé lists work experiences according to relevant achievements rather than by time as shown in Figure 6-5 on page 111. For example, if you have a skill as a programmer, but your last job was as a restaurant server, you might want the programming experience to be the first information seen by a potential employer. In that case, you would use a skills résumé to highlight your skills over your most recent work experiences.

# 6-4 Résumé Experience, Education, and Special Skills

**Directions:** Use the space provided to complete the activity or take notes. Alternatively, you can download the electronic version of this activity from the companion website.

1. Create a list of your work experience that you want a potential employer to see. Make sure it is accurate, complete, and follows the guidelines in the chapter. Later, you will transfer this information to your résumé.

2. List your education history. Put the most recent information first. You will transfer this information to your résumé.

3. Make a list of special skills you will include on your résumé. You will transfer this information to your résumé.

Download the electronic version of this activity.

For a skills résumé, omit the dates of employment. List your strongest experience or skills first, followed by the least-developed skills or experience. Use a skills résumé if there are gaps in your employment history. Another use for a skills résumé is to present the skills and experiences you are capable of utilizing, even though you have not used them in your most recent job.

## Combination Résumé

Use a combination of both the timeline and skills résumé when you want to express that your skills are your strengths against the backdrop of more recent work experience. A *combination résumé* is illustrated in Figure 6-6 on page 112. After the career objective and profile, list your achievements and skills. A brief listing of your work experience follows.

# Saving Your Résumé

Once you create a résumé, it is a good idea to save it as a master résumé document. Name your résumé file MasterResume or something similar. This will be the document to return to when customized versions are needed to apply for different positions. The master résumé is *not* the file to send to a potential employer. It is a working document to use as a basis for future submissions.

When you have finalized your résumé and are ready to post it or attach it to an e-mail, remember to save it as another file with a professional name. There are many naming conventions that can be used. Select the one you are comfortable with and stick to it. Include your name in the file name so the employer can identify your résumé. For example, Christopher Jeffries may save his master résumé file as ChristopherJeffriesResume before sending it to a potential employer. However, he may save three versions of his résumé for three different positions as:

- JeffriesMktMgrResume.docx
- JeffriesComMgrResume.docx
- JeffriesProMgrResume.docx

## Saving as a Plain Text File

When applying online to job boards and when copying and pasting information from your résumé into application forms on employer websites, formatting may become distorted. Therefore, you will need to prepare a version of your résumé with special formatting, such as bulleted lists, removed. This can be accomplished by saving a plain text version of your résumé. When you save a plain text version of a Word file, the file name will appear with a .txt extension. To create a plain text résumé, select the **Save As** option in Word to display a dialog box. Select **Plain Text** from the list of options.

When a plain text document is launched, it will often open in Notepad. An example of a plain text résumé is shown in Figure 6-7 on page 113. You will notice that all of the formatting is removed. This will make it easy to cut and paste information into an online form.

## Saving as a PDF File

There will be many times when you will attach a résumé to an e-mail when applying for a position. You may choose to attach the résumé as a Word document. However, you might choose to send it as a .pdf file. A .pdf file will keep your file intact, including the formatting, and protect it from changes. You can save the document as a .pdf file in Word. Select the **Save As** option in Word to display a dialog box, and then choose **PDF** from the list of options.

## Saving as a Web Page File

When preparing a résumé for your e-portfolio or personal website, you can save the document as a web page in Word. Select the **Save As** option in Word to display a dialog box, and then choose **Web Page** or **Single File Web Page** from the list of options. This creates an HTML version of your résumé document, which will open in a web browser when launched. This web-based résumé will look similar to the Word version, as it will retain the formatting you applied in Word. If you decide to save your résumé as a web page, upload it to your e-portfolio site.

## 6-5 Master Résumé

**Directions:** Use the space provided to complete the activity or take notes. Alternatively, you can download the electronic version of this activity from the companion website.

1. Create your master résumé in Word using the drafts from Activity 6-3 and Activity 6-4. When you are finished, run a spell check and proofread the document.

2. Ensure that the master résumé file is saved as a Word document.

3. Next, save the master résumé file as a plain text document.

4. Return to the Word version of the master résumé file, and then save it as a PDF document.

5. Return to the Word version of the master résumé file, and then save it as a web page document.

Download the electronic version of this activity.

Rather than just saving your résumé as a web page, you may choose to create a separate, additional web-based résumé. This type of résumé can be highly designed and can include various types of content, such as images, sound clips, and video clips. A job seeker can use a web-based résumé to display his or her design abilities, technical skills, or other talents and experience. For example, a musician can include sound or video clips of past performances on his or her web-based résumé. Similarly, a web developer can include a demo of a program he or she created. There are many free web-based résumé templates available online that can help you get started.

Before you create this type of résumé, conduct research to make sure this format is appropriate for the job you seek. It is a good idea to have both types of résumés available for potential employers. If you use a web-based résumé, add a link to it in your professional e-mail signature block.

## Custom Résumés

As you apply for positions, you will find the need to customize your résumé to fit the job for which you are applying. You may apply for more than one type of job or job title at any given time. For example, a qualified marketing professional might find several positions for which to apply. One position may be for a marketing manager, a second might be for a communications manager, and another may be for a promotions manager. He or she is qualified for all three, so three résumés will need to be created. Each version will have different keywords, objectives, and profiles, but the core material will likely remain the same.

Apply the information you learned in this chapter to customize your résumé for specific job openings. Keep in mind that customizing may simply mean changing a few keywords. On the other hand, it could mean major rewrites to sections of your résumé. Be flexible and cognizant about what an employer wants.

A creative way to customize your résumé is to create a visual résumé. A **visual résumé** is one that presents information in a graphically appealing format. One type of visual résumé is an infographic résumé. An **infographic résumé** is a résumé in which the content is displayed

**The Best App for that**

*JobCompass* is an app that locates job postings in your area. By using the geographic location of your mobile device, JobCompass shows available jobs within a radius of 5 to 100 miles. How could this app provide an edge for job seekers?

using a combination of words and graphics to present information clearly and quickly. Others can view your information without having to read through many lines of text.

There are many websites that offer templates for infographic résumés for free or at a minimal cost. This makes it practical for anyone to create a visually appealing document. No graphic design experience is necessary. Similar to other templates, information can be pulled from your master résumé into a new format using charts, tables, and other graphic elements, as shown in Figure 6-8 on page 114. By customizing your résumé to be visually appealing, it may give you an edge on the competition. However, it is important to note that most infographic résumés look appealing but are not scannable for keywords. When you post your résumé online, include both the text and visual versions.

Finally, remember to conduct a final check to make sure every detail of your résumé is complete. Proofread and run a spell check, as well as read each line for sense. Make sure the file is formatted correctly and all other guidelines have been followed. Using the checklist in Figure 6-9 on page 115 will help you as you finalize the document.

# 6-6 Infographic Résumé

**Directions:** Use the space provided to complete the activity or take notes. Alternatively, you can download the electronic version of this activity from the companion website.

1. Conduct an Internet search for visual or infographic résumés. Review the examples that you found.

2. Which résumé do you prefer? Why?

3. Next, create your own visual or infographic résumé. Use the information in your master résumé to create this new version.

Download the electronic
version of this activity.

# JALIA CORTEZ

111 First Street, Redwood City, CA 94061                              (650) 555–1234
jcortez@e-mail.com                                            www.linkedin.com/in/jalia-cortez

## CAREER OBJECTIVE
College graduate seeking concierge position in the hotel lobby to utilize customer service skills and create the ultimate guest experience.

## CAREER PROFILE
Bilingual, top contributor, and provider of consistent information to guests. Responds to queries, gives directions, and makes detailed reservations and recommendations. Utilizes and shares knowledge of local events and venues in addition to local transportation options. Personable and engaging in casual conversation with guests.

## EXPERIENCE
College of San Mateo, Redwood City, CA
August 2014 to present
Administrative Assistant to the Director of Education
- Screen the director's correspondence and assist with preparation of responses
- Prepare e-mails, memorandums, and letters
- Assist with research, editing, and final preparation of reports
- Manage the calendars of five staff members and the director
- Schedule meetings and make special arrangements, such as catering and A/V equipment
- Maintain up-to-date personnel data for staff members

Jefferson High School, Redwood City, CA
June 2013 to August 2014
Receptionist and Administrative Assistant, Principal's Office
- Scheduled appointments for student, faculty, and parents
- Maintained calendars
- Answered telephones, screened, and directed calls
- Greeted visitors, faculty, and students and provided assistance as needed

## EDUCATION
Associate of Arts in Office Administration, 2014
Lincoln Community College, Redwood City, CA

## SPECIAL SKILLS
Computer: Microsoft Office Suite
Language: Spanish, intermediate-level speaker
General: Excellent verbal and written communication, superior organizational skills, and multitasking

**Figure 6-4** A timeline résumé lists work experiences in reverse chronological order with the most recent information first.

# Brandon Barta

New York City Area 10002                              (212) 555 1356
bbarta@e-mail.com                           www.linkedin.com/in/brandonbarta

## CAREER OBJECTIVE

Publishing professional seeking a managing editor position to use editorial leadership skills to develop top-selling titles.

## CAREER PROFILE

Leader in the development of trade books on scientific topics. Uses knowledge of the market and team-building skills to create profitable collections of book titles.

## KEY ACHIEVEMENTS

- Developed impeccable editing skills, including the ability to review content for accuracy, substance, sourcing, and the correct use of grammar.
- Managed the Greenhouse & Thomas lists of scientific and environmental titles, including environmental sciences reference books and collections of historical papers. Representative titles include *Conservation of Inland Wetlands, Animals of the Great Lakes Regions, Marine Sources of Organic Fuels,* and *The Role of Light in Evolution.*
- Recruited authors from leading faculty of major universities and from technical, research, and engineering staffs in the environmental sciences industry. Signed approximately 100 new titles.
- Delivered presentations to sales staff and to company management describing new books and editorial plans.
- Demonstrated leadership, collaborative nature, and flexible attitude.

## SPECIAL SKILLS

- Knowledgeable about editorial development, copyediting, copyright concerns, production, photo research, and artwork preparation for scientific and technical books.
- Successful with promotion methods for scientific and technical books, including direct mail, online advertising, cataloging, and professional publication sales.

## EXPERIENCE

- Greenhouse & Thomas, New York City, NY, Managing Editor
- Moss & Wallace Book Company, New York City, NY, Senior Editor
- Eldridge Press, Boston, MA, Special Projects Editor

## EDUCATION

Smith College, Northampton, MA, Bachelor of Science in Biology, minor in Journalism, 1998

**Figure 6-5** A skills résumé lists work experiences according to relevant achievements rather than by date.

# Peter Jesse Owosu

Greater San Diego Area

Phone: (619) 555–4023 • E-mail: pjowosu@e-mail.com

www.linkedin.com/in/peter-jesse-owosu

## CAREER OBJECTIVE

College graduate seeking a project coordinator position to use organizational expertise to manage complex projects for a fast-paced office.

## CAREER PROFILE

Detail-oriented professional with strong organizational skills and the ability to manage projects so they are completed on time and within budget. Provides accurate schedule estimation and funding reviews for projects.

## EDUCATION

Grandhill College, San Diego, CA, Associate of Arts in Communication, 2013

## SKILLS

### Project Coordinator Skills

- Utilized knowledge of project coordination software to input project data such as milestones, budget, expenses, internal team members, scope, subject matter experts, and due dates.
- Provided support by designing and producing project milestone charts with due dates and internal newsletter layout.

### Team Skills

- Communicated with employees to resolve discrepancies and to bring focus to specific responsibilities, roles in the project, duties necessary to complete the project, and accountability.
- Scheduled meetings with workers and followed up to promote smooth project work flow.
- Handled general questions with professional courtesy and diplomacy.

## EXPERIENCE

### Grandhill College, San Diego, CA

June 2013 to present

Office Assistant, Recruitment Office

- Manage projects; answer questions concerning recruitment department events and services from students, staff, community agencies, and the general public; and direct students to appropriate college resources concerning recruitment issues.
- Assist in the organization of Recruitment Day, including contacting college representatives, making room reservations, and designing floor plan logistics.
- Provide production support for the Recruitment Office counseling staff by developing flyers, brochures, and letterhead.

### Insightful Vision Center, San Diego, CA

May 2011 to June 2013

Customer Service

- Tactfully and professionally handled customer inquiries, complaints, and concerns regarding merchandise.
- Scheduled appointments with clients and followed up to promote continued business.

**Figure 6-6** A combination résumé lists skills and work experience in a way that presents the information in the most favorable fashion. This combination résumé was created using a template.

```
JALIA CORTEZ
111 First Street, Redwood City, CA 94061
(650) 555-1234
jcortez@e-mail.com
www.linkedin.com/in/jalia-cortez

CAREER OBJECTIVE
College graduate seeking concierge position in the hotel lobby
to utilize customer service skills and create the ultimate guest
experience.

CAREER PROFILE
Bilingual, top contributor, and provider of consistent information
to guests. Responds to queries, gives directions, and makes detailed
reservations and recommendations. Utilizes and shares knowledge of
local events and venues in addition to local transportation options.
Personable and engaging in casual conversation with guests.

EXPERIENCE
College of San Mateo, Redwood City, CA
August 2014 to present
Administrative Assistant to the Director of Education
* Screen the director's correspondence and assist with preparation of
responses
* Prepare e-mails, memorandums, and letters
* Assist with research, editing, and final preparation of reports
* Manage the calendars of five staff members and the director
* Schedule meetings and make special arrangements, such as catering
and A/V equipment
* Maintain up-to-date personnel data for staff members

Jefferson High School, Redwood City, CA
June 2013 to August 2014
Receptionist and Administrative Assistant, Principal's Office
* Scheduled appointments for student, faculty, and parents
* Maintained calendars
* Answered telephones, screened, and directed calls
* Greeted visitors, faculty, and students and provided assistance as
needed

EDUCATION
Associate of Arts in Office Administration, 2014
Lincoln Community College, Redwood City, CA

SPECIAL SKILLS
Computer: Microsoft Office Suite
Language: Spanish, intermediate-level speaker
General: Excellent verbal and written communication, superior
organizational skills, and multitasking
```

**Figure 6-7** A plain text résumé makes it easy to copy and paste information into an online form.

# Stephen K. Sunwoo

**E-mail:** sksunwoo@e-mail.com
**LinkedIn:** http://www.linkedin.com/in/stephen-k-sunwoo
**Phone:** (253) 555–1098
Seattle area 98103

Seeking full-time, part-time, and freelance graphic design work that is both challenging and engaging.

## Essential Information

### Work History

2012–Present — Junior Graphic Designer
Synergy Communications, Tacoma, WA

2011–2012 — Contract Graphic Designer
Definition Designs Seattle, Seattle, WA

2009–2011 — Contract Layout Artist
The Independent Daily, Seattle, WA

### Industry Experience

 **5** years

### Education

 Washington State University
Art (Digital Media), BA, 2010
Seattle, WA

### Technology I Use

 PSD  EPS  AI  PNG  PDF  PPT  XLS  DOC  JPG  HTML CSS

## Information About Me

### Where I'm From

Portland, Oregon

### Hobbies

- Tennis
- International cinema
- Fantasy baseball

### Duties Performed

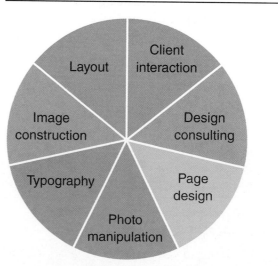

Layout, Client interaction, Design consulting, Page design, Photo manipulation, Typography, Image construction

Goodheart-Willcox Publisher; Images: tele52/Shutterstock.com

**Figure 6-8** A job seeker can use an infographic résumé to showcase skills and talents in a visually appealing manner.

# Résumé Checklist

## Heading
___ Full, formal name
___ City and state for e-résumés or full address for hard-copy résumés
___ Phone number
___ E-mail address
___ Personal LinkedIn URL

## Specific Information
___ Career objective
___ Career profile

## Experience
___ Beginning and ending dates of employment
___ Company name
___ General location of company, such as city and state
___ Position held
___ Specific descriptions of work performed
___ Keywords that match the position

## Education
___ Official college name
___ City and state
___ Degree obtained or degree title that is in process with expected date of graduation

## Optional Information
___ Skills, languages, special accomplishments, awards, or achievements
___ Personal website or blog address
___ E-portfolio link
___ Twitter account name

## Formatting and Editing
___ Single page
___ Ample white space
___ Keyword check
___ Spell check
___ Punctuation check
___ Grammar check

## Saving
___ Master version of the résumé
___ Customized versions of the master résumé for specific job application

Goodheart-Willcox Publisher

**Figure 6-9** Check the final draft of your résumé against the résumé checklist, and edit as needed.

## Chapter Summary

- A résumé can be the first impression that most employers will have of who you are. Its chief purpose is to sell yourself to a potential employer by showing how your experiences and skills match the qualifications of the job. It can be easier to use a résumé template rather than starting from scratch.

- Keywords are words that specifically relate to the functions of the position for which the employer is hiring. Using keywords in a strategic manner can help you land an interview. Research what keywords are trending to better customize your job search to your needs.

- Résumés have standard sections that employers expect to see. Standard sections include the heading, experience, education, and special skills. A career objective and profile can be included as well.

- Two common résumé formats are a timeline résumé and skills résumé. Some candidates find that the best strategy is to combine the two formats, which is commonly referred to as a combination résumé.

- It is a good idea to create a master copy of your résumé as a Word document. Using the master document, you can save the file as a plain text file, as a PDF file, or as a web page file.

- You may find the need to customize your résumé to fit different jobs for which you are applying. A creative way to customize your résumé is to develop a graphically appealing visual résumé.

## E-Flash Card Activity: Career-Related Terms

Review the career-related terms that follow. Then visit the G-W mobile site to practice vocabulary using e-flash cards until you are able to recognize their meanings. If you do not have a smartphone, visit the G-W Learning companion website to access this feature.

| | |
|---|---|
| résumé | career profile |
| résumé template | timeline résumé |
| trending | skills résumé |
| heading | visual résumé |
| career objective | infographic résumé |

## Review Your Knowledge

1. Explain the purpose of a résumé.

2.  What is a résumé template? What are the advantages to using one?

3.  Discuss the importance of keywords.

4.  What is ADT software used for?

5.  Define the term *trending*.

6.  List and explain each section of the résumé.

7.  List and describe three types of résumés.

8.  Describe three ways to save a résumé.

9.  Explain the benefits of a web-based résumé.

10.  Discuss the importance of customizing a résumé for specific positions.

## Apply Your Knowledge

1.  Read one of the résumés featured in this chapter as though you are a hiring manager. What did you learn about the applicant from reading his or her résumé? What questions would you have for this person after reading it?

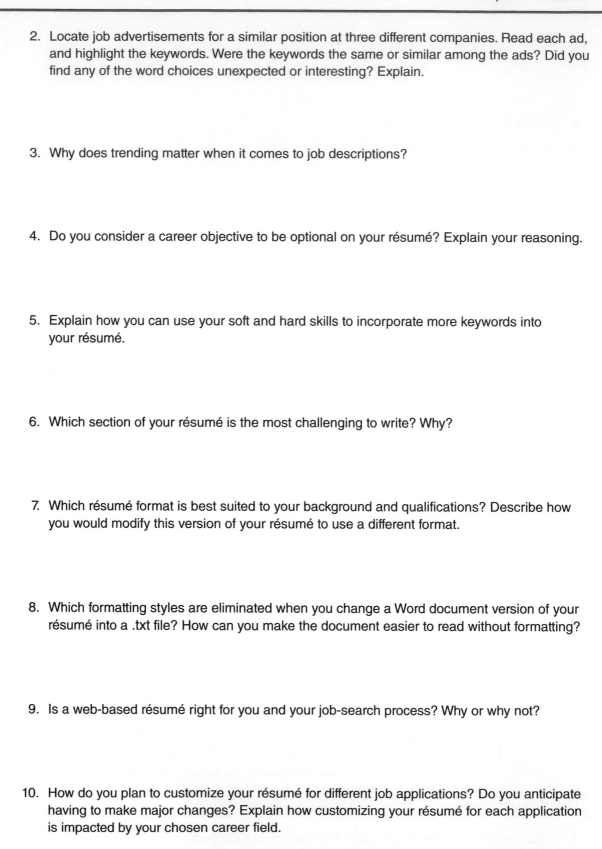

2. Locate job advertisements for a similar position at three different companies. Read each ad, and highlight the keywords. Were the keywords the same or similar among the ads? Did you find any of the word choices unexpected or interesting? Explain.

3. Why does trending matter when it comes to job descriptions?

4. Do you consider a career objective to be optional on your résumé? Explain your reasoning.

5. Explain how you can use your soft and hard skills to incorporate more keywords into your résumé.

6. Which section of your résumé is the most challenging to write? Why?

7. Which résumé format is best suited to your background and qualifications? Describe how you would modify this version of your résumé to use a different format.

8. Which formatting styles are eliminated when you change a Word document version of your résumé into a .txt file? How can you make the document easier to read without formatting?

9. Is a web-based résumé right for you and your job-search process? Why or why not?

10. How do you plan to customize your résumé for different job applications? Do you anticipate having to make major changes? Explain how customizing your résumé for each application is impacted by your chosen career field.

## Exploring Certification

### Career Certification Skills—Using Reading Skills

You are a cashier at a locally owned grocery store. Your manager has asked all cashiers to review the company's Return and Exchange Policy to avoid customer confusion. Read the Return and Exchange Policy, and respond to the questions that follow.

> **Return and Exchange Policy**
> Unopened items in new condition returned within 60 days will receive a refund. Perishable items, such as dairy products and meats, have a conditional return policy. Receipts for these items will show an employee stamp with a "return by" day range at the bottom. The "return by" day is seven days from the date of purchase. Items that do not have a receipt will be denied a refund but can be exchanged for another product equal to the value of the product at the time of the return. Bundled items must be returned with all pieces for a refund. Some items, such as gift cards, are never returnable.

1. What information must you give a customer who purchases milk?

2. A customer wishes to return an item, but does not have a receipt. He says he paid $9 for it; however, the product is currently on sale for $5. According to the Return and Exchange Policy, how would you handle this return?

### Career Certification Skills—Applying Math Skills

You believe you have found the perfect position. However, you live 40 miles away from the office. You decide to commute to your office on the train. If the commuter train travels at 75 miles per hour (mph), estimate how long the commute will be to your new office. Select the correct answer. Show your calculations.

A. 15 minutes

B. 22 minutes

C. 40 minutes

D. 32 minutes

## Career Certification Skills—Finding Information

At your new job, you oversee the processes used to manufacture products. You have created a document that outlines the sequential process that must be followed. However, you often get questions from the team about the steps.

Using the process document, answer the questions.

### Process Document

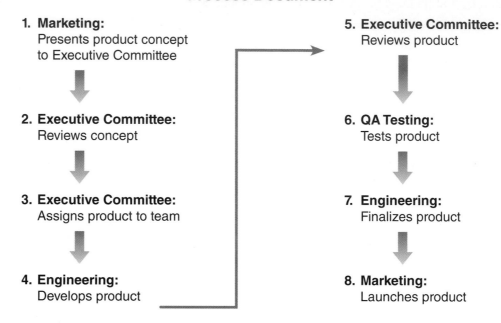

1. **Marketing:** Presents product concept to Executive Committee

2. **Executive Committee:** Reviews concept

3. **Executive Committee:** Assigns product to team

4. **Engineering:** Develops product

5. **Executive Committee:** Reviews product

6. **QA Testing:** Tests product

7. **Engineering:** Finalizes product

8. **Marketing:** Launches product

1. What happens to the product immediately after the quality assurance testing?

2. What is the last step in the process?

3. Which department is responsible for step three of the process?

## Chapter 7

# Cover Letters

## Outcomes

- **Explain** the purpose of a cover letter.
- **Identify** the sections of a cover letter.
- **Discuss** three ways to submit a cover letter to apply for a position.

## Career-Related Terms

| | |
|---|---|
| cover letter | networking cover letter |
| application cover letter | inquiry cover letter |

You will see icons at various points throughout the chapter. These icons indicate that interactive activities are available on the *Connect to Your Career* companion website. Selected activities are also available on the *Connect to Your Career* mobile site. These activities will help you learn, practice, and expand your career knowledge and skills.

 Companion Website
www.g-wlearning.com/careereducation/

 Mobile Site
www.m.g-wlearning.com

# Overview

Writing a cover letter is an important part of the application process. A cover letter is an opportunity to market yourself and convince the reader to grant you an interview. Your goal is to convince the employer that you are the best person for the position.

A good cover letter presents your personal qualifications in a way that attests to your ability to be a good employee. It shows that you have a genuine interest in the company as well as the position.

Once you have captured the reader's attention with your cover letter, make it count. Make an impression that will ensure an invitation to interview.

# Cover Letter

A **cover letter** is a formal written communication that accompanies a résumé or a job application to introduce the applicant and express interest in a position. The cover letter is about you, the type of job that you want, and an explanation of why you are the best candidate for the job. It must create an immediate, positive impression of your persuasive communication skills. The cover letter must be brief and no longer than one page. It should be written to invite potential employers to read your résumé. If your cover letter is ineffective, you will not be considered a viable candidate.

A compelling cover letter includes your personal brand statement and reason for contacting the employer. It includes your goal of obtaining a position and your interest in that particular company and position. The letter should also describe why you would be an asset to the employer. Use research you have conducted about the company to support your statement of interest in it.

When creating a cover letter, consider using a template to get the process started. Similar to a résumé template, a cover letter template is a pre-formatted word processing document that contains a standard layout with adequate margins of white space. Using a template will help your letter look balanced and reflect a professional look and feel. Consider using a template and customizing it for your personal needs rather than to start from scratch.

You may need to create different types of cover letters during the course of your job search process. The type of letter you write depends on how you learned about the position for which you are applying. The three basic types of letters typically used include application, networking, and inquiry cover letters.

The **application cover letter** may be used for all inquiries about a position that has been posted. Most candidates use the application cover letter.

A **networking cover letter** is used when someone with influence has suggested that the person apply for a position. This letter should introduce yourself with a brief statement about who in your network recommended you apply for the position.

An **inquiry cover letter** is used to learn if any potential positions are available, for which the job seeker would like to be considered. Generally, these are positions that have not been posted publicly. This is also known as *prospecting*. In this letter, you are asking to be considered for a specific position if an opening becomes available. The hope is that the company will keep your cover letter and résumé on file for future opportunities.

Cover letters are dynamic. The information in each letter changes slightly to match specific job requirements. Create one foundational cover letter, and save it as a master document, similar to creating a master résumé. You can modify this cover letter each time you submit your résumé or a job application.

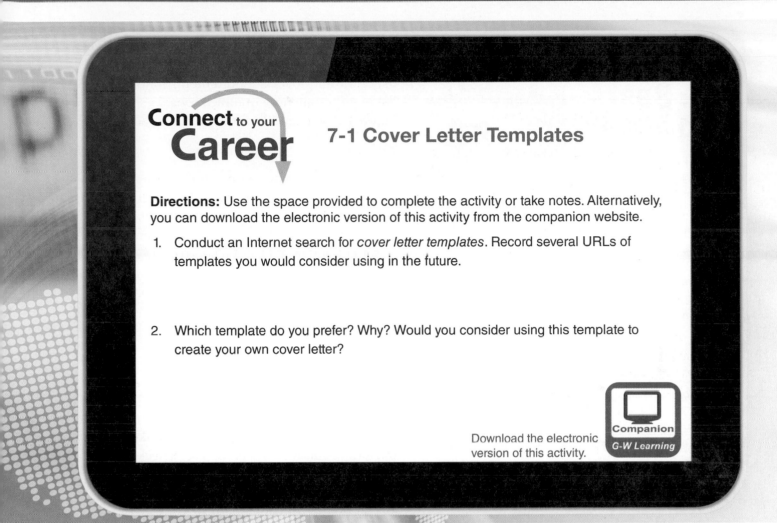

**Connect** to your **Career**

## 7-1 Cover Letter Templates

**Directions:** Use the space provided to complete the activity or take notes. Alternatively, you can download the electronic version of this activity from the companion website.

1. Conduct an Internet search for *cover letter templates*. Record several URLs of templates you would consider using in the future.

2. Which template do you prefer? Why? Would you consider using this template to create your own cover letter?

Download the electronic version of this activity.

Companion *G-W Learning*

# Parts of a Cover Letter

When writing a cover letter, follow standard letter formats. A standard cover letter will include the following sections, as shown in the cover letter in Figure 7-1 on page 129.

## Heading

Your letter should include a heading that states your contact information at the top of the page. Format it so that it looks similar to letterhead, but keep it simple. Include your complete contact information similar to your résumé.

## Date and Inside Address

Next, key the date followed by the inside address. The *inside address* is the address of the person receiving the letter. It includes the recipient's name, title, company, and mailing address.

## Greeting

Use a formal greeting for every cover letter. A formal greeting begins with "Dear" followed by "Mr." or "Ms." and the last name of your contact. Begin the letter with "Dear Sir or Madam" if you do not have a contact name.

## Introduction

Begin the letter with a direct opening paragraph that explains exactly why you are sending the communication. For example, "I am applying for the position of hotel concierge." In the next sentence, state how you heard about the available position. Indicate if you learned about the position from an instructor, for example. Next, add a sentence that describes your enthusiasm and desire to hold this position. If you have created a personal brand statement, add it next.

**The Best App for that**

*Dropbox* is an app that works as a virtual folder on your mobile device. You can drag and drop files, such as your résumé and cover letters, into Dropbox. Having these files on your mobile device allows you to be prepared for unexpected employment opportunities.

The following is a sample cover letter introduction with a personal brand statement as the closing line.

*I am applying for the position of hotel concierge at your company. I saw your ad for this position on your corporate website. As a catalyst for positive interaction, I have a history of engaging guests so that they are comfortable. A concierge has the responsibility to make a difference for guests in the hotel. Whether providing recommendations for restaurants, entertainment, or transportation, the key is to create positive interaction. My passion is to guide and to serve.*

## Body

The body is the longest part of the letter. Its purpose is to demonstrate that you meet or exceed the qualifications of the job. Do not restate the information in your résumé. Instead, show why you are qualified for the position. Use pertinent keywords from the job requirements to show the strength of your qualifications. Describe why you are a good long-term fit for the company.

The body of your cover letter may be written in paragraph form, as shown in the cover letter in Figure 7-1. Or, you may choose to use a bulleted list of the employer's requirements followed by a list of your matching qualifications, as shown in Figure 7-2 on page 130. Either format is acceptable.

## Closing

One of the main reasons for sending a cover letter is to ask for an interview. In the closing paragraph, request an opportunity to discuss your qualifications with the reader in a sincere and confident sentence. Detail when you are available, and express that you look forward to hearing from him or her. Include your contact information so the reader can get in touch with you.

# Ways to Submit a Cover Letter

Before submitting a cover letter, it is important to do one final review for accuracy. Make sure the letter is perfect and error free. Check for correct grammar, punctuation, and spelling. The checklist in Figure 7-3 on page 131 will help you as you finalize the document.

Once perfected, there are a variety of ways to submit a cover letter to apply for a position.

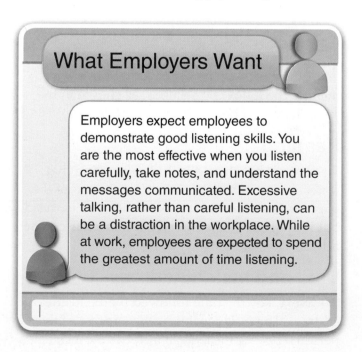

**What Employers Want**

Employers expect employees to demonstrate good listening skills. You are the most effective when you listen carefully, take notes, and understand the messages communicated. Excessive talking, rather than careful listening, can be a distraction in the workplace. While at work, employees are expected to spend the greatest amount of time listening.

# 7-2 Draft Cover Letter

**Directions:** Use the space provided to complete the activity or take notes. Alternatively, you can download the electronic version of this activity from the companion website.

1. Using the Internet or other source, search for and select an advertisement for a position that interests you. Record the position title, name of the company, name of the contact person, and the mailing address.

2. Create a new Word document or use the template you selected in Activity 7-1. Write the heading that you will use for the letter. Write an appropriate greeting to begin the letter.

3. Create a draft of your introductory paragraph.

4. Write the body of the cover letter. Keep it succinct and to the point. Remember to use keywords as you describe your qualifications.

5. Write the closing paragraph. Remember to request the opportunity for an interview.

Download the electronic version of this activity.

The most common methods are submitting by e-mail, uploading to a job board, or submitting a hard copy.

## Submit by E-mail

When submitting a cover letter and résumé via e-mail, use your professional e-mail account. It is a best practice to use the cover letter as the formal content in the body of the e-mail. You can copy and paste the information from your master cover letter into the e-mail message. However, omit the heading from the cover letter that includes your contact information. This information should be included in the signature block you created for your professional e-mail account. You may also choose to include an electronic signature after the closing line of the cover letter.

Omit the date and inside address as well. Since the e-mail is dated and time-stamped, there is no need to add a date. In the subject line, include the title of the job for which you are applying. Create a subject line announcing that you are applying for a posted job. Keep the subject line brief, professional, and clear. The proper way to state the subject is to use your last name, the words "application for," followed by the title of the position. The following is a sample of a subject line.

*Cortez Application for Front Desk Concierge.*

Many candidates make one or more of the following common mistakes in their subject lines:

- omit the subject line
- use exclamation points
- key a subject line in all caps
- create a subject line that is confusing or generic
- use a lengthy subject line that becomes truncated

A well-written and formatted cover letter in an e-mail is shown in Figure 7-4 on page 132.

# Career Portfolio

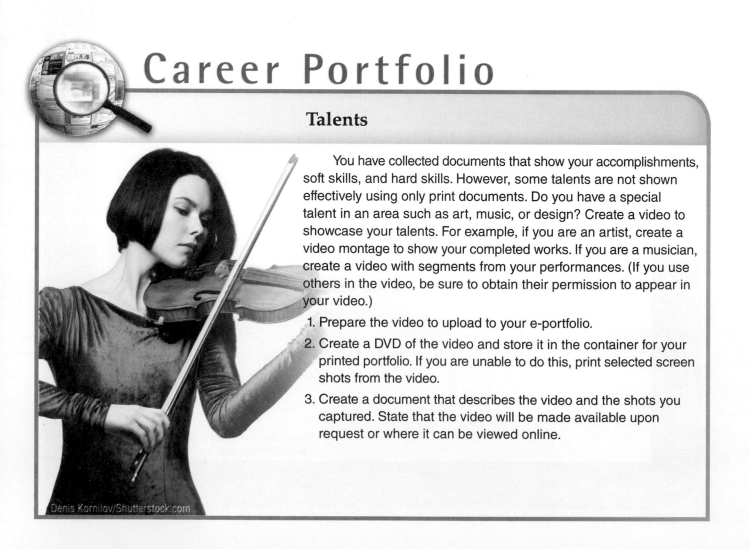

## Talents

You have collected documents that show your accomplishments, soft skills, and hard skills. However, some talents are not shown effectively using only print documents. Do you have a special talent in an area such as art, music, or design? Create a video to showcase your talents. For example, if you are an artist, create a video montage to show your completed works. If you are a musician, create a video with segments from your performances. (If you use others in the video, be sure to obtain their permission to appear in your video.)

1. Prepare the video to upload to your e-portfolio.
2. Create a DVD of the video and store it in the container for your printed portfolio. If you are unable to do this, print selected screen shots from the video.
3. Create a document that describes the video and the shots you captured. State that the video will be made available upon request or where it can be viewed online.

Denis Kornilov/Shutterstock.com

## 7-3 Master Cover Letter

**Directions:** Use the space provided to complete the activity or take notes. Alternatively, you can download the electronic version of this activity from the companion website.

1. Create your master cover letter using the cover letter draft from Activity 7-2. When you are finished, run a spell-check and proofread the document.

2. Save the master cover letter file as a Word document.

3. Next, save the master cover letter file as a plain text document.

4. Return to the Word version of the master cover letter file and then save it as a PDF document.

5. Return to the Word version of the master cover letter file and then save it as a web page document.

Download the electronic version of this activity.

Some e-mail services include the option to mark an e-mail as *priority*. You can use this option if you are sending your résumé and cover letter immediately before the submission process is scheduled to close.

You may opt to attach the cover letter to the e-mail message. However, not all employers open cover letter attachments. If you choose to attach the letter, insert your signature as an electronic file in the Word document. Save the letter as a PDF file before attaching it to the e-mail.

## Upload to a Job Board

You may apply for a position through an online job board. *Online job boards* are websites that host job postings for employers and allow applicants to apply for jobs seamlessly. Job boards will be covered in the next chapter. If you are applying through a job board, you may be required to upload your résumé and cut and paste your cover letter into a web form. The website will give directions on how to complete these tasks. Always follow the directions as specified. It may be necessary to use plain text for your cover letter as the form may omit formatting. Therefore, it is better to be safe and use unformatted text.

## Submit a Hard Copy

Some employers will require you to submit a hard copy of your cover letter and résumé to be considered for a position. Hard copy cover letters and résumés should be printed on high-quality white paper. Do not staple the documents together. However, you may secure them with a paper clip. Place the documents, unfolded, into a folder or large manila envelope with the person's name clearly indicated on the outside. If you are mailing the documents, take the manila envelope containing the documents to the post office and have it weighed so the appropriate amount of postage can be affixed to the package.

Once you secure an interview, you will take copies of your documents to present to the interviewer. In this case, it is not necessary to put the name of a person on the outside of the folder or envelope. However, be prepared with an adequate number of documents for those who may be part of the interview team.

# Social Media for Your Career

Tumblr is a free microblogging and social networking website owned by Yahoo. Tumblr allows users to create, share, and follow short blogs. In addition, Tumblr supports and runs multimedia uploads, such as photos and videos. As a user, you can create professional microblogs and follow those posted by others, including leaders in your career field. Such resources can be beneficial when searching for employment. For example, view blogs led by executives in your field who might be in a position to help you with your career search. Tumblr hosts more than 150 million blogs as of this writing.

# Peter Jesse Owosu

1006 Mountain View Parkway, San Diego, CA 91932

(619) 555–4023 • pjowosu@e-mail.com • www.linkedin.com/in/peter-jesse-owosu

September 24, 20--

Susan Taylor
Standard Manufacturing Company
553 Cleveland Street
San Diego, CA 91911

Dear Ms. Taylor:

Marie Franklin at Dynamics Supply Company informed me that you have a position open for a project coordinator. After reviewing the job description and requirements, it was clear that my experience and skills are a perfect match for this open position. My degree and work experience have focused on communication and project management. A position as project coordinator is the ideal job opportunity for which I am seeking. I help companies make the most of their talent by using proven, systematic project coordinator methods.

As a person who is known for organization and problem solving, I am able to set achievable goals and complete projects on schedule. My reputation for following up on unresolved issues and working well with clients has helped me succeed in project management. Being results oriented leads me to success.

Please find my résumé enclosed with this communication. I would appreciate an interview to discuss this position. Please contact me at your convenience at the phone number or e-mail above. I look forward to the opportunity of meeting with you for an interview for this position.

Sincerely,

*Peter Jesse Owosu*

Peter Jesse Owosu

Enclosure

**Figure 7-1** A cover letter should be well written and include all of the standard sections.

# Jalia Cortez

111 First Street, Redwood City, CA 94061

(650) 555–1234 • jcortez@e-mail.com • www.linkedin.com/in/jalia-cortez

November 30, 20--

Human Resources
Great Corporation
12344 Main Street
Redwood City, CA 94061

Dear Sir or Madam:

I am applying for the position of hotel concierge at your company. I saw your ad for this position on your corporate website. As a catalyst for positive interaction, I have a history of engaging people so that they are comfortable. A concierge has the responsibility to make a difference for guests in the hotel. Whether providing recommendations for restaurants, entertainment, or transportation, the key is to create positive interaction. My passion is to guide and to serve.

I have reviewed the qualifications posted for this position. I am certain that my skills and talents match the requirements for which you are looking.

**Your Requirements**:
• Proven professional with excellent verbal communications skills
• Outgoing personality
• Ability to create and edit written materials
• Self-motivated
• Ability to multitask

**My Qualifications**:
• Appointed lead speaker for staff meetings held each month
• Recognized as employee of the month
• Researched and edited professional reports
• Initiated a program that highlights student accomplishments
• Expanded contacts with key people at local businesses by 20 percent

Working with the guests at a well-known hotel is appealing and challenging. I would appreciate an opportunity to discuss this position with you. My résumé is attached for your review. I will follow up with an e-mail to request an appointment. Thank you for your time and consideration.

Sincerely,

*Jalia Cortez*

Jalia Cortez

Enclosure

**Figure 7-2** You can communicate your qualifications as a bulleted list in the body of the cover letter.

# Cover Letter Checklist

## Heading
___ Included full name
___ Stated mailing address
___ Included phone number
___ Added e-mail address
___ Added personal LinkedIn URL

## Date and Inside Address
___ Used correct date
___ Included recipient's name, title, company, and mailing address

## Greeting
___ Added formal greeting
___ Included name of contact if known

## Introduction
___ Stated reason for sending the communication
___ Included how you heard about the position
___ Showed enthusiasm for position
___ Used personal brand statement

## Body
___ Demonstrated qualifications for this position
___ Displayed career successes
___ Used job requirement keywords
___ Emphasized accomplishments

## Closing Paragraph
___ Requested an interview
___ Stated availability
___ Included contact information

## General
___ Customized for this position
___ Limited to one page
___ Formatted attractively and professionally
___ Used professional tone throughout
___ Proofread and spell-checked
___ Reviewed by instructor or peer
___ Printed on high-quality white paper

Goodheart-Willcox Publisher

**Figure 7-3** Check the final draft of your cover letter against the cover letter checklist, and edit as needed.

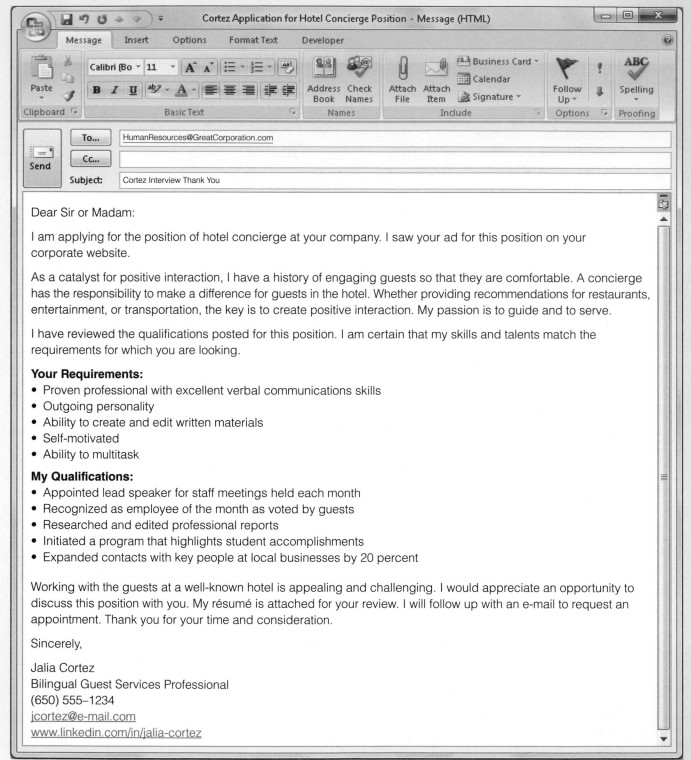

**Figure 7-4** A cover letter submitted by e-mail should include an appropriate subject line.

## Chapter Summary

- A cover letter is a formal written communication that accompanies a résumé or a job application to introduce yourself and express your interest in a position. Cover letters follow standard letter writing formats. There are three basic types of cover letters: application, networking, and inquiry cover letters.

- Cover letters use a standard letter format. They should include a heading, then the date and inside address. A formal greeting should be used. An introduction will be followed by the body of the letter. The closing should include a request for an interview.

- When applying for a position, cover letters may be submitted by e-mail, uploaded to a job board, or delivered as a hard copy.

## E-Flash Card Activity: Career-Related Terms

Review the career-related terms that follow. Then visit the G-W mobile site to practice vocabulary using e-flash cards until you are able to recognize their meanings. If you do not have a smartphone, visit the G-W Learning companion website to access this feature.

cover letter                                                          networking cover letter

application cover letter                                     inquiry cover letter

## Review Your Knowledge

1. Describe the purpose of a cover letter.

2. Identify the three types of cover letters.

3. What is prospecting?

4. Name the parts of a cover letter.

5. There are two ways the body of a cover letter can be written. What are they?

6.  What should you include in the closing paragraph of your cover letter?

7.  Describe the three common ways a cover letter can be submitted.

8.  Describe how to submit a cover letter via e-mail.

9.  Why use unformatted text when submitting a cover letter to an online job board?

10.  How should hard copy cover letters be prepared for submission?

## Apply Your Knowledge

1.  When applying for a job without specific requirements, what is the best way to communicate in your cover letter that you are the best candidate for the job?

2.  What strengths will you emphasize in your cover letters to employers?

3.  What would an employer's impression be if he or she received your résumé without a cover letter?

4.  A classmate shows you a job ad for a position that would be a good fit for your qualifications. What type of cover letter would you write?

5.  Review the Cover Letter Best Practices Checklist in Figure 7-3. How would you modify this checklist for your personal job search process?

## Exploring Certification

### Career Certification Skills—Using Reading Skills

Your classmate would like to get your feedback as she writes her résumé. She presented you with a portion of her résumé to review. Read the education section of her résumé, and respond to the questions that follow.

---

**Education**
- ABC College 2009 to 2010 Engineering Major
- XYZ College 2008 to 2009 Culinary Arts Major
- Community College 2005 to 2006 General Studies

---

1. Are there any gaps in this classmate's education? What are the possible reasons for gaps?

2. Education is a partial picture of a complete candidate profile. What advice would you give your classmate regarding the rest of her résumé to change the dynamics of the education presented?

### Career Certification Skills—Finding Information

You have taken a job as an assistant in a preschool. You presented the children with a lesson about whales. Read the data in the graph below. Using this data, which whale is the largest?

| Whale Length and Weight Chart | | |
|---|---|---|
| **Type of Whale** | **Length** | **Weight** |
| Indo-Pacific humpback | 6½ to 9¼ feet | 440 pounds |
| Blue whale | 80 to 90 feet | 132 tons |
| Killer whale | 18 to 30 feet | 10 tons |

Source: American Museum of Natural History

### Career Certification Skills—Applying Math Skills

You landed a part-time job working from home. You work five hours each week, and your hourly rate is $25. It is critical that you have access to the Internet to perform your work. A local Internet provider gives you a rate of $60 per month for an Internet connection. What percentage of your monthly salary will you spend on your Internet connection? Select the correct answer. Show your calculations.

A. 10%

B. 12%

C. 15%

D. 11%

## Chapter 8

# Applying for Jobs

## Outcomes

- **Explain** how to complete a job application.
- **Describe** how to apply for jobs in person.
- **Explore** how to apply for jobs online.
- **Implement** the Sunday Evening Plan.
- **Manage** the application process.
- **Organize** the application process.

## Career-Related Terms

| | |
|---|---|
| job application | online job board |
| job-search list | aggregate job board |

You will see icons at various points throughout the chapter. These icons indicate that interactive activities are available on the *Connect to Your Career* companion website. Selected activities are also available on the *Connect to Your Career* mobile site. These activities will help you learn, practice, and expand your career knowledge and skills.

Companion Website
www.g-wlearning.com/careereducation/

Mobile Site
www.m.g-wlearning.com

kurhan/Shutterstock.com

# Overview

The job application process does not stop with the résumé and cover letter. You will probably be asked to complete a formal job application form. This form provides information the employer needs during and after the employment process. The application may be a hard copy or online form. Both require the same amount of preparation and care when completing them.

In some cases, you may apply for a job in person. However, you are likely to apply for a job online—one that you might find on a job list or a job board. Both types of websites provide current, up-to-date job advertisements. You can make these resources work for you by adopting the Sunday Evening Plan. This plan involves updating your application documents every week. In addition, managing and organizing the application process will help ease your job search.

## Job Applications

You have completed a résumé and a cover letter so that you may start the application process. However, it is likely that you will be required to complete one more document. At some point, many companies require that a candidate complete a job application. A **job application** is a form used by some employers to gain more information about the applicant. A portion of a sample job application is shown in Figure 8-1.

Job applications take time to complete. In order to respond to every requirement, you will need to gather information before you begin. Your résumé will have most of the information required, so this is a good document to use as a resource.

The application requires personal information, names and addresses of the schools you have attended, and degrees earned. You will record addresses of your previous employers, supervisors' names, and contact information. The application may ask if previous employers may be contacted. If a former supervisor is no longer employed where you worked, state that the person is no longer at the company and provide contact information for the human resources department. You will also be asked to provide the names and contact information for professional references. Some job applications require additional information beyond your work experience. Be truthful for each question and answer honestly. Do not leave any lines blank. If the information is not applicable to you, write "N/A" in the space.

After the job application is complete, proofread it and compare it with your résumé. If either document contains conflicting information, edit the documents so they match.

### Hard-Copy Application

It may be necessary to print an application from the Internet and complete it by hand. At other times, a visit to a business may be necessary to pick up a printed application. When completing a hard-copy application, use blue or black ink and write legibly. Consider photocopying or obtaining more than one copy of the blank form. If you make an error that cannot be corrected, start with a new form. Your final form should be clean, neat, and accurate. Sign and date the completed form. If you are required to mail an application, include a hard copy of your résumé and cover letter.

### Online Application

Many companies require that job candidates complete online job applications. Resist the temptation to hurry through the form. Spelling, complete sentences, and the rules of good writing still apply. Make sure you have proofread everything carefully before you press the **Submit** button. Once the application is submitted, you will not be able to make revisions or corrections.

# Job Application

## Personal Information

| Last Name | | First Name | Middle Initial |
|---|---|---|---|

| Address | City | State | Zip |
|---|---|---|---|

| How long at present address? | Phone Number | Social Security Number |
|---|---|---|

What date will you be available for work?

Type of employment desired:

_____ Full-time only          _____ Part-time only          _____ Full- or part-time

If hired, can you furnish proof that you are legally entitled to work in the United States?

If hired, can you furnish proof of age?

| What position are you applying for? | What are your salary requirements? |
|---|---|

Hours you will be available to work:

Have you ever been convicted of a felony?

If yes, please explain

The XYZ Company is a drug-free employer and you will be required to pass a drug screening as a condition of employment. I understand and agree to participate in testing. (        ) initials

## Educational Information

| Name and Address of School | Course of Study | Diploma or Degree |
|---|---|---|
| High School | | |
| College Education | | |
| Graduate Education | | |
| Other Education/ Training | | |

**Figure 8-1** Companies require candidates to complete a job application to gain more information about the applicant's qualifications.

# 8-1 Job Application

**Directions:** Use the space provided to complete the activity or take notes. Alternatively, you can download the electronic version of this activity from the companion website.

1. Print the job application found in Activity 8-1 on the *Connect to Your Career* companion website. Or if you prefer, conduct an Internet search for *sample job application*. Select one and print it. Complete the application. Refer to your résumé, list of references, or other documents if necessary. Use blue or black ink and your best handwriting. The application must be neat, clean, and error free.

2. Proofread your application. Compare it to your résumé and cover letter. If there is any conflicting information, revise your documents to match. If you need to correct the job application, print a new copy and start again. Sign and date the form.

3. Next, practice completing the job application electronically by keying your responses directly into the form.

4. Print the completed application. Sign and date the form. Submit it to your instructor.

Download the electronic
version of this activity.

In some cases, you can download and print the online application and complete it by hand before you record your final information online. This can help you complete and submit a well-prepared document.

## Applying for Jobs in Person

You do not always have to wait for a business to advertise employment opportunities. For some businesses, such as retail, it is appropriate to visit and ask for a job application. Some businesses request that you complete the application off-site and return it when it is complete.

If you do not know the process of the particular business you plan to target, prepare to stay on-site to complete the application. Bring a quality blue or black ink pen with you to complete the application so you will not have to ask to borrow one. Make sure you have all of the information with you necessary to complete an application. Although filling out an application on-site is not a formal interview, dress professionally. Plan to demonstrate that you are not only qualified but professional as well.

Before your visit, customize a résumé and an inquiry cover letter that best matches the business to which you are applying. Create a separate document that clearly lists professional references and their contact information. Print each document and place in a folder or envelope that you can leave with the human resources manager. If applicable, bring a copy of your portfolio to leave behind.

After you complete the application, assemble the application, cover letter, résumé, and references in order, and place them in the envelope or folder

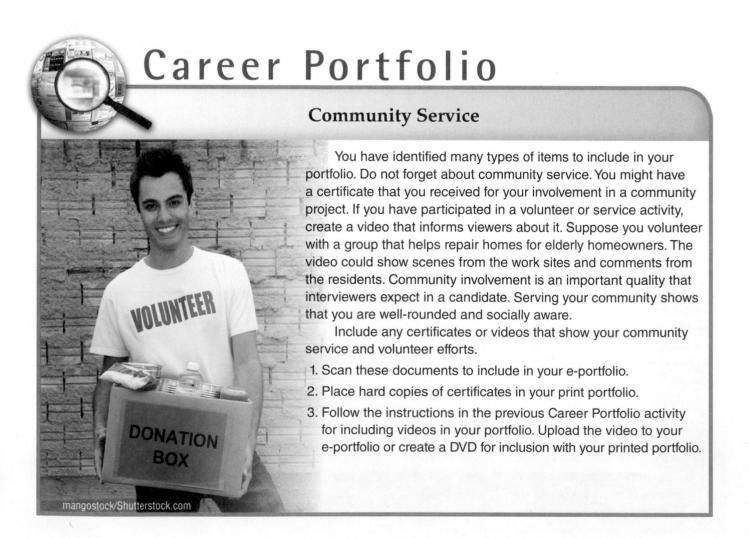

# Career Portfolio

## Community Service

You have identified many types of items to include in your portfolio. Do not forget about community service. You might have a certificate that you received for your involvement in a community project. If you have participated in a volunteer or service activity, create a video that informs viewers about it. Suppose you volunteer with a group that helps repair homes for elderly homeowners. The video could show scenes from the work sites and comments from the residents. Community involvement is an important quality that interviewers expect in a candidate. Serving your community shows that you are well-rounded and socially aware.

Include any certificates or videos that show your community service and volunteer efforts.

1. Scan these documents to include in your e-portfolio.

2. Place hard copies of certificates in your print portfolio.

3. Follow the instructions in the previous Career Portfolio activity for including videos in your portfolio. Upload the video to your e-portfolio or create a DVD for inclusion with your printed portfolio.

mangostock/Shutterstock.com

you brought. Make a note in your smartphone or notebook. Include the name of the person who took your documents, along with the day and time.

Within one week of dropping off the application, if you have not heard from the company or the manager, it is appropriate to call one time and explain that you want to follow up regarding the application you submitted. From that point, wait for the business to contact you.

While you are waiting, continue to apply for as many jobs for which you are qualified. The process of connecting to your career is ongoing. Always apply for jobs and only cease when you are employed.

# Applying for Jobs Online

The process of applying for jobs online is almost entirely reading and sorting through available job postings. Read online job postings carefully. You will not apply for all jobs posted online, just those that are the closest match to your skills, qualifications, and physical location.

When applying for jobs, keep in mind that the *required* qualifications must be met. However, it is not often that you will meet 100 percent of the *desired* job requirements. You need to set a benchmark to help you determine if you would have a chance at the job or if you are completely out of your league. The *benchmark* is how many of the job requirements you believe are necessary to meet before you apply for a position. For example, your benchmark may be to meet 80 percent of the advertised desired requirements in a job posting.

As you begin applying for jobs online, you will find that different job postings will take you to various websites on the Internet. Some job advertisements take you directly to a corporate website, while others link you to a recruiting agent who screens résumés.

There are hundreds of new jobs posted online each day. This can seem overwhelming. However, the steps to search for available jobs online follow a pattern. The home page of most job-search websites features a text box to enter search criteria. The first step is to enter a job title, keywords, or a company name. The next step is to select the desired location for the position.

Some job sites offer options for an advanced search. In these cases, criteria that are more specific can be selected to narrow your search. For example, you may be able to set search parameters to find full-time jobs only.

In order to stay on top of new opportunities, you can create a filter to alert you to specific jobs. This strategy allows you to be able to apply immediately after specific jobs are posted. You can program the alert to arrive in your professional e-mail inbox. If your mobile device is set up to retrieve your e-mail, you will receive the notifications there. When you do, in many cases, you can use your mobile device to apply for jobs.

There is no limit to the number of available jobs for which one applicant might apply. With each application, include a cover letter. After you click the **Submit** button for an online job post, do not use the **Back** button on your browser. The **Back** button returns the browser to the previous window and might cancel your online submission.

In general, there are three types of websites you can use for your job search: job-search lists, online job boards, and aggregate job boards.

## Job-Search Lists

One way to find available jobs is by using an online job-search list. **Job-search lists** are websites where multiple employers post job openings on a daily basis. LinkedIn, Twitter, and Craigslist are examples of websites that host job-search lists. Using job-search lists are free and intended for public viewing. These sites allow users to view available jobs anywhere in the world. Be aware, however, that these websites often contain invasive ads that appear as part of the lists of available jobs. Read the content carefully so that you do not click on advertisements inadvertently.

Job-search lists are not sites where the job applicants can create accounts or receive alerts for available jobs. These sites are for finding a job post and responding directly to the employer or agency that posted the opening. In most cases, users are not required to sign up or create a user name or password to take advantage of these sites. However, some sites, such as Twitter, do require people to sign up for an account to access job posts.

To begin searching for a job, the first step is to select a job title and the desired location for the job. Once you find a job of interest, it is necessary to find a contact name and e-mail address. Then you can apply directly to the individual who created the online post. Be careful of job ads that sound too good to be true. Research each company name or individual who posts a job advertisement and determine if you have found a legitimate company or individual before you send personal information.

Each job site updates information frequently. This means if you see a job for which you want to apply, apply today. If you wait until tomorrow, you might not find that exact job posting again. The number of available jobs varies according to seasons and market fluctuations.

## Online Job Boards

**Online job boards** are websites that host job postings for employers and allow applicants to apply for jobs seamlessly. Applicants do not contact the employer directly. Instead, these sites offer a one-click method, whereby the applicant's documents are forwarded by the site directly to the employer or hiring agent. Examples of online job boards are Monster.com and Dice.com.

Online job boards require job seekers to set up an account and career profile as described in Chapter 1. Once the account is created, some online job boards invite applicants to upload and store cover letters and résumés. After the account and profile information is complete, it is important to customize the account and privacy settings to reflect your preferences. Job boards offer multiple settings such as private, visible, or limited. Be certain that you understand the options before making your decision as this will limit the employers or recruiters who have access to your information.

Similar to using a job-search list, the first step is to enter a job title, keywords, or company name. The next step is to select the desired location for the position. Some job-search sites offer an option for an advanced search. More specific criteria can be selected to narrow your search. Once you achieve the search combination that returns jobs for which you are interested,

research the companies that posted the jobs. If you are interested in working for a particular corporation, or want to return to the site, bookmark it. If the company and job description meet your requirements, you are ready to begin the application process.

If you find multiple job postings to which you want to apply but are unable to do so immediately, forward the job postings to your professional e-mail account. This action sends the company name, job title, job description, and submission details to your e-mail.

## Aggregate Job Boards

**Aggregate job boards** are websites that collect data from multiple online job boards and combine the results. Instead of searching through job boards individually, an aggregate job board collects and compiles posted jobs into one site. Examples of aggregate job boards include Indeed.com and SimplyHired.com.

When you select a job advertisement on an aggregate job board, the listing will include where the original advertisement for the position was posted. The advertisement may have been a local newspaper, individual job board, job list, or other source. You can go to the original site of the advertisement and apply there. Alternatively, if you prefer, you may apply for jobs directly from the aggregate site.

An advantage of using aggregate sites is that job seekers have access to multiple jobs that match positions for which they are seeking. The disadvantage of using aggregate sites is that many do not store applicant résumés. As a result, the process to apply for a position from aggregate sites may require several more steps than when applying from singular sites that store résumés.

# The Sunday Evening Plan

Every Monday morning, recruiters comb job boards with the advanced search criteria for new and updated résumés. Monday morning is a critical day in the job-search process for potential employees. Recruiters begin each week by sorting through résumés with keywords that match the criteria they seek.

## 8-2 Job-Search Lists and Online Job Boards

**Directions:** Use the space provided to complete the activity or take notes. Alternatively, you can download the electronic version of this activity from the companion website.

1. Conduct an Internet search for job-search lists. Record the URLs for several websites you would consider using.

2. Which job-search list are you most likely to use? What criteria did you use to make your selection?

3. Conduct an Internet search for online job boards. Select one you would consider using for your job search. Record the URL for the website you selected.

4. Create an account on this job board by following the instructions on the website.

5. Record the information for your profile completely and professionally.

6. Upload your master résumé and master cover letter.

Download the electronic version of this activity.

In order to get your résumé viewed by recruiters on Monday morning, update your information on Sunday night. Use the *Sunday Evening Plan*. Every Sunday evening while you are a job seeker, update, edit, and proofread your résumé. Then upload it to the job boards you are actively using. If you find that no edits are necessary for your résumé, delete the current one on the job board and upload the same résumé so that it is flagged as new. Recruiters are notified of new and updated résumés.

The same strategy holds true as a method to get noticed on professional networking sites that you have joined. Every Monday morning, LinkedIn and Twitter feeds shape the entire week. Get in on the Monday morning action by commenting in a group on Sunday evening. When others log in and read their Monday morning news feed, your post will be near the top. In addition, on Sunday night tweet about your potential career asking if anyone knows of any open positions.

The Sunday Evening Plan should take you fewer than 30 minutes each week. Plan to spend, at a maximum:

- 10 minutes to review and re-upload your résumés
- 10 minutes to post on LinkedIn
- 10 minutes to Tweet

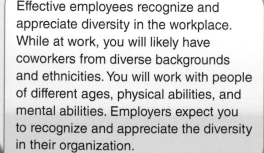

## What Employers Want

Effective employees recognize and appreciate diversity in the workplace. While at work, you will likely have coworkers from diverse backgrounds and ethnicities. You will work with people of different ages, physical abilities, and mental abilities. Employers expect you to recognize and appreciate the diversity in their organization.

Be consistent. Using just 10 minutes for each online media will yield exponential results by keeping your name near the top of online media search results.

# Managing the Application Process

Managing the application process is a job in itself. Writing a résumé and cover letter are just two of the many tasks that are necessary to find a position. The workplace is more competitive than ever. You have to put effort into finding a job that fits your needs and interests.

## Time Management

Time management is crucial when looking for a job. Time slips away quickly. The process must be managed so you can find the right position in an amount of time that works for you. Create a schedule that includes an end goal of when you need to be employed. Then, fill in the days with the activities that are needed to reach the goal.

Calendar software works well as a time management tool. It will allow you to set notices that will remind you that you have responsibilities on certain days. You may prefer a paper calendar. Use what works best for you.

Some of your responsibilities will include the tasks you have learned in this text. You will add others as you progress. Examples of tasks to schedule are:

- create professional networking accounts
- manage your online presence
- develop a portfolio
- draft a career plan
- draft a technology plan
- develop a personal brand statement
- create a résumé
- draft a cover letter
- complete an application
- prepare for interviews

Without a schedule, it could be challenging to accomplish all the activities needed to become employed.

## Stay Current

Your résumé and portfolio, along with other documents, should always be up-to-date to reflect your current situation and abilities. This information will be constantly revised and customized to be appropriate and current for job applications. Be proactive and look for reasons to revisit your employment documents. Add an alert to your calendar to review items on a regular basis.

## Keep in Touch with Your Network

It is important to keep in touch with the people in your network. Note when you contact each person, and if you should follow up in the future. If you need to follow up, add an alert in your calendar.

Record each person's name, contact information, and any important notes or tips you receive. For example, Katie works at Procter & Gamble and knows the human resources director. This information should be on your smartphone or tablet so that you can access it whenever necessary. A spreadsheet stored only on your computer at home will not be useful if you need to refer to someone in your network and you are not at home.

## Set Job Alerts

Some websites offer the service of electronic job alerts. Once you register as a job seeker and make your career preferences, you may be offered the opportunity to set job alerts. These websites will push an e-mail or text message to you notifying you of available jobs that meet your criteria. If a job you applied for is re-posted, some websites will inform you that you have already applied to the same job. This saves valuable time that you would spend looking for opportunities.

## Download Apps

Download the apps for any websites and social media accounts you use regularly for your

**The Best App for that**

Download mobile job-search apps to your digital device to stay connected during your job application process. These apps allow you to access your accounts as well as apply for jobs. *Monster.com Job Search* is one example of an online job board that provides a mobile app for its users.

job search. Loading the app on your smartphone or tablet will save you time when you want to visit the site when you are not at a computer.

# Organizing the Process

The job-search process can continue for some time. As you submit applications and start interviewing, it will be important to keep track of the details. Mixing up details like the names of companies or contact people, job descriptions, or dates and times of scheduled interviews could cost you an opportunity.

## Applications

Create a spreadsheet to record the jobs for which you apply. You will apply for many positions throughout this process. After a while, it will be difficult to keep track of them if you have not kept an accurate record. When you submit a job application, record the following information.

- title of the position
- name, address, and URL of company
- name, title, phone number, and e-mail address of the contact person

- source of the lead
- date of application

If you are responding to an advertisement, keep a copy of the job posting. If it is a printed advertisement, use a folder or envelope to store the ad. If the advertisement is online, copy it into a folder on your computer.

In many cases after applying online, applicants receive an e-mail response to the submission. Some online job boards, such as Careerbuilder.com, automatically track application activities and send an e-mail response. Some businesses also send an automatic e-mail response to applicants acknowledging the application. Create a folder in your e-mail and label it "Job Responses" or something similar. Move these e-mails into that folder as you receive them.

If you do not get a response to your application, do not take it personally. It does not mean you are not qualified. There are many people who apply for posted jobs. Most recruiters and employers select a predetermined number of responses, such as ten or twenty that stand out. As you will recall, most of the applications are screened through ADT software. A human may not even see the applications until they have been sorted and selected. These are more reasons why your résumé and cover letter should be outstanding and include keywords for which the software is looking.

## Leads

Once you start getting responses to applications, these become *job leads*. When someone actually contacts you for more information, record this on your spreadsheet. Record the following information.

- title of the position
- name, title, phone number, and e-mail address of the person who contacted you
- date of the communication
- other pertinent information

After you have been contacted, this will give you an opportunity to follow up with that person to pursue the position. Persistence is important. If someone has recognized you as a qualified applicant and you are still interested in the position, keep the communication going.

## Interviews

Tracking interviews is an important step in the process. When a potential employer decides to make contact with you for an interview, he or she will call or e-mail you. You should closely monitor your calls and e-mail messages. Make certain that you manage all incoming cell phone calls, e-mails, and voice-mail messages promptly and professionally while in the job hunting process.

As you begin to schedule interviews, continue using your spreadsheet. Your spreadsheet will grow as interview opportunities arise. In addition to the information you initially recorded about the lead, you will include pertinent facts about the interview. This additional information includes the following.

- name and contact information of the person who scheduled the interview
- interview date
- interview location
- name and title of the person(s) with whom you will interview
- title of the position
- any other pertinent information for the interview

Copy this information to your smartphone or tablet.

## 8-3 Job Application Tracker

**Directions:** Use the space provided to complete the activity or take notes. Alternatively, you can download the electronic version of this activity from the companion website.

1. As you apply for jobs, a tracking document will help manage the process. Create a tracking document. One method is to use a spreadsheet program with multiple sheets for each phase of the process. Open a spreadsheet and name each sheet accordingly.
   - Sheet 1, Applications
   - Sheet 2, Leads
   - Sheet 3, Interviews

2. On Sheet 1, *Applications*, insert names for the columns using the steps outlined in *Track Applications* in this chapter.

3. On Sheet 2, *Leads*, insert names for the columns using the steps outlined in *Track Leads* in this chapter.

4. On Sheet 3, *Interviews*, insert names for the columns using the steps outlined in *Track Interviews* in this chapter.

Download the electronic version of this activity.

# Chapter Summary

- A job application is a form used by some employers to gain more information about the applicant. It must be filled out neatly and completely. Job applications can be either hard copy or electronic.

- You do not have to wait for businesses to advertise job openings. In many cases, it is acceptable to visit the company in person and ask to apply. Plan on staying on-site to complete an application. Be prepared with a résumé and cover letter tailored to the company and a copy of your portfolio.

- Applying for jobs online begins with a search by job title, keywords, or company name. Three types of websites you can use for your job search are job-search lists, online job boards, and aggregate job boards.

- Most recruiters look for qualified applicants on Monday morning. The *Sunday Evening Plan* involves updating your electronic résumés and posting on professional networking sites on Sunday evening so that your résumé and other postings are flagged as new on Monday.

- Managing the application process involves time management, staying current, keeping in touch with your network, setting job alerts, and downloading mobile apps to your digital device. Successful management of the application process will keep you in control of your job search.

- Organizing the application process involves tracking applications, tracking leads, and tracking interviews. Create spreadsheets or similar documents to keep application dates, company names, and contact information neatly organized.

## E-Flash Card Activity: Career-Related Terms

Review the career-related terms that follow. Then visit the G-W mobile site to practice vocabulary using e-flash cards until you are able to recognize their meanings. If you do not have a smartphone, visit the G-W Learning companion website to access this feature.

job application

job-search list

online job board

aggregate job board

## Review Your Knowledge

1. What is a job application? What information is typically required on a job application?

2. How should you prepare to apply for a job in person?

3. Describe the steps involved when searching for a job online.

4. Explain how the use of a benchmark can aid your job search.

5. Compare and contrast job-search lists and online job boards.

6. What is an aggregate job board? Give an example.

7. Summarize the Sunday Evening Plan.

8. What does managing the application process involve?

9. Describe how to practice good time management during the job-search process.

10. How can you stay organized throughout the job-search process?

## Apply Your Knowledge

1. Why is it important that hard copy applications be clean, neat, and accurate? What message does a messy application send to a potential employer?

2. Are there any businesses in your community to which you would apply in person? List the businesses and note the positions in which you might be interested.

3. It is important to set a benchmark of how many advertised job requirements you meet before you apply for a job. Review several job advertisements for open positions in your field. What benchmark will work for you?

4. Types of websites that you can use for your job search include job-search lists, online job boards, and aggregate job boards. Which type do you plan on utilizing in your personal job search? Explain why.

5. Applying for jobs online involves a keyword search. List the keywords you will use to search for jobs online.

6. Searching for jobs online allows you to set search parameters that include location, salary range, and full- or part-time status, among others. What search parameters will you use when searching for desirable jobs?

7. The Sunday Evening Plan involves updating your professional online presence on Sunday evening in anticipation of hiring managers reviewing applications on Monday morning. How will you implement the Sunday Evening Plan in your personal job search?

8. There are many facets to managing the application process, such as time management, keeping in touch with your network, and setting job alerts. Which is the most challenging to you? How do you plan to meet this challenge?

9. It is important to keep in touch with your network. Reach out to someone in your professional network. How did you contact this person? What did you talk about with him or her? Summarize your interaction here.

10. Staying organized is one of the most important aspects of the application process. Describe how you will use technology to stay organized.

## Exploring Certification

### Career Certification Skills—Using Reading Skills

From the job searches that you conducted, you found a potential job that was of interest. After reading the description, you concluded you are not qualified for that specific job, but decided to apply. Fortunately, you landed a screening interview. During the interview, the interviewer asked why you should be hired and what you would bring to the company. You are requested to hand-write a paragraph of your explanation.

1. Make a list of the reasons that you think you should be hired. Include the skill that you would bring to the company.

2. Using the list you prepared, write the paragraph that you would submit to the interviewer. Use correct English and grammar as you compose one handwritten paragraph. Be certain to explain why you would be an asset to a company, even if you do not possess all the job requirements. Show sufficient evidence to support your reasoning.

## Career Certification Skills—Finding Information

You are a new employee in the human resources department. You are given the company organizational chart. An organizational chart displays each job position within the reporting structure for a company.

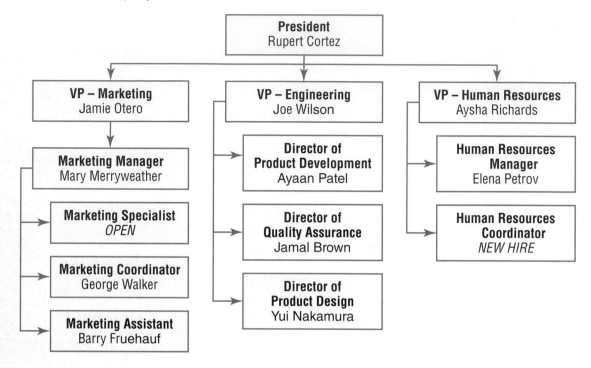

Using the organizational chart, answer the following questions.

1. What is the title of the person that heads the engineering department?


2. Who reports to Joe Wilson?


3. If you need to report an incident to the head of marketing, whom would you contact?


## Career Certification Skills—Applying Math Skills

In your new job as a carpenter, you are preparing to install a wooden floor in a rectangular room that is 25 1/2 feet by 20 1/2 feet in size. The pieces of wood are sold in boxes that contain enough pieces to cover 25 square feet. How many boxes must you order to complete the job? Select the correct answer. Show your calculations.

A.   20

B.   21

C.   72

D.   287

## Connecting to Your Career

### Why It Matters

Congratulations! You have been offered an interview. Next, you must prepare. Your preparation should include your research about the company, job responsibilities, and much more. The interview may be formal or informal, in person or virtual. Planning is the key to a successful interview that hopefully will generate a job offer.

After the interview process is complete, take time to reflect on what transpired. Use post-interview techniques at the conclusion of each interview to help put things in perspective.

If you are offered a position, take your time and evaluate the compensation package. It is your choice to accept or reject the offer. If you are not offered the position, keep moving forward with the job-search process until you find the right job for you.

Once you accept a job, learn to be a good employee. You have a long and productive future ahead, so be the best you can be.

# Preparing for the Interview

## Outcomes

- **Discuss** the three types of interviews.
- **Describe** how to conduct research about a potential employer.
- **Prepare** responses to potential questions that may be asked during an interview.
- **Create** a list of questions to ask during an interview.
- **Compare and contrast** in-person and virtual interviews.

## Career-Related Terms

| | |
|---|---|
| netiquette | hypothetical question |
| screening interview | blue-sky question |
| structured interview | signal phrase |
| unstructured interview | panel interview |
| behavioral question | |

You will see icons at various points throughout the chapter. These icons indicate that interactive activities are available on the *Connect to Your Career* companion website. Selected activities are also available on the *Connect to Your Career* mobile site. These activities will help you learn, practice, and expand your career knowledge and skills.

Companion Website
www.g-wlearning.com/careereducation/

Mobile Site
www.m.g-wlearning.com

# Overview

A job interview is the employer's opportunity to ask questions to see if you are qualified for the position. This is your opportunity to sell yourself as a potential employee. Keep in mind that your answers to interview questions are important in the employer's decision-making process. In addition, your ability to ask the interviewer insightful questions is also important.

The interview may be formal or informal. It may be an in-person interview or a virtual interview. All interview opportunities require preparation and careful planning in order to make a positive impression. The first step in preparing for a job interview is to learn as much as you can about the job and the company.

# Job Interview

A *job interview* is the employer's opportunity to inquire about details included in your résumé and to assess you as a potential employee. During this meeting, you are the focus. The interviewer will ask questions to uncover information about you as a job candidate. At the same time, it is your opportunity to exhibit your personality, while discussing the skills and abilities you possess as a potential employee.

The interview is one of the most important steps in the job application process. You have captured the interest of an employer, and this is your chance to convince that person to hire you. The job interview is the employer's opportunity to discuss the details in your résumé and assess your qualifications for the position. It is also an opportunity for you to learn if the company and position are the right fit for you.

When your résumé catches the eye of a hiring manager, you might receive an e-mail or a phone call requesting an interview. If you receive an invitation to interview via e-mail, netiquette dictates that you respond immediately. **Netiquette** is etiquette used when communicating electronically, especially via the Internet. If a time for the interview was not indicated in the message, request that information in your reply. Confirm the location of the interview and with whom you will be meeting. If you receive a phone call, be polite and express interest in the opportunity. Confirm the details of the appointment and location of the meeting during the call.

Your first interview may be a screening interview. A **screening interview** is a preliminary, informal interview designed to determine if a candidate's skills qualify him or her for a formal interview. Screening interviews are brief and involve questions about your skills, experience, and availability. These interviews are typically conducted by a recruiter or hiring manager via phone or e-mail. This type of interview helps employers narrow the list of potential candidates who will be scheduled for formal interviews.

If all goes well, the next step in the process is a formal interview. **Structured interviews**, also known as *directive interviews*, are formal interviews in which a predetermined list of questions is posed to each candidate interviewing for a position. All job candidates are asked the same questions so responses can be compared objectively to evaluate each candidate. These questions range from general to specific.

**Unstructured interviews** are interviews that are less formal and might or might not consist of a specific list of questions. The questions asked will typically change from one candidate to the next. Unstructured interviews are usually used to get to know a candidate's personality in a relaxed situation, such as over lunch or dinner.

**9-1 Informal Interviews**

**Directions:** Use the space provided to complete the activity or take notes. Alternatively, you can download the electronic version of this activity from the companion website.

1. The first step in the interview process may be a screening interview. Conduct an Internet search for *screening interview tips*. List five tips you find most helpful.


2. You may be invited to interview at a restaurant while having a meal with the interviewer. Many unstructured interviews are at mealtime, held during lunch or dinner. Conduct an Internet search for *mealtime interview tips.* List five tips you find most helpful.

Download the electronic version of this activity.

# Company Research

Once you have scheduled a formal interview date and time, you should become familiar with the company, its products, services, size, and potential for growth and expansion. Your first source of information is the company website. Navigate to the company's official website, and search for the *About Us* section. Read the contents carefully. Review information about the products and services the company offers. Make notes on everything you find. If the website includes employees' names, search for your interviewer by name to learn more about him or her.

After learning about the company from its website, enter the company name in a search engine. Locate news articles, press releases, and comments from its customers. Note how the company promotes its brand in social media.

If possible, research the company's competitors. This information will help you to determine how the company measures up against its competition. Your research will help prepare you to talk about the company and its mission.

# Interviewer Questions

Have you ever been asked a question that you did not know how to answer? To avoid such a scenario during an interview, you should plan, prepare, and practice potential interview questions. Review the description of the job for which you are interviewing. Make a list of the qualifications and skills required. Next to each requirement, list your matching experience, qualifications, and skills. Be certain you have read the details on any specific duties or other requirements so that you are prepared to answer questions.

# 9-2 Company Research

**Directions:** Use the space provided to complete the activity or take notes. Alternatively, you can download the electronic version of this activity from the companion website.

1. Conduct an Internet search for a job that interests you. List the position and company name.

2. Conduct research on the company you selected by visiting the company's official website. Read the *About Us* or equivalent section carefully. Continue reviewing the site to learn about the products and services the company offers. List any important information you find.

3. Next, key the name of the company in a search engine. Avoid returning to the company's official website. Look for press releases, articles, comments from customers, and social media posts in your search results. Record the URLs of five sites that reveal important information you could use to prepare for an interview.

Download the electronic version of this activity.

Interview questions are intended to assess your qualifications for a position. By asking questions, the interviewer can evaluate your qualifications as well as your personality and your fit with other employees in the company. Many commonly asked questions are posed so the hiring manager can learn more about the experience, education, and skills presented in your résumé.

The types of interview questions asked can vary depending on the type of interview you attend. However, there are common interview questions for which you can prepare answers ahead of time.

# General Information Questions

*General information questions* are aimed at gathering facts about you such as your education and work experience. Some examples of general information questions and answering strategies include the following.

- What can you tell me about yourself?
  *Suggested strategy:* Succinctly summarize your abilities as they relate to the job qualifications. Do not provide a general life history. Begin with your degree and any related courses. Walk through your pertinent duties at each previous job.

- What other jobs have you held?
  *Suggested strategy:* Provide your job title, the name of the company, and a brief summary of the duties involved. Focus on jobs with skills that relate to the position you are seeking. Use keywords from the job posting if possible.

- What interested you most about this position?
  *Suggested strategy:* Focus on the duties that piqued your interest in the job and how they align with your previous experience and career goals.

- Why do you want to work for this company?
  *Suggested strategy:* This is a good opportunity to share some information you learned about the company during your research. Relate what you know about the company to your career goals as well.

- What is your major strength?
  *Suggested strategy:* Select one of your strengths that relates to the requirements of the position, and provide an example of an occasion where you used it in a previous job.

- Are you comfortable using the technology required by this position?
  *Suggested strategy:* Share any experience you have with the technology required including the number of years you have used it and whether you consider yourself a novice, intermediate, or expert user. You can also provide some examples of how and when you used the technology.

# Behavioral Questions

Interviewers may ask questions that relate to your behavior or how you might typically conduct yourself. **Behavioral questions** are questions that draw on an individual's previous experiences and decisions. Using behavior-based questions in an interview is known as a *behavioral interview*. Your answers to these types of questions indicate past behavior, which may be used to predict future behavior patterns. These questions are typically more focused than general information questions. They require job seekers to provide a specific example of when they used a skill to successfully complete a task. Answers should include what the task was, the action that was taken, and the results of the action. While you cannot prepare specific answers to these questions, remain poised, answer honestly, and keep your answers focused on the question. Some examples of behavioral questions include the following.

- Tell me about a situation in which you needed to persuade your supervisor to make a change in a process or procedure.

- Tell me about a time when you needed to assume a position of the leader of a group. What were the challenges, and how did you help the group meet its goals?

- Describe a time when you missed the opportunity to provide the best service possible. How would you have changed your approach for a more successful outcome?

# Career Portfolio

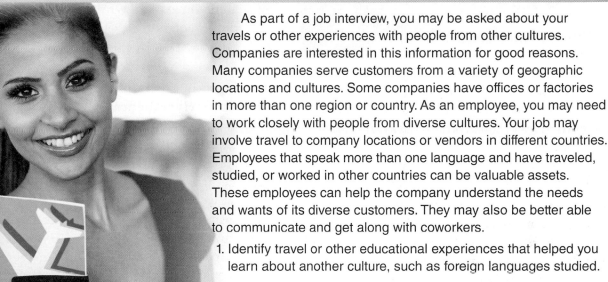

## Cultural Competence

As part of a job interview, you may be asked about your travels or other experiences with people from other cultures. Companies are interested in this information for good reasons. Many companies serve customers from a variety of geographic locations and cultures. Some companies have offices or factories in more than one region or country. As an employee, you may need to work closely with people from diverse cultures. Your job may involve travel to company locations or vendors in different countries. Employees that speak more than one language and have traveled, studied, or worked in other countries can be valuable assets. These employees can help the company understand the needs and wants of its diverse customers. They may also be better able to communicate and get along with coworkers.

1. Identify travel or other educational experiences that helped you learn about another culture, such as foreign languages studied.

2. Write a paragraph that describes the experience. Explain how the information you learned might help you better understand customers or coworkers from this culture.

3. Make a list of any languages in which you are fluent.

4. Save the document file in your e-portfolio. Place a printed copy in the container for your print portfolio.

michaeljung/Shutterstock.com

---

• Describe a situation in which you needed to be creative in order to help a customer with a problem. What was the problem and how did you solve it?

• Describe a situation when you made a mistake. Tell me how you corrected the mistake and what measures you put in place to ensure it did not happen again.

## Stress Questions

*Stress questions* are posed to candidates to see how a person reacts to pressure. These questions indicate whether candidates can "think on their feet." Stress questions are subjective, and it is difficult to predict the interviewer's preferred response. This type of question might shake a candidate's confidence. Some people become

defensive when they do not have an answer. Others become embarrassed or tongue-tied. It is critical to remain cheerful and professional. Answer such questions in a positive manner, and do not panic or lose your composure. These questions may be uncomfortable to answer but should not be illegal.

When presented with a stress question, take time to process it and formulate a coherent answer to respond articulately. To gain more time to answer a challenging question, consider using reflective techniques that acknowledge the question while giving you time to think of an answer. Some reflective technique responses are:

• "That is a great question."

• "I had not considered that angle."

• "Exactly. That happens sometimes."

**The Best App for that**

To become acquainted with virtual conferencing software, download selected virtual conference apps to your mobile device. These apps allow you to have quick access to software that interviewers use for virtual interviews. The *Skype* mobile app is an example of one popular program used by many employers.

You should anticipate some difficult questions. Your résumé and portfolio contents might trigger some tough questions. For example, if you have a gap in your work history or if your college major and your work experience are not consistent, recognize these inconsistencies. Be prepared for questions on these topics from your interviewers. If you have gaps in your employment, have an explanation as to why those gaps exist. When presented with stress questions, it is your responsibility to transform an awkward moment into a positive one. Some examples of stress questions and answering strategies include the following.

- What is your biggest weakness?

  *Suggested strategy:* Choose something you are honestly challenged by but will not jeopardize being considered for the position. For example, someone interviewing for a bank teller job would not offer counting money as his or her biggest weakness. After you have provided a response, explain what you are doing to improve your weakness.

- Why are you looking to leave your current job?

  *Suggested strategy:* Avoid saying anything negative about your current employer. Direct your responses toward your own growth and career goals you have set.

- Can you explain why there is a gap in your employment?

  *Suggested strategy:* Provide an honest answer, focusing on the positive.

Stress questions also include hypothetical questions. **Hypothetical questions** are questions that require a person to imagine a situation and describe how he or she would act. Frequent topics of hypothetical questions relate to working with and getting along with coworkers. For example, "What would you do if you were waiting on a customer and a coworker was constantly interrupting you?"

You cannot prepare specific answers to these questions, so you need to rely on your ability to think on your feet. For these types of questions, the interviewer is aware that you are being put on the spot. In addition to what you say, he or she considers other aspects of your answer as well. Body language is first and foremost. Avoid fidgeting and looking at the ceiling while thinking of your answer. Instead, look at the interviewer and calmly take a moment to compose your thoughts. Keep your responses brief. If your answer runs too long, you risk losing your train of thought. Try to relate the question to something that is familiar to you, and answer honestly. Maintain a professional and calm demeanor. Showing that you can remain poised and project confidence carries a lot of weight, even if your answer is not ideal.

Another type of stress question is the blue-sky question. A **blue-sky question** is one where the interviewer describes a scenario that may or may not be related to the job duties and requires a response from the candidate. This type of question is posed to test the candidate's life values and priorities. An example of a blue-sky question is, "If you had $10 million, what would you do with it?" Answers to these types of questions reveal personal character. Being cognizant of that, answer the question with honesty and brevity.

 **9-3 Interview Questions**

**Directions:** Use the space provided to complete the activity or take notes. Alternatively, you can download the electronic version of this activity from the companion website.

1. Write a response to each of the following general information questions often asked during job interviews.

   • What can you tell me about yourself?

   • What other jobs have you held?

   • Why do you want to work for this company?

2. Write a response to each of the following stress questions often asked during job interviews.

   • What is your biggest weakness?

   • Why are you looking to leave your current job?

   • How do you handle rejection?

Download the electronic version of this activity.

# Questions to Ask

During the interview, the hiring manager will provide you with an opportunity to ask questions. Therefore, you should prepare a list of intelligent questions to pose if asked. Study the job description and the company to formulate your list. Understand that this portion of the interview is a moment to demonstrate leadership potential.

Ask questions when requested to do so, but do not be aggressive or overbearing. Remember, the interviewer is in charge. Avoid redundant inquiries or previously addressed topics. Keep in mind that questions you ask reveal your personality. The following are some questions you may want to ask.

- What are the specific duties of this position?
- To whom will I report?
- What is company policy or criteria for employee promotions?
- Do you have a policy for providing on-the-job training?
- What are the working hours?
- When do you expect to make your hiring decision?
- If I am hired, what is the anticipated start date?

When asking questions, preface each with a signal phrase. A **signal phrase** is a preplanned beginning phrase that enhances a question. These phrases add professional polish to the question and show that you have been listening closely to the information the interviewer has shared. Some examples of signal phrases include:

- You mentioned that…
- You referred to…
- I noted that you said…
- I appreciate the way you addressed…
- You were clear in the expectations, but I have one additional question…

Do not ask salary questions during the first interview. Salary will be addressed if an offer of employment is presented. It is inappropriate to ask about money before then as doing so can give the impression that you are more concerned about money than the position. Attend the first interview on good faith that the salary offer will be acceptable.

You should *avoid* the following questions during an interview.

- What is the hourly pay for this job?
- How many other people will you interview?
- May I come back so that we can talk about this position again?
- What did you think about your interview with me?
- Are you going to hire me?

If the interview was exhaustive, all potential questions were answered, and there are no further questions about the position or the company, a candidate may ask a question about the hiring process. An example might be, "What is the next step in this process?" Another closing question could be, "When might I expect to hear from you regarding your decision?" If all questions have been addressed, offer a phrase such as, "You have answered all of my questions. Thank you. I have no additional questions to ask at this time."

The offer from an interviewer to the candidate to ask questions becomes the best time for the candidate to thank the interviewer as well. This demonstrates leadership potential and recognition of the interviewer's time.

# Interview Location

Companies are no longer confined to face-to-face interviews. Technology provides the flexibility of conducting virtual interviews. Both in-person and virtual interviews require careful planning and preparation.

## In-Person Interview

An *in-person interview* is one that is conducted with all of the participants at the same location. Usually, a job candidate is invited to the company office to meet with the hiring manager. In-person interviews can also take place away from company property. *Remote-location interviews* are in-person interviews held at an off-site location, such as on a college campus or at a job fair. For some remote-location interviews, it is common to prearrange an interview time, just as you would if you were visiting the company office.

## 9-4 Questions to Ask

**Directions:** Use the space provided to complete the activity or take notes. Alternatively, you can download the electronic version of this activity from the companion website.

1. There are standard questions you will ask about any job for which you are interviewing. Those questions will be about topics such as on-the-job training and hours worked. Make a list of five common questions that you would ask about any job.

2. Conduct an Internet search for questions to ask during a job interview. List five questions that resources suggest you ask.

3. Conduct an Internet search for questions *not* to ask. List five questions that resources recommend you avoid asking.

Download the electronic version of this activity.

You may be interviewed by one person or multiple people. A **panel interview** is an interview in which a candidate talks with multiple interviewers in a room. Each member of the panel might present different angles or questions related to the candidate's ability and the job for which he or she is being interviewed. If you know you will be interviewed by a panel, ask questions about the details before you arrive, such as how many members there will be and the names of each. Some candidates are required to deliver a brief demonstration or presentation for panel interviews. If so, you will have advance notice and time to prepare.

Plan to arrive at least 15 minutes before the appointment time. Allow plenty of time for traveling. Take into consideration weather, traffic, or other factors that might delay your arrival.

Be sure you know exactly where the interview is being conducted. Some companies have several locations, and you must be sure that you arrive at the correct place on the day of your interview. This information is usually provided by the person with whom you arranged the interview date and time. However, if is it not, contact the human resources department at the company for the location and directions. An e-mail is an appropriate way to reach human resources to get this information. Be respectful in your query. An example message would be, "I want to confirm the location of the interview. Will you please provide me with the exact street address and suite number?"

If possible, before your interview, visit the location to gain a sense of the time it takes to get there. Use a map or an online map program to guide you. Once you arrive, park and walk to the building where the interview will take place. You need to learn how long it takes to park, walk from the parking area to enter the building, and check in. If you are unable to visit the company in person before the interview, use an online map program, such as Google maps, that allows you to see the building, parking locations, and other surrounding areas online.

Make sure you have an understanding of the company's visitor protocol. If the information has not been provided by the hiring manager, locate a general number for the company. Call the main number, and ask about its protocol for visitors. Is there visitor parking? Will you need a visitor pass? Some companies require identification to proceed past the lobby for an interview. Other companies need only the name of the person with whom you have an appointment.

## Virtual Interview

A virtual interview is also known as a *technology-based interview.* One of the advantages of a virtual interview is that the candidate is not required to commute to the employer's location. However, the potential for technical difficulties is a disadvantage. It can be difficult to create a strong first impression when troubleshooting technical problems. Be certain to be in an area where you have a solid connection before the interview.

A virtual interview might be conducted via the phone or the Internet. Therefore, it is important that your e-résumé, online presence, and e-portfolio are up-to-date and readily available. This may include completing your LinkedIn profile and updating your blog or your e-portfolio site with work samples that are relevant to the job for which you are interviewing.

### Telephone Interview

For an interview conducted over the phone, the interviewer will arrange to call you, or you will be asked to place the call. If the interviewer is calling you, make sure you are by the phone at least five minutes early. You should answer the call yourself. If you are placing the call, you will be calling the interviewer's direct line or calling into a conference-call number. Place the call no earlier than five minutes before the scheduled appointment time. For conference calls, call in and hold for the moderator.

## What Employers Want

Employers expect ethical communication. An ethical communicator uses honesty and accuracy to guide all communication. Communication must be truthful and presented in an unbiased manner. Facts should be given without distortion. If the information is an opinion, label it as such. Do not take credit for ideas that belong to someone else—always credit your sources.

Even though you cannot be seen, it can be helpful if you are sitting up straight at a desk or a table for the phone call. Be sure you have all the materials you would take with you to an in-person interview, such as your résumé and company research notes. Your materials should be easily accessible to reference during the interview. Avoid the sound of shuffling papers or the clicking of keys on a keyboard during the interview. Silence the interview area to eliminate background noise. The interview dialogue should not compete with television, radio, and barking dogs, for example. Such occurrences can ruin an interview. Secure the room against noise disruptions and concentrate on the interviewer only.

## Skype Interview

Real-time video conferencing using Skype or other technologies requires using a web camera and an Internet connection for both parties to make visual contact. If you are not familiar with the video conferencing software being used, take time before the day of the interview to get acquainted with it. Some video conferencing software requires users to download and install a program, which can be time-consuming. On the day of the interview, log on at least five minutes early. It is considered unprofessional to log on at the start time of the interview. In all cases, be the first to the virtual interview so that when your interviewer arrives, you are in position and ready to greet him or her.

A video interview requires the same amount of care and preparation as an in-person interview in terms of attire and personal details. In addition, you should prepare the physical surroundings where the interview will take place. Find a quiet place away from traffic noise, the radio, or other distractions. It is imperative to direct your web camera view so that the interviewer's view reflects a work environment. For example, if your laptop is in your kitchen and the web camera gives the other party a view of dirty dishes, this would give the wrong impression. Virtual work environments from a web camera's point of view should be as simple as a plain wall or a wall with framed pictures and a bookcase.

Pay special attention to the lighting in the room. The lighting in the room should be flattering to you. Consider the time of day of your interview, and practice using different light sources.

The virtual interview follows the same pattern as an in-person interview. The conversation might begin with a brief, pleasant question about the connection before starting. The interviewer will then most likely take the lead. At the end of the conversation, he or she will offer you a chance to ask questions. You will have a chance to respond, close the interview, and thank him or her.

## 9-5 Virtual Interviews

**Directions:** Use the space provided to complete the activity or take notes. Alternatively, you can download the electronic version of this activity from the companion website.

1. One type of virtual interview is interviewing via the telephone. Conduct an Internet search for *how to interview over the telephone*. Make a list of details that should be considered when interviewing via the telephone.

2. Many employers who conduct virtual real-time video interviews use software such as Skype. Visit the Skype website to learn more about this technology. Make a list of things you will need if an employer suggests a Skype virtual interview.

Download the electronic version of this activity.

## Chapter Summary

- A job interview is an employer's opportunity to inquire about details included in your résumé and to assess you as a potential employee. The interview is one of the most important steps in the job application process. Three types of interviews include a screening interview, a structured interview, and an unstructured interview.

- As part of the preparation process, you should become familiar with the company, its products, services, size, and potential for growth and expansion. This information will enable you to answer questions as well as ask questions during the interview.

- Interview questions are intended to assess your qualifications for a position. Three types of interview questions commonly used are general information questions, behavioral questions, and stress questions. Prepare for these types of questions before the interview.

- During the interview, the hiring manager will provide you with an opportunity to ask questions. Come prepared with a list of questions to which you would like responses.

- Companies are no longer confined to face-to-face interviews. Technology provides the flexibility of conducting virtual interviews. Two common types of virtual interviews are telephone interviews or real-time video conferencing. Both types of interviews require careful planning and preparation.

## E-Flash Card Activity: Career-Related Terms

Review the career-related terms that follow. Then visit the G-W mobile site to practice vocabulary using e-flash cards until you are able to recognize their meanings. If you do not have a smartphone, visit the G-W Learning companion website to access this feature.

netiquette

screening interview

structured interview

unstructured interview

behavioral question

hypothetical question

blue-sky question

signal phrase

panel interview

## Review Your Knowledge

1. Explain how an interview is an opportunity for both the interviewer and the candidate.

2. Describe the purpose of a screening interview.

3. Define *structured interview*. What makes a structured interview different from an unstructured one?

4. Give examples of how to research a company that has invited you to an interview.

5. What types of questions are commonly asked during a job interview? Describe the purpose of each.

6. Explain the purpose of a signal phrase.

7. Where do in-person interviews typically take place?

8. What is a panel interview?

9. Briefly describe the two types of virtual interviews.

10. How should you prepare for a video interview?

## Apply Your Knowledge

1. It is important to use netiquette when communicating with potential employers. Research the rules of netiquette. What did you learn?

2. If possible, you should research the competitors of the company with which you are interviewing. Explain why this is important information to have for an interview.

3. There are different types of questions that a hiring manager might ask. One type of question is general information. Select one general information question that was presented in this chapter, and read its suggested strategy. How would you answer this question?

4. Your résumé and portfolio contents could trigger stress questions posed by the interviewer. Are you prepared if this happens to you? What are some stress questions you might be asked during an interview? How will you answer them?

5. An example of a blue-sky question is, "If you had $10 million, what would you do with it?" How would you answer this question in a job interview? Explain what your answer reveals about you as a potential employee.

6. What questions are most important for you to ask during an interview based on your career goals and your chosen career field?

7. Review the list of questions to avoid during an interview. Why is it unwise to ask certain types of questions during an interview?

8. A panel interview is an interview in which a candidate talks with multiple interviewers in a room. Describe how you would prepare for a panel interview.

9.  Imagine you have an interview with a company located 50 miles away from your home. Describe how you would prepare for commuting to the interview location.

10. Would you prefer a telephone or video interview? Explain your reasoning.

## Exploring Certification

### Career Certification Skills—Using Reading Skills

1.  Select a job board and locate its policy on posting cover letters. Read the policy carefully. State the name of the job board, and summarize its cover letter policy.

2.  Based on the information you read, determine how many cover letters you will store on that site. Make a list of the factors you would use to determine how to create ideal cover letters that would be appropriate to be viewed by employers who post jobs that would be of interest to you. Using the list you created, write a paragraph describing why you made the decision to select the cover letter or letters that will be displayed. Use valid reasoning to support your choice.

### Career Certification Skills—Applying Math Skills

You are working in a retail store as a cashier. The customer has a cash purchase that totals $8.37 and gives you a $20 bill. How much change would you return to the customer? Select the correct answer. Show your calculations.

A.  $11.50

B.  $12.00

C.  $11.63

D.  $11.11

## Career Certification Skills—Finding Information

The policy at your new job is to refrain from using first or second person when writing office correspondence. You research English grammar. Your research reflects information about first, second, and third person when writing sentences. So that you do not forget this information, you create the following chart that you can use on the job.

|  | Singular | Plural |
|---|---|---|
| **First person** | I | we |
| **Second person** | you | you |
| **Third person** | he/she/it | they |

Goodheart-Willcox Publisher

Using the chart, rewrite these first- and second-person sentences using third person construction.

1.  I find it difficult to count calories when I eat in restaurants every day.


2.  You need to find your bike helmet before riding.


3.  I learned that most people have difficulty saving money because they spend too much.


4.  Your financial statement contained some errors, and I think that you should revise it.


5.  Do you think that eating blueberries is healthy?

## Chapter 10

# The Interview

## Outcomes

- **Describe** ways to prepare for an interview.
- **Discuss** how to make a positive first impression at an interview.
- **Identify** materials necessary to take to the interview.
- **Describe** the interview event.
- **Explain** the purpose of a second interview.

## Career-Related Terms

subjective elements

formal seated position

body language

second interview

You will see icons at various points throughout the chapter. These icons indicate that interactive activities are available on the *Connect to Your Career* companion website. Selected activities are also available on the *Connect to Your Career* mobile site. These activities will help you learn, practice, and expand your career knowledge and skills.

Companion Website
www.g-wlearning.com/careereducation/

Mobile Site
www.m.g-wlearning.com

# Overview

The last step in preparing for an interview is to practice responses to questions that are likely to be asked. There are two suggested methods of preparing: practice in front of a mirror and conduct a mock interview. Both approaches will help you feel more confident when you arrive for your appointment.

At the interview, be prepared for introductions, questions, and the closing segment. Dress appropriately and come with the necessary documents. Have your questions prepared for the interviewer and allow time, if needed, for pre-employment tests. If you are successful, the opportunity for a second interview might be extended at a later date.

## Practice for the Interview

All successful interviews begin with preparation. A successful interview is more likely if you take time to rehearse prior to the appointment. It is important to become familiar with possible answers and responses that you might provide, as well as the questions you might ask.

You can benefit from practicing in front of a mirror. This activity allows you to see what the interviewer will see. Dress professionally when you practice to become comfortable with your attire. As you rehearse your responses, pay special attention to your facial expressions and posture. Decide how you will introduce yourself to the interviewer. If possible, record your voice so that you can monitor your tone and inflection. It is natural to be nervous during an interview, but learn to sound as relaxed as possible. Practicing in front of a mirror and recording your voice will help you feel more prepared.

Conducting a mock interview is another way to prepare for a formal interview. A *mock interview* is a practice interview conducted with another person. During a mock interview, one person will role-play the interviewer and the other the job candidate. This gives you a chance to uncover potential mistakes and to determine if you are ready for the interview process. Take mock interviews seriously. This practice strategy provides training necessary to polish your performance in front of another person.

If you attend a college or university, check with the administration or career services office as they may have personnel dedicated to perform mock interviews. Alternatively, you may decide to ask a friend or family member to participate.

Select a quiet place to conduct the mock interview. Prepare a table or desk and chairs to simulate an office environment. If possible, record yourself as the interviewee. If you have one available, a camera on a tripod works well for this purpose. You will gain insight into how others perceive you when reviewing the video.

After you conduct your first mock interview as the interviewee, switch roles. This experience will allow you to see the job candidate from the interviewer's position. Observe how another person responds to your questions. Try to gain an understanding of what to do and what not to do during your interview. Regardless of the role you are assuming, be sure to stay in character for the entire mock interview.

## First Impressions

During an interview, subjective elements can influence the perception of a hiring manager. **Subjective elements** are factors that contain bias and are more emotional than logical. Subjective elements are the psychological nuances that occur

**Connect** to your **Career**

## 10-1 Mock Interview

**Directions:** Use the space provided to complete the activity or take notes. Alternatively, you can download the electronic version of this activity from the companion website.

1. Prepare for a mock interview. List ten questions to be used for the mock interview. You can refer to Chapter 9 for questions an interviewer might ask, or create your own list of questions. After each question, write your response.

2. Practice your answers in front of a mirror. Afterward, record your thoughts on the experience.

3. Ask a friend to assume the role of interviewer and conduct a mock interview. This person should use the questions you prepared. Remember to introduce yourself and shake hands with the interviewer. If possible, ask another friend to film the interview.

4. Next, watch the video and critique your performance. If this had been a real interview, do you think you would have impressed the interviewer? Why or why not?

5. What did you learn from this experience?

Download the electronic version of this activity.

when an interviewer and interviewee meet for the first time. Often unintentionally, an interviewer will make split-second judgments about you. This determination is the first impression. The first impression usually comes from outward appearances, such as the way you dress, smile, walk, and even your handshake. Make eye contact with the interviewer. This initial impression occurs when the interviewer greets you. These first moments should count in your favor.

Conveying a positive first impression starts with a plan. From within the first few seconds of meeting your interviewer, he or she will decide a great deal about you based on the way you look. While this practice may not be a fair assessment of a candidate's skills and qualities for the job, the first visual impression makes a powerful impact on potential employers. Make sure your appearance is appropriate for your interview. A clean and professional appearance is a good way to start a chain of events leading to a job offer.

Each work environment has an unspoken system of operations based on the company's philosophy and objectives. The work environment sets the tone and mood within the boundaries of an organization. If possible, visit the company where you have applied for a position. Become an anonymous customer of the business where you wish to work. Get an impression of the working environment and note what the employees wear. Once you understand the work environment of your desired employer, identify appropriate attire in that setting, and elevate it slightly for the interview.

## Dress

Dressing to gain employment at a surfboard retailer can be completely different from dressing to interview for a position as a bank employee. Your appearance and attire should match the workplace environment. However, there are safe interview clothing choices that work across many types of professional environments.

An appropriate way to dress for an interview is to wear conservative, neutral clothes. A business suit is appropriate for both men and women. If the weather is inclement, plan for outer garments as well. A single outer garment that you can easily remove, such as an overcoat or raincoat, is an asset to a professional wardrobe. Suggestions for appropriate interview attire for men and women are shown in Figure 10-1.

Do not wear anything to the interview that will disrupt or distract a potential interviewer from focusing on your skills. The goal is to help the interviewer focus on your strengths as an employee.

## Personal Details

Details are important when preparing for an interview. Clothes should be neat, clean, and in good condition. Shoes should be clean and free of any scuffmarks or obvious wear. A nice timepiece, such as a wristwatch, can impress potential employers. For other jewelry choices, choose conservative, not flashy, items.

Pay attention to personal grooming, hygiene, and cleanliness. Refrain from wearing cologne. A neat hairstyle is preferred by most hiring

**The Best App for that**

Using your mobile device, search for the *Job Interview Question-Answer* app. This interactive video app helps you prepare for interview questions in a mock interview format. An interviewer poses questions, and you film yourself answering them. The app then coaches you on how best to answer the questions.

## Appropriate Attire for a Job Interview

**Women**

- Wear a suit or dress with a conservative length.
- Choose solid colors over prints or flowers.
- Wear pumps with a moderate heel or flats.
- Keep any jewelry small.
- Have a well-groomed hairstyle.
- Use little makeup.
- Avoid perfume or apply it very lightly.
- Nails should be manicured and of moderate length without decals.

**Men**

- Wear a conservative suit of a solid color.
- Wear a long-sleeved shirt, either white or a light color.
- Tie should be conservative.
- Wear loafers or lace-up shoes with dark socks.
- Avoid wearing jewelry.
- Have a well-groomed haircut.
- Avoid cologne.
- Nails should be neatly trimmed.

Goodheart-Willcox Publisher; images: Shutterstock.com

**Figure 10-1** Wearing conservative, professional attire helps the interviewer focus on your strengths as a potential employee.

managers. Your hands and jewelry are important aspects of the impression you make at an interview as well. Make certain that fingernails are clean and not broken or uneven. In addition, downplay piercings and tattoos. Your smile should be inviting. One of the single most effective personal details is a genuine, warm smile.

# Materials for the Interview

As final preparation for the interview, create a professional interview bag, such as a briefcase, backpack, or satchel. Place only the essentials in the bag including a binder with pockets. Place dividers in the binder to keep your information organized. Make sure you have the following items in your interview bag.

- hard copies of your résumé that are unfolded and without holes or staple marks
- pad of paper for taking notes
- pen with which to write
- notes from your company research
- the list you created of job requirements compared to your experience, qualifications, and skills
- prepared questions for the interviewer
- list of references
- appointment calendar
- business cards
- bottle of water

If you have created a portfolio, bring a copy to leave with the interviewer. If you have an e-portfolio, write the link on your business card.

# The Interview

Arrive 15 minutes early. Attend the interview alone—do not bring someone with you. Turn your cell phone off and place it out of sight. When you arrive in the building, introduce yourself to the receptionist. State who you are, why you are there, and whom you have come to see. Ask the receptionist to let the person know you have arrived.

# 10-2 Interview Checklists

**Directions:** Use the space provided to complete the activity or take notes. Alternatively, you can download the electronic version of this activity from the companion website.

1. On a separate sheet of paper or in a word processing document, create a checklist that you will use for your interview attire. Include each article of clothing, shoes, etc. This will help you prepare for the interview and remember important details.

2. Create a separate checklist you will use for materials to take with you to the interview.

Download the electronic version of this activity.

---

Someone will greet you and escort you to the room where the interview will take place. The greeter may be the interviewer or someone from the human resources department. Be pleasant and professional to everyone.

## Introduction

The first connection that takes place with the interviewer is the initial introduction. Once you arrive in the interview room, wait to be seated. It is appropriate to extend your hand when the interviewer approaches you to deliver a firm handshake. A firm handshake and good posture, along with a pleasant greeting, is the beginning of making a positive connection with the interviewer.

The interviewer might say, "Please, have a seat." Most interviewers use a hand gesture to indicate the appropriate seat for the interview candidate. At that time, it is advisable to sit in a formal seated position. A **formal seated position** entails sitting upright, with both feet on the floor and both hands comfortably resting either on chair armrests or in the lap. This is the opposite of slouching. The seated position will change slightly during the interview process as the conversation begins to unfold; however, try not to fidget during your conversation.

In all interview situations, be aware of your body language. **Body language** is how gestures and facial expressions communicate feelings. Be aware of your facial expressions, gestures, body movement, and body position. Make eye contact with the interviewer.

If this is a virtual interview, greet the interviewer with a smile and an introduction. Look directly into the camera as if you are making eye contact. Your posture will be seen on the camera, so it is important to sit in a formal seated position.

Often the interviewer will begin with preliminary comments and a greeting that might include brief questions such as, "Did you have any difficulty finding our offices?" The preliminary questions are meant to break the ice and allow the interviewer to gain an impression of how the candidate handles new challenges. Avoid complaining about traffic, commute time, unclear directions, or other obstacles that you negotiated in order to arrive successfully. Instead, show that you listen and follow directions well. Consider saying, "I made a trial run yesterday based on the directions from your assistant, which made the drive today very easy."

If you have a portfolio, ask the interviewer if he or she would like to have a copy. Also, offer a hard copy of your résumé.

## Interviewer Questions

Your interview preparation will pay dividends as you answer the questions posed by the interviewer. Focus on the keywords of the available job when articulating personal qualifications. Language choices should be respectful and formal as well. For example, if the interviewer elicits a response where a "yes" is expected, do not offer "yeah" as a substitute. Do not be distracted by the person's outward appearance. Focus on answering interview questions to the best of your ability and selling yourself as the best candidate for the job.

### What Employers Want

*Flexibility* is the ability to alter your actions as a situation requires. Employers expect employees to be flexible in the workplace. Situations do not always go as planned. Employees who do not adjust their behavior based on the situation can create obstacles in the workplace. Do not be an employee who does not adapt when necessary. You could find yourself without a job.

## Social Media for Your Career

Vizualize.me is a graphic résumé-building program, which allows users to turn text into appealing charts for use in an infographic résumé. Users can import their career information directly from their LinkedIn or Twitter accounts. The Vizualize.me program auto-populates the graphic résumé with your information. Users can choose from free media options or pay a fee for designed templates and styles.

# Career Portfolio

## References

michaeljung/Shutterstock.com

The purpose of your portfolio is to help you get a job. You should build a network of people who can help you in your job-search process. People in your network might be instructors, employers, coworkers, or counselors who know about your skills and interests. The people you requested to serve as references are part of this important group. Those who participate with you in volunteer efforts, clubs, or other organizations can also be part of your network. These people can help you learn about open positions. They may also be able to give you information that will help you get an interview.

An important part of your portfolio is a list of references. A reference is a person who knows your skills, talents, or personal traits and is willing to recommend you. When applying for a position, consider which references can best recommend you for the position for which you are applying. Always get permission from the person before using his or her name as a reference.

1. Identify people who are part of your professional network.

2. Create a database to contain information about the people in your network. Include each person's name, contact information, and relationship to you. For example, the person might be a coworker, employer, or fellow club member.

3. Next, select a list of three to five people who have agreed to be professional references. Create a document with the heading of Professional References. List each person and his or her contact information. This list will be used in the application process.

Federal and state laws prohibit employers from asking questions that relate to a candidate's:

- age
- disability
- genetic information
- marital or family status
- ethnicity or national origin
- religion
- gender

If an interviewer asks you a question that does not relate to your ability to perform a job, politely decline to answer the question.

## Candidate Questions

After the interviewer has finished with his or her questions, you will be asked if you have any questions of your own. This is the time to ask the questions you have prepared. Be respectful of the interviewer's time. If you believe the interview is complete, do not extend time by asking additional questions that are unnecessary. However, make certain that you have asked for any important information that was not already covered.

## Closing

When the interview is complete, conclude the interview by summarizing your skills briefly. In advance, prepare a closing statement that you will share with your interviewer. Take the opportunity to restate your brand statement using one complete sentence. If during the interview you did not highlight a skill or some experience that fits the position, use your closing statement to highlight these positive qualities. Express to the interviewer that you are interested in the position and that you believe you would make many positive contributions in the organization. Ask for any follow-up activities that you should pursue. It is also appropriate to ask when a decision will be made to fill the position.

Thank the interviewer for his or her time. If convenient, extend your hand to give the interviewer a final, firm handshake. A firm handshake is as appropriate to conclude a meeting as it is to begin one. Remember that your closing statement and thank-you should be brief but positive. Ask the interviewer or interviewers for a business card, and if possible, offer your business card.

## Pre-Employment Tests

Often, employers screen potential job candidates by giving them pre-employment tests. These tests consist of questions to measure skills necessary for basic employment. Employers that give pre-employment tests generally do not always share the results with job candidates.

Some employers give simple math or grammar tests, while others administer personality tests. Government agencies use their own tests to measure a variety of skills, such as writing and reading comprehension. Businesses such as retailers, banks, utility companies, and staffing agencies are likely to administer a test that measures the integrity of a candidate when interviewing for a position related to money, public safety, or merchandise.

If you know you will be taking a test, be certain to get plenty of rest the night before and eat a healthy breakfast. If possible, take practice tests online so that you are comfortable with the test-tasking process.

## Second Interviews

Occasionally, some employers request a second interview. In general, a **second interview** is another formal interview that occurs after it has been determined that the candidate is qualified and more information is needed about him or her.

If you are called for a second interview, prepare for the event as diligently as you did for the first interview. The same protocol is in order. Maintain a clear mindset that you are a top candidate, and arriving unprepared could leave the employer with a poor impression. Again, pay attention to your wardrobe and which documents to bring with you. If possible, do not wear the identical outfit worn at the first interview. Vary your attire, even if you only wear something slightly different, such as a different color or type of shirt.

A second interview can also be a time for you to address questions that you did not have an opportunity to ask during the first interview. When called back for a second interview, a candidate has a chance to ask additional questions and to discuss specific working expectations and benefits. Some of your additional questions might include travel expectations, telecommuting, flextime, job sharing, overtime expectations, and work attire. Make a list of questions ahead of the interview and order the list according to priority. You might only have a chance to ask a few questions, so you need to ask the most important ones first.

# 10-3 Pre-Employment Tests

**Directions:** Use the space provided to complete the activity or take notes. Alternatively, you can download the electronic version of this activity from the companion website.

1.  Conduct an Internet search for *pre-employment tests*. List five of the most common pre-employment tests used to evaluate job candidates. Describe what each test evaluates.

2.  Conduct an Internet search for *pre-employment test tips*. Select several of the most helpful tips and techniques suggested for preparing for these tests. Summarize what you learned.

Download the electronic version of this activity.

## Chapter Summary

- Successful interviewing is the result of planning. Practice your rehearsed responses to questions in front of a mirror. Conduct a mock interview by having a friend play the role of the interviewer. Practice, practice, practice.

- First impressions usually come from outward appearances, such as the way you dress, smile, and walk. Make sure your attire and personal details are interview appropriate.

- Come prepared with materials that will be required during the interview. Use a professional briefcase, backpack, or satchel to carry these necessary items.

- On the day of the interview, arrive 15 minutes early. A firm handshake and good posture, along with a pleasant greeting, is the beginning of making a positive connection with the interviewer. When the interview is complete, conclude by summarizing your skills briefly. Be prepared and allow time in the event that you will be given a pre-employment test.

- A second interview is another formal interview that occurs after it has been determined that the candidate is qualified and more information is needed. If you are called for a second interview, prepare for the event as diligently as you did for the first one.

## E-Flash Card Activity: Career-Related Terms

Review the career-related terms that follow. Then visit the G-W mobile site to practice vocabulary using e-flash cards until you are able to recognize their meanings. If you do not have a smartphone, visit the G-W Learning companion website to access this feature.

| | |
|---|---|
| subjective elements | body language |
| formal seated position | second interview |

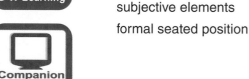

## Review Your Knowledge

1. Describe the importance of practicing for an interview.

2. What happens during a mock interview? Explain why this strategy is good practice for interviews.

3. Define *subjective elements*. Give some examples.

4. Discuss how subjective elements can impact your first impression at an interview.

5. Identify a safe choice for interview attire.

6. List the materials necessary to take to the interview.

7. What is a formal seated position? Why is it important during an interview?

8. Explain the limitations set by federal and state laws regarding illegal questions an employer should *not* ask during an interview. If you are asked an illegal question, how should you respond?

9. How can you prepare for a pre-employment test?

10. What does it mean to be given a second interview?

## Apply Your Knowledge

1. You can benefit from practicing for an interview. Will you practice in front of a mirror, conduct a mock interview, or both? Describe how you plan to practice for an interview.

2. What can you learn from playing the role of an interviewer when conducting a mock interview?

3. Conveying a positive first impression starts with a plan. Explain how you plan to make a positive first impression at interviews. Include information about your dress and other personal details.

4. Not all candidates apply for an office job. Is it ever appropriate to wear something other than a suit to an interview? Explain your reasoning.

5. Consider a job title of interest to you. If you were invited to interview for the position, which personal documents would you bring to the interview and why? How do you plan to carry your materials to an interview?

6. In all interview situations, it is important to be aware of your body language. Write a paragraph that describes the ways your body language can help or hurt an interview's outcome.

7. Write a closing statement that you will give at the conclusion of an interview. Be sure to include your personal brand statement.

8. Describe how you will prepare for the possibility of pre-employment tests that may be given at the end of the interview process.

9. What criteria will you use to evaluate your performance in an interview?

10. If you were preparing for a second interview, would you do anything differently from your first interview?

## Exploring Certification

### Career Certification Skills—Using Reading Skills

You are at a mock interview and your potential "new boss" has a dilemma. She wants to get your opinion about the memo she composed. She will use this to help her determine your level of reading comprehension and logical decision making. Following is a copy of the memo that she provides for you to read. Read the message and then determine the best responses.

**Internal Memo**

Employees have been noted for taking excessive breaks over the last three months. A management company has been hired to determine best practices for employee break times. Each employee may take one 10-minute break during any shift that is shorter than six hours. Each employee may take one 10-minute break in the morning and one 10-minute break in the afternoon during any shift six or more hours in length. These breaks may be scheduled at the employees' discretion. Each employee may request up to two additional breaks, if needed, at any given point in the day. Each additional break must be approved by a manager. All breaks must be taken in the employee break room or off company property.

1. What is the greatest number of breaks that an employee may take in any one day?

2. Who must approve additional breaks?

### Career Certification Skills—Applying Math Skills

The store where you are employed is selling a set of headphones for 15 percent off the original price. The price of the set of headphones is $39 before the discount. What is the total price for the set of headphones after the discount? Select the correct answer. Show your calculations.

A. $33.15

B. $39.00

C. $35.47

D. $42.50

## Career Certification Skills—Finding Information

You are in charge of tracking project budgets in your new job. You are provided with a pie chart that shows how much of the total budget is allocated for each department involved in the project. Using the pie chart, answer the following questions.

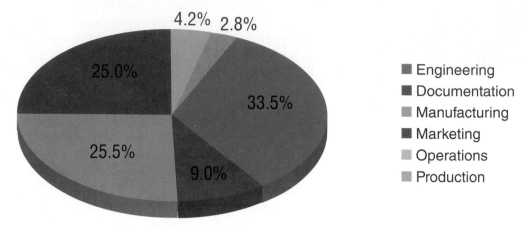

1. What percentage of the budget is allocated to the marketing department?

2. Which department has the smallest portion of the overall budget?

3. The engineering department is projecting that they will run over budget by 7 percent. The documentation department is willing to give up 2.5 percent of the money allocated to them. The manufacturing department will relinquish enough of their budget money to cover the rest of the engineering department's overage. What are the new percentages for the three departments?

# Evaluating the Interview

## Outcomes

- **Identify** post-interview techniques.
- **Describe** the employment process after a job offer had been extended.

## Career-Related Terms

| | |
|---|---|
| job offer | employment verification |
| compensation package | background check |

You will see icons at various points throughout the chapter. These icons indicate that interactive activities are available on the *Connect to Your Career* companion website. Selected activities are also available on the *Connect to Your Career* mobile site. These activities will help you learn, practice, and expand your career knowledge and skills.

Companion Website
www.g-wlearning.com/careereducation/

Mobile Site
www.m.g-wlearning.com

# Overview

An important part of the interviewing process is to evaluate the interview once it has transpired. If you are successful and get the job, take time to reflect on the experience. If you do not get the job, do not feel defeated. You will not get every position for which you apply. Look at each interview opportunity as an experience to prepare you for the next one. Utilizing the post-interview techniques at the conclusion of each interview will help put things in perspective.

If you are offered a position, take time to evaluate all aspects of the job and compensation package before you accept or reject the offer. Negotiation may be necessary to get the salary that you desire. If you do accept the offer, be prepared for the employment processes that follow.

# Post-Interview Techniques

Post-interview techniques consist of a series of steps a job candidate should complete after the interview. Imagine you have successfully completed an interview with a potential employer. What do you do next? First, you should take the time to evaluate the experience. This will enable you to learn from the interview and move forward with confidence. Next, follow up in a professional way with a formal thank-you message. Finally, you should think positive and continue your job search. Common post-interview techniques include these steps:

- evaluate the interview
- follow up with a thank-you message
- manage emotions
- continue the job search

## Evaluate the Interview

After the interview, evaluate your performance as soon you can. It is common to feel doubt and anxiety, but it is important to accept that the interview was a one-time occurrence. Evaluate your experience, and develop a plan to move forward.

An effective post-interview technique is to identify how you felt afterward. Immediately after an interview, make notes about your overall impression of the company, interviewers, and process. Then, measure your desire to work for that company based on what you learned. If you were offended or had a negative feeling about the company, you might decide immediately that you do not wish to be an employee there.

Assess your performance and design a plan addressing how you would perform better during the next interview. Evaluate your performance with the attitude that the process was a learning experience. Ask yourself the following questions, and answer honestly.

- Did I articulate my prepared responses as planned?
- Did I answer the questions with thoughtful intelligence?
- How could I better prepare for the questions I was not expecting?
- Did I have all of the documents requested?
- Was I dressed appropriately?
- Did my voice project confidence but not arrogance?
- Was my smile pleasant and natural?
- Did I talk too much or not enough?
- Did I remember to shake the interviewer's hand when I arrived and when I left the interview?

Expand this list with your own set of questions to evaluate your interview skills. Every job interview is an opportunity to practice. Do not feel your time was wasted if you do not get the job offer or decide the job is not a good fit for you.

# 11-1 Interview Evaluation

**Directions:** Use the space provided to complete the activity or take notes. Alternatively, you can download the electronic version of this activity from the companion website.

1. Post-interview techniques help prepare you for the next opportunity to interview for a position. The first step is to evaluate the interview. Create a list of at least 10 questions you will use to evaluate your first job interview. Use the questions in the chapter as a starting point, and then add any additional questions that will be important for you.

2. Use the Internet to research questions that will help you evaluate your interview experience in an objective manner. Which resources were most beneficial to you? Why?

3. Prioritize your final list of questions with the most important ones at the top of the list.

Download the electronic version of this activity.

Companion
*G-W Learning*

## Send a Thank-You Message

After an interview, follow up with the interviewer in the form of a thank-you message. The *thank-you message* is the unsolicited communication demonstrating professional courtesy, from you to the interviewer. This communication can also affirm your interest in the position and exhibit your ability to be professional. Regardless of your impressions of the interview, send a thank-you message. If possible, send it within 24 to 48 hours after the interview. You should send a separate thank-you message to each person with whom you interviewed. If you discussed any follow-up actions on your part during the interview, such as providing references or work samples, include them with this communication.

You may choose to send a hard copy of a formal letter. Figure 11-1 shows an example of a professional thank-you message. Write the letter using a standard letter format similar to your cover letter. Thank the interviewer for his or her time. Express your continued interest in the position, and close with the desire to hear back concerning the hiring decision. If any follow-up material was promised, enclose it with the letter. If you created business cards, insert one into the letter before mailing.

Thank-you messages can also be handwritten. Some candidates purchase thank-you cards to handwrite and send in the mail. Interviewers appreciate handwritten cards. If you decide to handwrite a thank-you, select a high-quality card or stationery, and be sure your handwriting is legible. Again, you can include one of your business cards in the card or letter before mailing.

An e-mail thank-you message is also acceptable. Figure 11-2 shows an example of a professional e-mail thank-you message. If the

# Career Portfolio

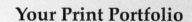

### Your Print Portfolio

You have collected multiple items for your print portfolio. Now you will organize those materials. Include captions or short summaries for items that are not self-explanatory. Include either a traditional résumé or infographic résumé, depending on the position for which you are interviewing. Consider adding your professional references list if appropriate.

A portfolio should include a table of contents and index. This will allow the person reviewing your information to find items easily. Remember to continue the process of updating your information and documents. Update the table of contents when you make changes to the portfolio.

Next, evaluate your finished portfolio. Try to view the portfolio as an interviewer would. Is the portfolio representative of your best work? Does it present a well-rounded and qualified individual? Consider having your instructor, a peer, or someone in your network review the portfolio and comment on its quality.

1. Create the table of contents.
2. Create the index.
3. Place the items in a binder, notebook, or other container. You also may want to create a title page for each subsection. Consider using tabbed dividers to separate the sections.

Andresr/Shutterstock.com

# Jalia Cortez

111 First Street, Redwood City, CA 94061
(650) 555–1234 • jcortez@e-mail.com • www.linkedin.com/in/jalia-cortez

December 3, 20--

Mr. Joshua Mitchell
Great Corporation
12344 Main Street
Redwood City, CA 94061

Dear Mr. Mitchell:

Thank you for the opportunity to interview for the position of hotel concierge with Great Corporation on Wednesday, December 2. The interview process provided me with a clear synopsis of the role and responsibilities for the position.

My enthusiasum for the position has grown after talking with you and members of your team.  My desire to work in the hotel business and serve customers is my passion. I would enjoy being a part of the company and having the opportunity to contribute to its success.

Thank you, again, for your time and consideration.  As requested, I am enclosing a copy of professional references.  I look forward to hearing from you soon.

Best regards,

*Jalia Cortez*

Jalia Cortez

Enclosure

**Figure 11-1** The standard letter format is appropriate for a thank-you message.

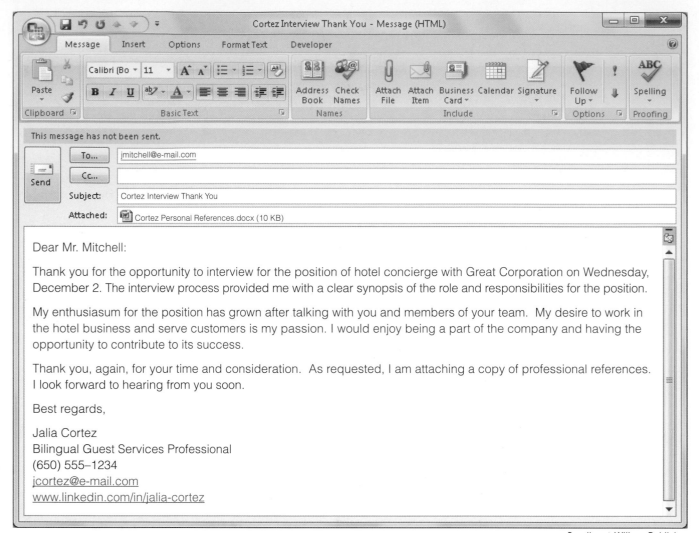

Goodheart-Willcox Publisher

**Figure 11-2** A thank-you message can also be sent as an e-mail.

thank-you message is in the form of an e-mail communication, attach any follow-up material to the e-mail.

## Manage Emotions

Most people have had the experience of interviewing for a job and not being selected for the position. This is part of the job-search process. Not every job for which you interview is the best match for you. If you do not hear from a representative of the company after a period of time, it often means another person was selected for the position. Some companies send communications to candidates to inform them that they were not chosen for the position.

However, many companies do not contact candidates at all if they are not selected.

Finding a job is far from a relaxing experience. Waiting for the results after an interview can be stressful. Not knowing how an interviewer perceived your performance might be unnerving. Recognize there are parts of the job-search process that you *can* control, such as positive or negative thoughts, what you include on your résumé, and how you perform at a job interview. One of the things you *cannot* control is who the company chooses to select for a position. Keep in mind that interviewing multiple times for various companies helps you gain confidence and much-needed experience in the job-search process.

## 11-2 Thank-You Message

**Directions:** Use the space provided to complete the activity or take notes. Alternatively, you can download the electronic version of this activity from the companion website.

1. Writing a thank-you message after an interview is expected, and it demonstrates professionalism. Using the example in Figure 11-1, write an introductory paragraph you might use to thank an interviewer for an opportunity to discuss a position.

2. The body of the letter should reiterate the interview experience. Write a paragraph you might use in your thank-you letter.

3. The last paragraph should thank the interviewer for his or her time. If any follow-up is required, the information should be stated here. Write a paragraph you might use as the last paragraph of a thank-you message.

Download the electronic version of this activity.

## Continue the Job Search

Some job seekers become confident after one interview, ending their search while waiting to hear from the interviewer. However, the best course of action is to continue to look for a position until you have a job. While you wait to hear the results from an interview, continue to seek additional employment opportunities. Be persistent in searching for the job that you want. Take charge of your job search.

# The Employment Process

At some point during this process, you will be offered a position. There is excitement and personal gratification that comes from being selected for a position for which you interviewed. However, once you receive the job offer, the process is not complete. First, you will evaluate the offer. Next, if necessary, you will negotiate the compensation. Then, you must respond to the job offer. If you accept the position, employment verification will conclude the process.

## Evaluate the Job Offer

After the interview process is complete, an employer may contact you by telephone or e-mail with a job offer. A **job offer** is a formal invitation to work under mutually agreed terms and conditions.

The job offer typically includes the title of the position, description of duties, expected hours, location of work, and the compensation package you will receive. The **compensation package** is everything an employee receives in return for his or her work. Part of the compensation is *salary*, which is the amount of money an employer agrees to pay an employee. A compensation package may include paid time off, such as vacation days and sick days, and retirement benefits, such as a 401(k) plan. Other types of compensation include:

- employer-paid medical, dental, and life insurance
- reimbursement for job-related travel
- salary increases per performance reviews
- overtime pay
- tuition reimbursement for continuing education
- annual bonuses tied to personal or company performance

When you finally receive a job offer, determine your next step. Consider whether it is the job you want. While it is flattering to be offered a position, you must make sure the job, benefits, and compensation fit your expectations. When you are offered a job, it is your responsibility to evaluate the offer. Examine the position and the expectations of the job. The decision to accept or reject a job offer is entirely yours.

Is the company one for which you would like to work? You should also determine if the job meets your career expectations. To evaluate any job offer, first carefully read all of the details. Then ask yourself questions, such as the following.

- Does the job offer meet the expectations I had at the interview?
- How does this position fit within my career plan?
- Is the job interesting?
- Does the salary offered represent a fair value for the skills I offer?
- Do I want to work for this company?
- Am I comfortable with the required duties?
- Will I need training or additional education right away?
- Does the growth potential for this position fit within my career plan?

Weigh the financial benefits offered with what it costs you to work each day. You should know what amount of money you will take home after commuting expenses and taxes are paid. To determine this, consider these questions.

- Will I be entitled to, or expected to, work overtime?
- If overtime work is expected, what is the rate of any hourly overtime pay?
- Does the employer offer health insurance? If not, what would I have to pay for health insurance?
- Will there be costs for clothing or uniforms?

# 11-3 Job Offer Evaluation

**Directions:** Use the space provided to complete the activity or take notes. Alternatively, you can download the electronic version of this activity from the companion website.

1. Conduct research on the Internet for salary calculators, salary comparison calculators, cost-of-living calculators, and other resources that will help you evaluate the salary offered to you. These calculators will help you determine if the salary meets your requirements. Record the URLs of the resources that are the most help to you.

2. After you have evaluated your salary requirements, there will be other questions to ask about the compensation package. In a separate document, create a list of 10 questions to ask the hiring manager. Your questions should pertain to the salary, benefits, and other aspects of the compensation package.

3. The compensation package is obviously an important part of a job offer. However, there are personal factors that you will consider. One subject of importance is that of expenses involved in working for the employer. Make a list of 10 questions you might ask yourself or the employer to help determine if the job is a good financial fit for you.

Download the electronic version of this activity.

- What will it cost to commute to the job location?
- What is the cost of gas and parking?

You will probably be offered a benefits package and salary. Discuss the details of the benefits with the employer, and make sure you understand what is being offered. If the salary is not acceptable, plan to express the salary that you require. Generally, the salary for minimum wage jobs and entry-level jobs is not negotiable.

It is important that you are comfortable with the offer and all details before you accept a position. If you accept the offer, you agree to all of the terms of employment.

## Negotiate

If the job meets your expectations, but the salary or compensation is not sufficient, consider negotiating. If you have been offered a salary and benefits package that does not meet your expectations, inquire about the opportunity to discuss a more appropriate package with the employer. Some items are negotiable, while others are not.

Remember that the employer may have multiple candidates willing to take the position at the salary offered. When you negotiate for salary, you are taking a risk. If your negotiation is baseless, the employer can withdraw the offer of employment.

**The Best App for that**

Part of evaluating a job offer includes calculating how your proposed salary translates into paychecks you will receive. A salary calculator app, like *My Salary Calc*, can help you determine how much you can expect in your paycheck. These programs are preloaded with tax information and allow you to input specifics about your pay.

If you decide to negotiate, establish a strong position by compiling the research to support your stance. For example, if you believe the job warrants a higher salary, research trends in your field for the same job title at various companies. Conduct an Internet search using phrases such as "salary comparisons" or "wages and jobs" to locate information to compare the salaries of people with similar job titles and responsibilities. Free online salary calculators can also help you project what salary you can expect based on the job title, your location, years of experience, and education.

Next, prepare a brief presentation with a script so that you can create a logical argument. Your presentation should include an introduction, the research you found noting the discrepancy in salary offerings, and a closing with a request for a moderate increase in your compensation package. Have a firm number in your mind and suggest it. Rehearse your presentation in front of family members or friends. Ask someone to role-play an employer in the situation to help you think about your request. Solicit feedback before you present it to an employer.

**What Employers Want**

As an employee, it is important that you maintain appropriate personal grooming habits for your new job. You looked your best at the interview; now you must look your best on the job. Wear clean, unwrinkled clothing. Maintain clean, manicured nails and have neatly combed hair. A smile also always helps you look your best.

## 11-4 Salary Negotiation

**Directions:** Use the space provided to complete the activity or take notes. Alternatively, you can download the electronic version of this activity from the companion website.

1. There will be job offers in which the salary is lower than you would like to accept. You may consider negotiating a more appropriate salary. Conduct Internet research on how to negotiate a salary. List five tips you found that might help you with the negotiation process.

2. The hiring manager will ask you the salary you require. Write five points you will make if given the opportunity to negotiate.

Download the electronic version of this activity.

---

Finally, contact the employer. Always begin with gratitude and acknowledgement of the position offered. Explain how you feel about the prospect of the new position and that you want to be compensated fairly. Ask if the salary is negotiable. If the response is a flat "no," thank him or her and say that you will consider the matter further. If the response indicates the salary or benefits package is negotiable, present your information. Close with your counter offer. Wait for the response, and proceed from there. Do not ask the employer to come up with a better number.

## Respond to the Job Offer

If the job meets your expectations, and you choose to accept the offer, respond as soon as possible to the employer. If you decide not to accept the position, a timely rejection is a professional courtesy.

## Accept a Job Offer

Once you are offered a job and you agree to the terms of employment and salary, formally acknowledge that you accept the position. The individual who contacts you with the job offer is the person with whom you will communicate regarding the acceptance of your position. A personal phone call is preferable. However, an e-mail may be necessary in order to submit a timely response. An example of an acceptance e-mail is shown in Figure 11-3.

If you accept the position, you will receive a *formal offer letter*. This document will include the salary and compensation package that was agreed upon after the job offer was made. It is important that you take your time to read the documents carefully. If there are any passages that you do not understand, ask for clarification.

Dear Ms. Boswell:

I am delighted to accept the position of Research Assistant for Becker Labs. I am excited about the opportunity of working with you and your team.

As soon as I receive the formal offer letter and additional forms you mentioned, I will complete and return them immediately. As we discussed, I will wait to hear from Mark Evans for further instructions about the medical exam and background check. I understand that there are required forms and processes that must be completed before I can start work.

Thank you again for the opportunity.

Sincerely,

**Figure 11-3** Acceptance of a job offer should be sent to the employer as soon as possible.

You will be required to sign the document, which affirms that you understand, agree, and accept the terms and conditions of employment.

## Decline a Job Offer

On the rare occasion that you must decline an offer of employment, contact the person who extended the job offer as soon as possible. Communicate that you are grateful for the opportunity, but it is necessary for you to decline the position. You do not need to state a reason, but be sure your communication is respectful. An example of a rejection e-mail is shown in Figure 11-4.

If the potential employer telephones you, express your decision on the phone, but follow up the conversation with a written notice. You may use e-mail for this message.

Handling the rejection of a job offer in a professional manner is important. You never know when, during the course of your career, you will cross paths with the company or its representatives in the future. Therefore, leave a positive, professional impression if you must decline a job offer from a company.

## Employment Verification Process

There are processes that must be completed before you are officially hired. The employer will complete an employment verification using the information on your application or résumé. **Employment verification** is a process in which a job candidate's employment history is checked to confirm the accuracy of the information he or she submitted. Employers typically verify

Dear Ms. Boswell:

Thank you for offering me the position as Research Assistant for Becker Labs. I considered your offer, but I have decided that I must decline.

I am grateful for the opportunity you extended. I appreciate your confidence in my abilities to perform the tasks required for the position.

Sincerely,

**Figure 11-4** It is important to be timely, professional, and respectful when declining a job offer.

only the dates of employment, position title, and other objective data. Most past employers will not provide subjective information about their employees, such as whether the employer considered you a good worker.

Another important part of the employment process is a background check. A **background check** is an evaluation of personal data that is publicly available. This information is available from government records and other sources, including public information on the Internet. Not all companies perform background checks for new employees. In most cases, an employer will seek your permission, or at least inform you, before performing a background check.

For positions that require interaction with company finances, employers often will request a candidate's credit history. They must demonstrate a viable business need in order to access this

information. They also are legally required to obtain your permission before conducting a credit check. If you believe your credit score might impact a job offer, obtain a copy of your credit report first and try to resolve any negative entries.

If an employer decides not to offer employment to a job candidate based on a credit report, the employer should provide a copy of it to the individual. In addition, a summary of rights should be provided.

Some employers require drug screenings for new employees. The employer pays for the test as part of the hiring process. Candidates are required to use the lab facility designated by the employer. If a candidate passes the drug-screening test, the hiring process will continue. If a candidate does not pass the drug-screening test, he or she will no longer be eligible for employment with the company.

## 11-5 Job Offer Responses

**Directions:** Use the space provided to complete the activity or take notes. Alternatively, you can download the electronic version of this activity from the companion website.

1. You are ready to accept an offer for a position. However, the person who made the offer is in meetings all day and can only be reached via e-mail. Write a response you would include in an e-mail accepting the job offer for the position.

2. After careful consideration, you have decided the job offer presented does not fit your career plans. Write a response you would include in an e-mail declining the job offer for the position.

Download the electronic version of this activity.

## Chapter Summary

- Post-interview techniques consist of a series of tasks to complete after the interview. These steps include evaluating the interview, following up with a thank-you message, managing emotions, and continuing the job search.

- After a job offer has been extended, you must complete several steps before the employment process is complete. You must evaluate the job offer, negotiate if desired, respond to the job offer, and complete employment verification. Employment verification might include a background check and a drug test.

## E-Flash Card Activity: Career-Related Terms

Review the career-related terms that follow. Then visit the G-W mobile site to practice vocabulary using e-flash cards until you are able to recognize their meanings. If you do not have a smartphone, visit the G-W Learning companion website to access this feature.

job offer                                                    employment verification

compensation package                            background check

## Review Your Knowledge

1. Post-interview techniques consist of a series of steps to evaluate the interview process. What are these steps?

2. What are some ways you can evaluate an interview?

3. Why is it important to send a thank-you message to the person or persons who interviewed you?

4. How can you manage the emotions that come with not being offered a job for which you interviewed?

5. List the steps of the employment process that occur after a job offer has been made.

6. Explain what typically is included in a compensation package.

7. When should you consider negotiating a job offer? What risks are associated with negotiating with a potential employer?

8. Compare and contrast the steps involved when accepting a job offer and when declining a job offer.

9. Explain what occurs during employment verification.

10. What is a background check? How do employers access information when conducting one?

## Apply Your Knowledge

1. Why is it important to evaluate an interview after it has taken place?

2. Thank-you messages can be a formal letter, a handwritten note, or an e-mail message. Give your opinion as to when each of these formats is appropriate.

3. Managing emotions during the job search process can be a challenge. How will you put the interviewing process in perspective and manage the emotions and stress of the experience?

4. Describe how you plan to continue your job search even after you begin interviewing.

5. Salary is often only part of employee compensation. What other forms of compensation are you hoping to acquire? Are any of them "must-haves"?

6. List questions you will ask yourself when evaluating a job offer.

7. Do you agree that negotiating a job offer is a risk? Explain your reasoning.

8. Recall a time when you participated in a negotiation, such as when buying a car. What did you learn from this experience? What can you apply from this experience to negotiating compensation with a potential employer?

9. An important part of the employment process is a background check. Do you think background checks are ethical? Why or why not?

10. Why might some employers conduct credit checks on potential employees?

## Exploring Certification

### Career Certification Skills—Using Reading Skills

You have recently been hired for a new position. The human resources manager requests that you come into the office to complete some paperwork. You will be taking the train and have learned that weather conditions will change the timing of your commute. There is a snowstorm and, as a result, the train will not make its usual stop at Main Street. Your appointment with the human resources manager is at 1:00 p.m., and you cannot afford to be late. Use the following chart to answer the questions.

| Condition | Change |
|---|---|
| Ice storm | Trains do not run |
| No Main Street stop | Pick up at First Street |
| No Plaza stop | Pick up at First Street |
| Fern Street closed | Walk to Second Street stop |
| Hillside stop closed | City bus depot, top of hill |
| Snowstorm | Train runs early |

1. Where should you catch the train?

2. Write a paragraph on how to prepare for your appointment to complete your pre-employment paperwork. Identify at least three elements that will make this office visit a success.

### Career Certification Skills—Finding Information

As the new lab technician, you are tasked with periodically checking the pressure gauge on the tank in the lab. Your colleague suggests becoming acquainted with the device to help you get comfortable reading the gauge.

Using the pressure gauge, answer the following questions.

1. What is the current pressure?

2. What is the lowest pressure on the gauge?

3. At what amount is the pressure considered to be at a dangerous level?

## Career Certification Skills—Applying Math Skills

Big Phone charges $0.12 per minute for calls. Cut-Rate Communication totals your phone usage each month and rounds the number of minutes up to the nearest 30 minutes. It then charges $7.10 per hour of phone usage, dividing this charge into 30-minute segments if you used less than a full hour. If your office makes 6 hours 20 minutes worth of calls this month using the company with the lower price, how much will these calls cost? Select the correct answer. Show your calculations.

A. $46.15

B. $45.60

C. $41.87

D. $54.00

## Chapter 12

# Your Career

## Outcomes

- **Prepare** for your first day on the job.
- **Identify** employer expectations.
- **Practice** appropriate workplace ethics.
- **Identify** ways to be safe in the workplace.
- **Describe** the performance evaluation process.
- **Update** your professional networks.
- **Connect** to your career.

## Career-Related Terms

| | |
|---|---|
| punctuality | infringement |
| dependability | copyright |
| time management | plagiarism |
| interpersonal skills | proprietary information |
| respect | ergonomics |
| ethics | performance evaluation |
| intellectual property | professional development |

You will see icons at various points throughout the chapter. These icons indicate that interactive activities are available on the *Connect to Your Career* companion website. Selected activities are also available on the *Connect to Your Career* mobile site. These activities will help you learn, practice, and expand your career knowledge and skills.

Companion Website
www.g-wlearning.com/careereducation/

Mobile Site
www.m.g-wlearning.com

Jeanette Dietl/Shutterstock.com

# Overview

Congratulations—you have a job! Out of all the candidates considered, you were selected for a new role. This event ushers in a new chapter of your life.

As you begin your new career, your employer will require that you complete a variety of employment forms and processes. Once you officially start your job, be the best employee you can be. Employees have a responsibility to meet their employer's expectations. Performance evaluations will be conducted to make sure you are performing your job well.

Stay current in your profession, continue networking, and plan for your financial future. You can have a long, productive career.

# Your First Day on the Job

The first day on the job is both overwhelming and exciting. You will probably spend the first day meeting coworkers and getting to know the facility. It is important to your career to make a positive first impression with those you meet

Learn all you can about the company *before* your first day of work. During the interview process, you should have acquired information about the company culture, its mission, its customers, and other valuable details. Use this information to aid your transition as a new employee. Contact the human resources department to inquire whether you need a badge or a security code to enter the premises. Ask which building entrance you should use and who you should call when you arrive. If you are driving, find out where employees are expected to park and whether you need a parking pass.

Dress appropriately and be on time for the first day of work. Greet each new coworker with a smile and pleasant conversation. Exhibit a positive attitude and your excitement to be part of the team. Your first impression sets the stage for your working career. When you meet with your new supervisor, convey your enthusiasm to be an asset to the company. Ask for guidance on your activities, people you should meet, and other information to make your first few days productive.

## Employment Forms

You will spend a considerable amount of time in the human resources department completing necessary forms for your employment. Come prepared with the personal information or documentation that will be required for a multitude of forms. You will need your Social Security number, contact information for emergencies, and other personal information.

### Form I-9

Be prepared to complete a *Form I-9 Employment Eligibility Verification*. The Form I-9 is used to verify an employee's identity and that he or she is authorized to work in the United States. This form is from the Department of Homeland Security of the US Citizenship and Immigration Services. Figure 12-1 illustrates the portion of the form that shows citizenship status. Both citizens and noncitizens are required to complete this form.

You must complete and sign the Form I-9 in the presence of an authorized representative of the human resources department. Documentation of your identity must be presented at the time the form is signed. Acceptable documentation commonly used includes a valid driver's license, a state-issued photo ID, or a passport. A list of other acceptable documents is listed on the form. The human resources department will explain this form and answer any questions you may have.

**Department of Homeland Security**
U.S. Citizenship and Immigration Services

**Form I-9, Employment
Eligibility Verification**

Read instructions carefully before completing this form.  The instructions must be available during completion of this form.

**ANTI-DISCRIMINATION NOTICE:** It is illegal to discriminate against work-authorized individuals. Employers CANNOT specify which document(s) they will accept from an employee.  The refusal to hire an individual because the documents have a future expiration date may also constitute illegal discrimination.

**Section 1. Employee Information and Verification** *(To be completed and signed by employee at the time employment begins.)*

| Print Name:   Last | First | Middle Initial | Maiden Name |
|---|---|---|---|

| Address *(Street Name and Number)* | Apt. # | Date of Birth *(month/day/year)* |
|---|---|---|

| City | State | Zip Code | Social Security # |
|---|---|---|---|

**I am aware that federal law provides for imprisonment and/or fines for false statements or use of false documents in connection with the completion of this form.**

I attest, under penalty of perjury, that I am (check one of the following):

☐ A citizen of the United States

☐ A noncitizen national of the United States (see instructions)

☐ A lawful permanent resident (Alien #) _____

☐ An alien authorized to work (Alien # or Admission #) _____
until (expiration date, if applicable - *month/day/year*) _____

| Employee's Signature | Date *(month/day/year)* |
|---|---|

**Preparer and/or Translator Certification** *(To be completed and signed if Section 1 is prepared by a person other than the employee.)* I attest, under penalty of perjury, that I have assisted in the completion of this form and that to the best of my knowledge the information is true and correct.

| Preparer's/Translator's Signature | Print Name |
|---|---|

| Address *(Street Name and Number, City, State, Zip Code)* | Date *(month/day/year)* |
|---|---|

**Section 2. Employer Review and Verification** *(To be completed and signed by employer. Examine one document from List A OR examine one document from List B and one from List C, as listed on the reverse of this form, and record the title, number, and expiration date, if any, of the document(s).)*

| List A | OR | List B | AND | List C |
|---|---|---|---|---|
| Document title: | | | | |
| Issuing authority: | | | | |
| Document #: | | | | |
| Expiration Date *(if any)*: | | | | |
| Document #: | | | | |
| Expiration Date *(if any)*: | | | | |

**CERTIFICATION:** I attest, under penalty of perjury, that I have examined the document(s) presented by the above-named employee, that the above-listed document(s) appear to be genuine and to relate to the employee named, that the employee began employment on *(month/day/year)* _____ and that to the best of my knowledge the employee is authorized to work in the United States.  (State employment agencies may omit the date the employee began employment.)

| Signature of Employer or Authorized Representative | Print Name | Title |
|---|---|---|

| Business or Organization Name and Address *(Street Name and Number, City, State, Zip Code)* | Date *(month/day/year)* |
|---|---|

**Section 3. Updating and Reverification** *(To be completed and signed by employer.)*

| A. New Name *(if applicable)* | B. Date of Rehire *(month/day/year) (if applicable)* |
|---|---|

C. If employee's previous grant of work authorization has expired, provide the information below for the document that establishes current employment authorization.

| Document Title: | Document #: | Expiration Date *(if any)*: |
|---|---|---|

I attest, under penalty of perjury, that to the best of my knowledge, this employee is authorized to work in the United States, and if the employee presented document(s), the document(s) I have examined appear to be genuine and to relate to the individual.

| Signature of Employer or Authorized Representative | Date *(month/day/year)* |
|---|---|

Form I-9

US Department of Homeland Security

**Figure 12-1** A Form I-9 is one of the forms you will be required to complete when you start a new job.

## Form W-4

You will also complete a *Form W-4 Employee's Withholding Allowance Certificate*. A Form W-4 is used by the employer for the information necessary to withhold the appropriate amount of taxes from your paycheck. Deductions are based on your marital status and the number of dependents you claim, including yourself. Based on your elections, the amounts withheld from your paycheck are forwarded to the appropriate government agency. Figure 12-2 shows a completed Form W-4.

At the end of the year, the employer sends the employee a *Form W-2 Wage and Tax Statement* to use when filing income tax returns. This form summarizes all wages and deductions for the year for an individual employee.

### Benefits Forms

The human resources department will provide you with a variety of forms that are specific to the compensation package offered by the employer. You will complete forms to confirm whether you elect to participate or decline participation in the various programs. Be prepared to complete multiple forms on your first day.

One benefit of working for a company is that many offer insurance coverage for employees. The insurance coverage might include medical, dental, vision, or life insurance. Conditions and terms apply for employees who accept insurance from an employer. For example, premium payments for insurance might be deducted from each paycheck.

Compensation packages are different for every employer, so plan to spend time learning what benefits your new company offers. Inquire about 401(k) plans, tuition assistance, retirement benefits, and daycare assistance for dependents.

## New Hire Training

As a new employee, you will be a part of an orientation for new hires. If you are one of several people hired at the same time, you may participate in group training. If you are the only individual hired at that time, your training may be one-on-one. Human resources, supervisors, and other senior employees typically conduct the training.

Most companies have an employee handbook that will be part of the training materials. Topics such as the history of the company, its mission, and company policies will be introduced.

**Figure 12-2** A Form W-4 provides information to your new employer regarding the amount of money to be withheld from your check.

## 12-1 Employment Forms

**Directions:** Use the space provided to complete the activity or take notes. Alternatively, you can download the electronic version of this activity from the companion website.

1.  Download the Form W-4 Employee's Withholding Allowance Certificate from the US Internal Revenue Service website at www.irs.gov. Print a copy of the form to use for this activity.

2.  Complete the form as a practice exercise. Use blue or black ink and your best handwriting. The form must be neat, clean, and error free. However, do not fill in the Social Security information. This should only be completed when you are ready to submit the form to an employer.

3.  Download the Form I-9 Employment Eligibility Verification from the US Citizen and Immigration Services website at www.uscis.gov. Print a copy of this form.

4.  Complete the form as a practice exercise.

5.  Review the acceptable forms of identification. Record which documents you have in your possession that you will provide to your new employer. Does your eligibility come from List A, List B, List C, or a combination of the lists?

Download the electronic version of this activity.

Government-related mandates will be addressed, such as education about harassment in the workplace. Employee-related topics will also be covered, such as employee safety and security, compensation, attendance policies, and benefits.

After the company policies have been presented, your supervisor or someone on your team will train you on the processes and procedures for your specific job. Each team generally has specific guidelines for accomplishing tasks that you will need to learn. This is an opportunity to start learning the expectations for your new position.

# Employer Expectations

As an employee, you have many responsibilities. Employers expect their employees to help the business operate and make a profit. Employees are also expected to work to the best of their abilities and follow the rules put in place by the employer. Your employer will expect you to follow the appropriate dress code, have good personal grooming habits, be punctual, and use good time-management and organizational skills as well as interpersonal skills.

## Dress Code

Your appearance is a reflection of you. Your clothes are an important part of your personal appearance. Some businesses have dress codes that must be followed. A *dress code* is a set of rules or guidelines about the manner of dress acceptable in a certain place. In the workplace, dress codes can be used for safety reasons or to ensure a professional atmosphere.

Even if there is no official dress code, it is important to avoid extremes in your appearance at work. For example, multiple piercings and tattoos may impress your friends but might have a negative effect on supervisors, coworkers, or customers.

## Punctuality

**Punctuality** means being on time. Being late is inconsiderate and is not tolerated in the working world. Coworkers may have to take on the work of employees who are late or absent. It is important to show up ready for work every day and on time.

Punctuality is a good sign of dependability. **Dependability** shows a person's ability to be reliable and trustworthy. Being dependable means others can count on you to do what needs to be done. Dependable people keep their word, are honest, and carry their share of the workload. Dependable employees tend to be given the important jobs in a company.

## Time Management and Organization

"Work smarter, not harder" is a phrase frequently quoted in business and industry. Employees who understand how to organize both their time and job responsibilities can meet or beat deadlines. They are able to take on more responsibilities and eventually earn promotions.

**Time management** is the practice of organizing time and work assignments to increase personal efficiency. It is another very important skill in the workplace because work assignments may include a variety of tasks. Often, you will need to work on several tasks at the same time. You will be expected to prioritize those tasks by determining which ones should be completed before others. When uncertain as to which tasks are the most important, always ask your direct supervisor. The difference between average and excellent workers is often not how hard they work, but how well they prioritize assignments.

## Interpersonal Skills

**Interpersonal skills** are those skills that help people communicate and work well with each other. Your company or business will expect you to have good interpersonal skills. These skills are necessary to complete the job duties and ensure a positive working environment. The ability to communicate well, show respect for others, and work as part of a team are skills all employers want in their employees.

### Communications

Giving and receiving information efficiently is the key to effective communications. Time is limited in the workplace and all employees have many duties and responsibilities. Others appreciate it when a person gets to the point

**The Best App** for that

Once you create an online presence, it is important to stay active by posting information that promotes you as a professional. When you belong to multiple social media networks, it can be time-consuming to update each one. Apps like *HootSuite* enable you to update and manage your social networks from a single interface.

quickly and in a positive manner. Being able to state your needs or intentions clearly to others can be learned through practice.

Careful listening and responding are also hallmarks of good communication. If you do not understand what someone wants, ask the person to clarify the request. Make sure to follow directions carefully. Always ask questions when you do not understand how to do a certain task. As in every part of life, communicating in a positive manner gets better results than negativity or a bad attitude.

## Respect

**Respect** is the feeling that someone or something is good, valuable, and important. Be considerate of the feelings of coworkers. A smile and a few minutes of friendly conversation are good ways to promote good working relationships.

Work environments are usually diverse. There will be people of many different cultures, beliefs, and ages. Regardless of personal differences, show respect to your supervisors, coworkers, and any other person you interact with on the job. Make sure to remember the golden rule: treat others as you would like to be treated.

## Teamwork

Many employers consider teamwork skills to be necessary in the workplace. Employees may be asked to work in different teams as work needs arise. Being a team member of a company work group is similar to playing on a sports team. Success is measured in terms of the success of the team, not each player. Teamwork means putting the team goals ahead of personal goals.

# Workplace Ethics

**Ethics** is a guiding set of moral values that helps people make decisions. *Workplace etiquette* is a set of guidelines for appropriate behavior on the job. The employee handbook includes a code of conduct that outlines the manner in which employees should behave while at work. Companies may define specific issues as inappropriate, unethical, or illegal. For example, employers have rules for avoiding computer threats, using company equipment, and downloading software.

## Company Equipment

Company equipment is designated for business-related functions, not for personal use. Office equipment includes desktop computers, phones, and photocopy machines. This equipment is provided to employees to improve efficiency. In many cases, it would be impossible for an employee to perform his or her job without it.

Many codes of conduct also have guidelines for visiting websites and rules for downloading to company computers. These rules protect the business' computer system and its private information.

Company-owned mobile devices, such as smartphones or tablets, are also company property. Never use them for personal reasons. Follow the company policies for appropriate communication and workplace behavior.

## Software Downloads

It is unethical and illegal for an employee to download software that has not been purchased and registered by the employer. When buying software, a license is purchased. A *license* is the legal permission to use a software program. All software has terms of use that explain how and when the software may be used.

Some software may only be lawfully used if it is purchased. These programs are known as *for-purchase software*. Demo, short for demonstration, software may be used without buying. However, demos are either limited in functionality or duration of use. If you decide to keep using the software, it must be purchased. *Piracy* is the illegal copying or downloading of software, files, or other protected material. This includes scanning or downloading images or music.

## Intellectual Property

**Intellectual property** is something that comes from a person's mind, such as an idea, invention, or process. Intellectual property laws protect a person's or a company's inventions, artistic works, and other intellectual property. Any use of intellectual property without permission is called **infringement**.

A **copyright** acknowledges ownership of a work and specifies that only the owner has the right to sell the work, use it, or give permission for someone else to sell or use it. The laws cover all original work, whether it is in print, on the Internet, or in any other form or media. You cannot claim work as your own or use it without permission. **Plagiarism** is claiming another person's material as your own, which is both unethical and illegal.

**Proprietary information** is any work created by company employees on the job that is owned by that company. Proprietary information may be referred to as *trade secrets* because it is confidential information a company needs to keep private and protect from theft. Proprietary information can include many things, such as product formulas,

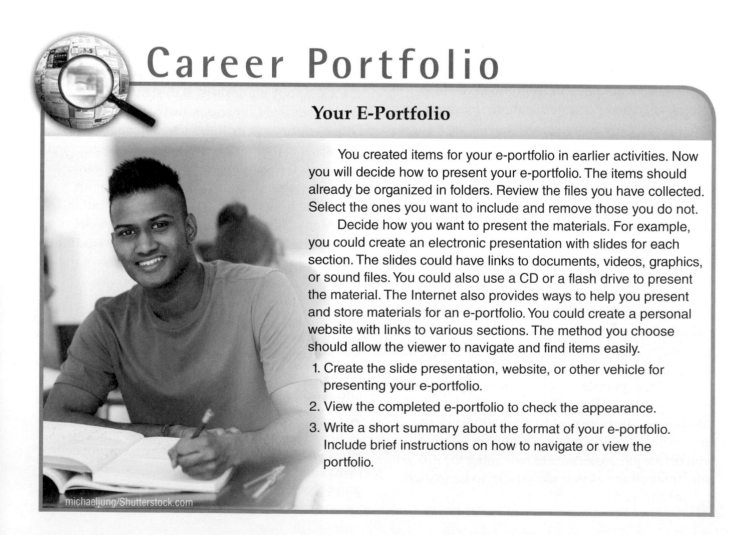

# Career Portfolio

### Your E-Portfolio

You created items for your e-portfolio in earlier activities. Now you will decide how to present your e-portfolio. The items should already be organized in folders. Review the files you have collected. Select the ones you want to include and remove those you do not.

Decide how you want to present the materials. For example, you could create an electronic presentation with slides for each section. The slides could have links to documents, videos, graphics, or sound files. You could also use a CD or a flash drive to present the material. The Internet also provides ways to help you present and store materials for an e-portfolio. You could create a personal website with links to various sections. The method you choose should allow the viewer to navigate and find items easily.

1. Create the slide presentation, website, or other vehicle for presenting your e-portfolio.

2. View the completed e-portfolio to check the appearance.

3. Write a short summary about the format of your e-portfolio. Include brief instructions on how to navigate or view the portfolio.

michaeljung/Shutterstock.com

customer lists, or manufacturing processes. All employees must understand the importance of keeping company information confidential. The code of conduct should explain that company information may only be shared with permission from human resources. Employees who share proprietary information with outsiders are unethical and, possibly, breaking the law.

## Netiquette

*Netiquette* is etiquette used when communicating electronically. Netiquette includes accepted social and professional guidelines for Internet communications. It applies to e-mails, social networking, blogs, texting, and chatting. For example, it is unprofessional to use texting language in a business environment. Always proofread and spell-check e-mails before sending them. When communicating electronically, it is important to follow the same common courtesy used in face-to-face discussions.

Internet access provided by the company should be used only for business purposes. Checking personal e-mail or shopping online is not acceptable. When using the Internet, you are a representative of the company.

# Workplace Safety

Workplace safety in the United States has continuously improved since the beginning of the 20th century. Gradually, injury, death, and illness related to working conditions have declined. This is due to a change in the type of work done today and in the safety precautions that have been put in place.

## Accident Prevention

Falling hazards, lifting hazards, and material-storage hazards account for most of the workplace accidents that occur in offices. Falls are the most common workplace accident in an office setting. Preventing workplace falls is relatively simple:

- close drawers completely
- do not stand on a chair or box to reach an object
- secure cords, rugs, and mats

Lifting hazards are sources of potential injury from improperly lifting or carrying items. Most back injuries are caused by improper lifting. To avoid injuries resulting from lifting:

- make several small trips with items rather than one trip with an overly heavy load
- use dollies or handcarts whenever possible
- lift with the legs, not the back
- never carry an item that blocks vision

Material-storage hazards are sources of potential injury that come from the improper storage of files, books, office equipment, or other items. A cluttered workplace is an unsafe workplace. Material stacked too high can fall on employees. Paper and files stored on the floor or in a hall are a fire risk. To prevent material-storage injuries:

- do not stack boxes or papers on top of tall cabinets
- store heavier objects on lower shelves
- keep aisles and hallways clear

Maintaining a safe workplace is the joint responsibility of the employer and employee. The employer makes sure the facility and working conditions are such that accidents are unlikely to occur. The employee uses common sense and care while at the office. Always read and understand equipment safety manuals, follow safety instructions, and abide by safety requirements.

## Workplace Ergonomics

**Ergonomics** is the science concerned with designing and arranging things people use so they can interact both efficiently and safely. In the workplace, it can include designing workstations to fit the unique needs of the worker and the equipment used. Applying ergonomic principles results in a comfortable, efficient, and safe working environment.

There are many types of ergonomic accessories that may improve a computer workstation, including wrist rests, specially designed chairs, and back supports. In addition, Figure 12-3 identifies actions that can be taken to create a comfortable environment and help prevent injury or strain to the worker's body.

# 12-2 Employer Expectations and Workplace Safety

**Directions:** Use the space provided to complete the activity or take notes. Alternatively, you can download the electronic version of this activity from the companion website.

1. As an employee, you will be expected to meet your employer's workplace expectations. What will an employer in your career field expect of its employees?

2. Workplace safety is different in every industry. What are some of the safety concerns in your career field?

3. What are the ergonomic concerns for the equipment commonly used in your career field? Examples of equipment include computers, desks and chairs, machinery, and automobiles. Describe these ergonomic concerns and how equipment is designed to be more comfortable and efficient for employees.

Download the electronic version of this activity.

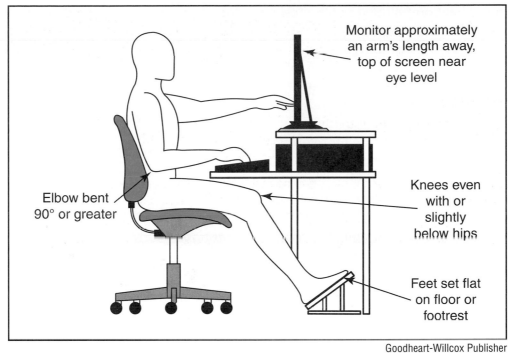

Goodheart-Willcox Publisher

**Figure 12-3** An ergonomic workstation is one that is safe and comfortable.

# Performance Evaluations

During your career, your performance on the job will be evaluated. A **performance evaluation** is a formal process designed to evaluate an employee's work with productive outcomes. The evaluation will take into account not only your actual job performance and how you execute your duties, but also how well you interact with your coworkers as a team player.

Performance evaluations are generally formal meetings with a manager or supervisor. He or she will review the evaluation with you and discuss the results. These meetings are an opportunity for you to conduct self-evaluations about what you want from your job and where you will advance yourself.

A *performance evaluation form* will be used in the evaluation. Ask to have a copy of the form early in your employment. Review the criteria often and execute each category to the best of your ability. At any time, if you feel that you are

not meeting the minimum criteria as detailed on the performance evaluation form, ask your immediate supervisor for guidance. He or she should be able to help remove obstacles that stand in the way of your success.

Remember you created a two- to four-year career plan. During a performance evaluation, it is up to you to decide if the outcome of your meeting is what you want for your career.

# Update Your Professional Network

When you begin your new job, update your LinkedIn, Twitter, and professional networking accounts to reflect your employment status. Enter your new title, the month and year that you begin your job, and the name of the company at which you are employed. After you add your new company to your profile, join the company's group and social networks. "Like" their pages.

It is important that you follow up with those in your network who agreed to be personal references for you during the employment process. Place a phone call or send an e-mail to each person with the good news. Provide each person with your new company's name and your job title, and let each one know that you appreciate the reference they provided for you. Offer to return the favor and provide them with a professional reference when needed.

Visit the employment websites and job boards where your résumé is posted. Change your job-seeking status from "searching" to "not searching." Otherwise, you will continue to get new job postings in your e-mail. Refer to your tracking documents if you do not remember all of the places your résumé is posted.

# Your Career

You will spend many hours of your life at work, so you must take charge of your career. Start planning for your future as soon as possible. There are many ways to have a long, productive, and happy career.

Be the best employee you can be. Nurture relationships with your supervisor as well as your coworkers. Keep personal problems separate from work as much as possible. While it is acceptable to engage in casual conversations, keep the conversations positive and brief. Conscientious employees maximize career retention by exhibiting effective leadership skills, even when they are not in a leadership position. Do your best each day.

Be wise with your money. Start saving for your retirement as soon as possible. Saving money early can make your retirement years more comfortable and easier to attain. Research the retirement benefits your new employer offers and take full advantage of them.

**What Employers Want**

Once you are hired, employers expect you to work within the company's policies and procedures. They are in place to make sure that the workplace functions efficiently and the company reaches its business goals. Employers want you to adapt to their systems. Take your time and get to know your work routines.

Grow and maintain your professional network as you progress in your career. The individuals you meet and work with along the way can help you throughout your career in many different ways. Additionally, being in touch with other professionals in your field will make you aware of new developments and opportunities in your career field.

Continue your professional development by staying up-to-date in your field. **Professional development** is training that builds on the skills and knowledge that contribute to personal growth and career development. Successful employees continually seek opportunities to improve the skills important to their careers. There are many options for professional development. Many businesses are willing to pay to provide professional development training for their employees. By keeping abreast of the most current expectations in your field, you can earn success in the workplace and exhibit leadership qualities.

## 12-3 Career Success

**Directions:** Use the space provided to complete the activity or take notes. Alternatively, you can download the electronic version of this activity from the companion website.

1. Describe the steps you will take to update your professional networking profiles on social media, follow up with your professional references, and update your job-seeking status on employment websites and job boards.

2. What does "be the best employee you can be" mean to you? Explain how you plan to carry this out in your career.

3. Now that you have a job, it is time to update your personal career plan. Update the career plan that you created in Chapter 5 to reflect your current status.

4. Is professional development important or necessary for your career? If yes, write what will be expected as you begin your new job.

Download the electronic version of this activity.

## Chapter Summary

- Your first day on the job, you will need to complete important documentation for human resources. You will be asked to complete a Form I-9, a Form W-4, and other documents related to your compensation package. You will also begin training for your new job.

- Employers have specific expectations of all employees. In the workplace, you will be expected to follow a dress code, be punctual, manage your time, and stay organized. Important interpersonal skills to have on the job include communication, respect, and teamwork.

- Workplace ethics affect employee decisions every day. It is important to act with ethics in mind when using company equipment and downloading software. Respect your coworkers' intellectual property and the company's proprietary information. Practice good netiquette at all times.

- The safety of employees is important in the workplace. Follow simple safety guidelines to avoid workplace accidents and keep everyone safe. Use ergonomics to ensure your workstation is comfortable and functional.

- Performance evaluations are an important part of your new career. These evaluations take into account your job performance and how well you interact with other coworkers.

- When you begin a new job, it is important to update your professional networks. Revise your social media profiles to reflect your new employment. Follow up with your professional references to thank them for serving as your references. Be sure to also update your employment status on job-search websites.

- You are now ready for a successful career! Be the best employee you can be. Be wise with your money and maintain your professional networks for continued success. Continue your professional development by staying up-to-date in your field.

## E-Flash Card Activity: Career-Related Terms

Review the career-related terms that follow. Then visit the G-W mobile site to practice vocabulary using e-flash cards until you are able to recognize their meanings. If you do not have a smartphone, visit the G-W Learning companion website to access this feature.

| | |
|---|---|
| punctuality | infringement |
| dependability | copyright |
| time management | plagiarism |
| interpersonal skills | proprietary information |
| respect | ergonomics |
| ethics | performance evaluation |
| intellectual property | professional development |

## Review Your Knowledge

1. What is the purpose of the Form I-9?

2. What is the purpose of the Form W-4?

3. Who typically conducts the training of new hires?

4. What do employers expect of employees?

5. Explain why it is important to be punctual.

6. List three interpersonal skills that all employers want in their employees.

7. Define *ethics*.

8. What are the two most important aspects of workplace safety?

9. Explain the purpose of performance evaluations.

10. What three things should you do in order to update your networks?

## Apply Your Knowledge

1.  What information is important for you to know before the first day on the job?

2.  Why is employee training necessary for new hires?

3.   Describe the typical dress code commonly used in your career field.

4.  What comes to mind when you hear the word "ethics"? What does it mean for an employee to be ethical?

5.  Explain how the material you create at your job is the property of the company, not your own.

6.  Describe the typical safety requirements and precautions in your chosen career field.

7.  Do you think performance evaluations are necessary? Explain your reasoning.

8.  Why is it so important to update your professional network about your employment status?

9.  Why is it important to start saving for retirement early?

10. What kind of professional development is important to you and your career? Why is it necessary?

## Exploring Certification

### Career Certification Skills—Using Reading Skills

You have been tasked with ensuring the company's website is following the trademark guidelines for Cut-Rate Communication, your phone service provider. Read Cut-Rate Communication's Product and Services Trademark Guidelines and respond to the questions that follow.

---

**Cut-Rate Communication's Trademark Guidelines**

When referring to exclusive Cut-Rate Communication products by name, you must adhere to the trademark guidelines.

Any time a Cut-Rate Communication trademarked product or service appears in a communication, a trademark symbol must be used. Communications include, but are not limited to, brochures, advertisements, and websites. Refer to Cut-Rate Communication's Trademark List for the correct spelling of trademarked products. Cut-Rate Communication's ownership of the trademark must be stated in the credit notice section of your communication.

Products covered under this policy include, but are not limited to, No-Cost Customer Service, Rapid Response Voice Messaging, and Clear-As-A-Bell Calling. For a complete listing, refer to Cut-Rate Communication's List of Proprietary Products.

---

1. The company website mentions Rapid Response Voice Messaging. How does this product name need to be represented on the company website?

2. Where should the company website include an attribution of Cut-Rate Communication's ownership of its trademarks?

### Career Certification Skills—Finding Information

In the workplace, you will need to read various forms of data. Data presented in a graph or chart are easier to understand than data displayed in sentence form. Data in graphs and charts fall into two main categories: discrete data and continuous data.

*Discrete data* represent numbers that are fixed. For example, if 27 customers entered a store on any given day, the number 27 is fixed. It is impossible to state that 27 1/2 customers entered the store. The data must represent that 27 or 28 customers were counted.

*Continuous data* can be any number within a range and are not fixed. For example, air temperature is not limited to either 80 degrees or 81 degrees, it can be any number in between such as 80.2 degrees, or 80.9 degrees.

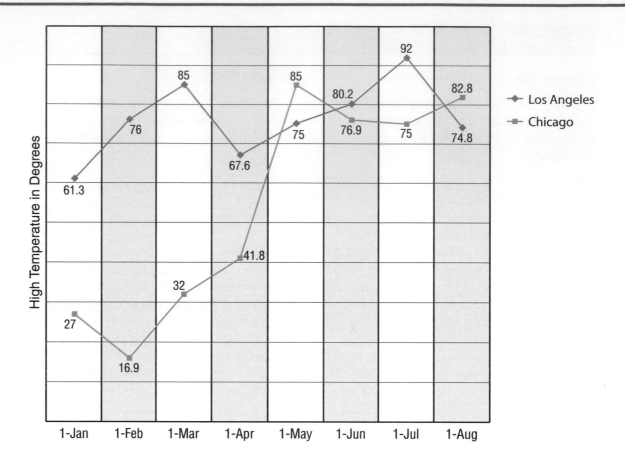

Use the graph to answer the questions that follow.

1. Which type of data is represented?

2. During which month were the temperatures of the two cities the most similar?

3. What was the temperature in Chicago on April 1?

## Career Certification Skills—Applying Math Skills

Chairs need to be lined up around the perimeter of the conference room at your office for a special presentation. You need to let the building manager know how many chairs are needed. The room is 60 feet wide and 54 feet long. Each chair requires 1.9 feet of width and you need to leave 3.8 feet of space for the doorway. How many chairs should you request to meet your needs? Select the correct answer. Show your calculations.

A. 111

B. 120

C. 26

D. 116

# Glossary

## A

**ability.** Mastery of a skill or the capacity to do something. (5)

**aggregate job board.** Website that collects data from multiple online job boards and combines the results. (8)

**application cover letter.** Cover letter used for all inquiries about a position that has been posted. (7)

**aptitude.** Characteristic that an individual has developed naturally. (5)

## B

**background check.** Evaluation of personal data that is publicly available. (11)

**basic skill.** Fundamental skill necessary to effectively function in society. (4)

**behavioral question.** Question that draws on an individual's previous experiences and decisions. (9)

**blue-sky question.** An interview question type in which the interviewer describes a scenario that may or may not be related to the job duties and requires a response from the candidate. (9)

**body language.** How gestures and facial expressions communicate feelings. (10)

## C

**career.** Long-term progression in one particular field with opportunities for growth and advancement. (5)

**career account profile.** Information that describes who a person is in his or her professional life. (1)

**career objective.** Brief statement in a résumé that explains an individual's career goals to an employer. (6)

**career plan.** Documentation of where a person is today in the job-search process and where he or she would like to be in two to four years. (5)

**career profile.** Part of a résumé that details an individual's accomplishments, skills, and current career level. (6)

**certification.** Professional status earned by an individual after passing an exam focused on a specific body of knowledge. (4)

**compensation package.** Everything an employee receives in return for his or her work (11).

## D

**dependability.** Ability to be reliable and trustworthy. (12)

## E

**electronic portfolio.** Contains data and content in analog form; also known as a *digital portfolio*. (1)

**emerging occupation.** New occupation that has developed or changed due to technological or other advancements. (5)

**employability skill.** Applicable skill used to help an individual find a job, perform in the workplace, and gain success in a job or career; also known as a *foundation skill* or *transferrable skill*. (4)

**employment verification.** Process in which a job candidate's employment history is checked to confirm the accuracy of the information he or she submitted. (11)

**ergonomics.** Science concerned with designing and arranging things people use so that they can interact both efficiently and safely. (12)

**ethics.** Guiding set of moral values that helps people make decisions. (12)

**etiquette.** Consideration for others. (3)

## F

**firewall.** Program that monitors information coming into a computer and helps assure that only safe information gets through. (2)

**follower.** Twitter member who views another user's Tweets in his or her own Twitter feed. (1)

## connection. (continued — column)

**connection.** On LinkedIn, a person in an individual's network who is added by invitation. (1)

**cookie.** Bit of data stored on your computer that records information about the websites a user has visited. (2)

**copyright.** Acknowledges ownership of a work and specifies that only the owner has the right to sell or use the work, or give permission for someone else to sell or use it. (12)

**cover letter.** Formal written communication that accompanies a résumé or a job application to introduce the applicant and express interest in a position. (7)

**formal seated position.** Sitting upright, with both feet on the floor and both hands comfortably resting either on chair armrests or in the lap. (10)

**freemium.** Users may utilize basic services without paying. (1)

## H

**hard skill.** Skill that is measureable and can be observed. (5)

**hashtag.** Searchable keyword on Twitter that links users to all Tweets marked with the same hashtag keyword. (1)

**heading.** Part of a résumé that provides a person's full name, phone number, e-mail address, and geographic location. (6)

**hypothetical question.** Question that requires a person to imagine a situation and describe how he or she would act. (9)

## I

**identity theft.** Illegal act that involves stealing someone's personal information and using that information to commit theft or fraud. (2)

**infographic résumé.** Résumé in which the content is displayed using a combination of words and graphics to present information clearly and quickly. (6)

**informational interviewing.** Strategy used to interview and ask for advice and direction from a professional, rather than asking for a job opportunity. (3)

**infringement.** Use of intellectual property without permission. (12)

**inquiry cover letter.** Cover letter used to learn if any potential positions are available, for which the job seeker would like to be considered; also known as *prospecting*. (7)

**intellectual property.** Something that comes from a person's mind. (12)

**Internet Protocol address.** Number used to identify an electronic device connected to the Internet. Also known as an *IP address*. (2)

**interpersonal skills.** Skills that help people communicate and work well with each other. (12)

## J

**job.** Short-term employment for compensation. (5)

**job application.** Form used by some employers to gain more information about the applicant. (8)

**job offer.** Formal invitation to work under mutually agreed terms and conditions. (11)

**job-search list.** Website where multiple employers post job openings on a daily basis. (8)

**job-specific skill.** Critical skill necessary to perform the required work-related tasks of a position. (4)

## K

**keyword.** A word that specifically relates to the functions of the position for which the employer is hiring. (5)

## M

**malware.** Term given to software programs that are intended to damage, destroy, or steal data on a computer. (2)

**microblog.** Short communication limited to a certain number of characters per post. (1)

**multi-level marketing (MLM).** Business strategy in which employees are compensated for sales they personally generate and for the sales of the other salespeople they recruit. (2)

## N

**netiquette.** Etiquette used when communicating electronically, especially via the Internet. (9)

**networking.** Talking with people and establishing relationships that can lead to career growth or potential job opportunities. (1)

**networking cover letter.** Cover letter used when someone with influence has suggested that the person apply for a position. (7)

## O

**Occupational Information Network (O*NET).** Resource that provides descriptions of in-demand industry areas in emerging occupations. (5)

**online job board.** Website that hosts job postings for employers and allows applicants to apply for jobs seamlessly. (8)

**online presence.** What the public can learn about a person from viewing his or her Internet activities. (1)

## P

**panel interview.** Interview in which a candidate talks with multiple interviewers in a room. (9)

**performance evaluation.** Formal process designed to evaluate an employee's work with productive outcomes. (12)

**people skill.** Skill that enables people to develop and maintain working relationships with others in the workplace. (4)

**personal brand.** Snapshot of who an individual wants to be as a professional. (5)

**personal commercial.** Rehearsed introduction that includes brief information about a person's background and a snapshot of his or her career goals; also known as an *elevator speech*. (3)

**personal quality.** Characteristic that makes up an individual's personality. (4)

**phishing.** Use of fraudulent e-mails and copies of valid websites to trick people into providing private and confidential personal data. (2)

**plagiarism.** Claiming another person's material as one's own. (12)

**portfolio.** Selection of related materials an individual collects and organizes to show his or her qualifications, skills, and talents. (1)

**professional development.** Training that builds on the skills and knowledge that contribute to personal grown and career development. (12)

**professional network.** People who support an individual in his or her career and other business endeavors. (3)

**professional reference.** Person who is ready and willing to recommend an individual for a job if requested. (3)

**proprietary information.** Any work created by company employees on the job that is owned by that company; also known as *trade secrets*. (12)

**punctuality.** Being on time. (12)

# R

**respect.** Feeling that someone or something is good, valuable, and important. (12)

**résumé.** Written document that lists an individual's qualifications for a job, including education and work experience. (6)

**résumé template.** Pre-formatted word processing document that contains a standard layout with adequate margins of white space. (6)

# S

**screening interview.** Preliminary, informal interview designed to determine if a candidate's skills qualify him or her for a formal interview. (9)

**search engine optimization (SEO).** Process of indexing a website so it will rank it higher on the list of returned results when a search is conducted. (1)

**second interview.** Formal interview that occurs after it has been determined that the candidate is qualified and more information is needed about him or her. (10)

**secure password.** A code used to access a private account or other private information, such as an e-mail account or computer network. (1)

**self-talk.** Internal thoughts and feelings about one's self. (1)

**signal phrase.** Preplanned beginning phrase that enhances a question. (9)

**skill.** Something an individual does well. (4)

**skills résumé.** Résumé that lists work experience according to categories of skills or achievements rather than by employer. (6)

**soft skill.** Behavior that a person uses to relate to others, and behavior that is not easy to measure. (5)

**software virus.** Computer program designed to negatively impact a computer system. (2)

**spyware.** Software that spies on a computer. (2)

**structured interview.** Formal interview in which a predetermined list of questions is posed to each candidate interviewing for a position; also known as *directive interview*. (9)

**subjective elements.** Factors that contain bias and are more emotional than logical. (10)

# T

**technology plan.** Documentation of software and other technology a person already knows today and needs to know in the future. (5)

**thinking skill.** Skill that helps a person solve problems. (4)

**time management.** Practice of organizing time and work assignments to increase personal efficiency. (12)

**timeline résumé.** Résumé that emphasizes employers and work experience with each; also known as *chronological résumé*. (6)

**trending.** Refers to keywords and phrases that have the highest number of searches in any given day. (6)

# U

**unstructured interview.** Interview that is less formal and might or might not consist of a specific list of questions. (9)

# V

**value.** Belief about the things that matter most to an individual. (5)

**visual résumé.** Résumé that presents information in a graphically appealing format. (6)

# Index